The
Lancashire,
Cumbria &
Manchester
Bus Handbook

Counties in this issue:

Cumbria

Lancashire

Greater Manchester

February 1996

British Bus Publishing

The Lancashire, Cumbria & Manchester Bus Handbook

The Lancashire, Cumbria & Manchester Bus Handbook is part of the Bus Handbook series that details the fleets of commercial and tendered bus operations together with express coach operators. Where space allows other significant operators in the areas covered are also included. These handbooks are published by British Bus Publishing and cover Scotland, Wales and England north of London.

Quality photographs for inclusion in the series are welcome, for which a fee is payable. The publishers unfortunately cannot accept responsibility for any loss and request you show your name on each picture or slide. Details of changes to fleet information are also welcome.

To keep the fleet information up to date we recommend the Ian Allan publication, Buses published monthly, or for more detailed information, the PSV Circle monthly news sheets.

The writer and publisher would be glad to hear from readers should any information be available which corrects or enhances that given in this publication.

Managing Editor: Bill Potter

Principal Editors for The Lancashire, Cumbria & Manchester Bus Handbook:
David Donati, Bill Potter and Brian Pritchard

Acknowledgements:
We are grateful to Martin Grosberg, Mark Jameson, Colin Lloyd, Gavin Robinson, Steve Sanderson, Simon Watts, the PSV Circle and the operating companies for their assistance in the compilation of this book.

The cover photographs are by Paul Wigan

Contents correct to January 1996
ISBN 1 890990 13 8
Published by British Bus Publishing Ltd
The Vyne, 16 St Margarets Drive, Wellington,
Telford, Shropshire, TF1 3PH
© British Bus Publishing Ltd, February 1996

CONTENTS

ABBOTT'S

J Abbott & Sons (Blackpool) Ltd, 95/97 Talbot Road, Blackpool, FY1 3QX

OFV467G	AEC Reliance 6U3ZR	Plaxton Elite	C57F	1969	
SFR127J	AEC Reliance 6U3ZR	Plaxton Elite	C53F	1970	
WFR147K	AEC Reliance 6U3ZR	Plaxton Elite II	C45F	1972	
WFR167K	AEC Reliance 6U3ZR	Plaxton Elite II	C45F	1972	
NFR487M	AEC Reliance 6U3ZR	Plaxton Elite III	C45F	1973	
NFR497M	AEC Reliance 6U3ZR	Plaxton Elite III	C53F	1973	
PBV637P	AEC Reliance 6U3ZR	Plaxton Supreme III	C53F	1976	
VFV907R	AEC Reliance 6U3ZR	Plaxton Supreme III	C53F	1977	
YRN507R	AEC Reliance 6U3ZR	Plaxton Supreme III	C53F	1977	
HCK847S	AEC Reliance 6U3ZR	Duple Dominant II	C53F	1978	
JCW517S	Volvo B58-56	Plaxton Supreme III	C53F	1978	
NCW747T	AEC Reliance 6U3ZR	Duple Dominant II	C53F	1979	
EFR97W	Leyland Leopard PSU5D/5R	Duple Dominant II	C53F	1981	
EFR107W	Leyland Leopard PSU5D/5R	Duple Dominant II	C53F	1981	
MSU611Y	Volvo B10M-61	Duple Laser	C57F	1983	Ex Duple demonstrator, 1983
A547HBV	Leyland Tiger TRCTL11/3R	Duple Caribbean	C51F	1983	
A777RBV	Leyland Tiger TRCTL11/3R	Duple Caribbean	C51F	1984	
B357UCW	Leyland Tiger TRCTL11/3R	Duple Laser	C55F	1984	Ex Duple demonstrator, 1985
D857XBV	Leyland Tiger TRCTL11/3RZ	Duple 340	C53FT	1987	
D327VVV	Quest J	Jonckheere Piccolo	C33FT	1987	
F727VAC	Volvo B10M-60	Plaxton Paramount 3500 III	C53F	1988	Ex Volvo Bus demonstrator, 1989
H687XBV	Volvo B10M-60	Plaxton Paramount 3500 III	C57F	1991	
K617SBV	Volvo B10M-60	Jonckheere Deauville	C53FT	1992	
M307KRY	Volvo B10M-62	Jonckheere Deauville	C53FT	1995	
M337KRY	Volvo B10M-62	Jonckheere Deauville	C53FT	1995	

Livery: Red and grey; WFR147K is operated by Blackhurst and YRN507R by Enterprise Motors.

Abbott's continue to operate eleven AEC Reliance coaches though these are gradually being replaced by Volvo B10Ms. The company has retained a tradition of purchasing new coaches that are retained throughout their life. Express services operate from the Fylde coast to Lancashire towns and on excursion and tour work from Blackpool. Seen here is the newest of the AECs, NCW747T, a number no longer supplied by the DVLA. *Paul Wigan*

APEX TRAVEL

W R Heslop, 41 Foundry Road, Parton, Whitehaven, CA28 6PB

RWM576T	Ford R1114	Plaxton Supreme IV	C53F	1979	Ex Stott, Oldham, 1995
SKB650T	Ford R1114	Plaxton Supreme IV	C53F	1979	Ex Stott, Oldham, 1995
CFR384V	Ford R1114	Duple Dominant II	C53F	1980	Ex Evag Cannon, Bolton, 1994
SYG437W	Ford R1114	Duple Dominant II	C53F	1981	Ex Irving, Dalston, 1995
NAO64W	Ford Transit 160	Dormobile	B16F	1981	Ex Winter, Bassenthwaite, 1995
D552MOK	Ford Transit VE6	Carlyle	B16F	1988	Ex Rochester & Marshall, 1994

Livery: Orange and red

The two vehicle fleet of Atherton Bus Company includes CNH171X seen here at the Bolton end of its route. The Eastern Coach Works B51 style is rapidly disappearing from the transport scene as many continue to be re-bodied or withdrawn.
Roy Marshall

ATHERTON BUS COMPANY

P G Hughes, 33 Landedmans, Westhoughton, Bolton, BL5 2QJ

GNS672N	Leyland Atlantean AN68/1R	Alexander AL	H45/31F	1975	Ex Partridge, Hadleigh, 1992
CNH171X	Leyland Leopard PSU3F/4R	Eastern Coach Works B51	C49F	1981	Ex United Counties, 1994

Livery: Blue, white and yellow.

B & D COACHES

R Dootson, 12 Northolt Avenue, Leigh, WN7 1TY

D178LTA	Renault-Dodge S56	Reeve Burgess	B23F	1986	Ex Cardiff Bus, 1994
D181LTA	Renault-Dodge S56	Reeve Burgess	B23F	1986	Ex Cardiff Bus, 1994
D502MJA	Iveco Daily 49.10	Robin Hood City Nippy	B19F	1987	Ex Midland Choice, Codnor, 1992
D511MJA	Iveco Daily 49.10	Robin Hood City Nippy	B19F	1987	Ex Midland Choice, Codnor, 1992
D615BCK	Iveco Daily 49.10	Robin Hood City Nippy	B21F	1987	Ex Ribble, 1993
F248KVU	Renault-Dodge S46	Northern Counties	B24F	1989	Ex City Nippy, Middleton, 1992
F249KVU	Renault-Dodge S46	Northern Counties	B24F	1989	Ex City Nippy, Middleton, 1992
H67WNN	Mercedes-Benz 814D	Carlyle	C29F	1990	Ex Skill's, Nottingham, 1994
N796XRA	Mercedes-Benz 709D	Plaxton Beaver	B23F	1995	

Livery: Blue and grey.

B&D operate around Atherleigh, and seen entering Leigh bus station is recently F220AKG, an Iveco new to the Red & White fleet. Three of this type are still operated, two of which were new to Greater Manchester while the third was with Ribble. Replacing this bus is new Mercedes-Benz 709, N796XRA.
Paul Wigan

BLACKBURN

Blackburn Borough Transport Ltd, Intack Garage, Whitebirk Road,
Blackburn, BB1 3JD

6-22

Leyland Atlantean AN68C/1R — East Lancashire — H43/31F — 1982

6	OCW6X	10	OCW10X	14	OCW14X	17	SBV17X	20	VBV20Y
7	OCW7X	11	OCW11X	15	OCW15X	18	VBV18Y	21	VBV21Y
8	OCW8X	12	OCW12X	16	SBV16X	19	VBV19Y	22	VBV22Y
9	OCW9X	13	OCW13X						

23-29

Leyland Atlantean AN68D/1R — East Lancashire — H43/31F — 1983

23	A23JBV	25	FCK25Y	27	FCK27Y	28	A28JBV	29	A29JBV
24	FCK24Y	26	A26JBV						

43	ABV43B	Leyland Titan PD2A/24	East Lancashire	H35/28R	1964
115w	PCW115P	Leyland Atlantean AN68A/1R	East Lancashire	H45/31F	1976
119w	CBV119S	Leyland Atlantean AN68A/1R	East Lancashire	H45/31F	1977

127-142

Leyland Atlantean AN68A/1R — East Lancashire — H43/31F — 1979-80

127	LFR127T	130	LFR130T	135	WRN135V	138	WRN138V	141	WRN141V
128	LFR128T	133	WRN133V	136	WRN136V	139	WRN139V	142	WRN142V
129	LFR129T	134	WRN134V	137	WRN137V	140	WRN140V		

143-147

Leyland Atlantean AN68C/1R — East Lancashire — H43/31F — 1981

143	DBV143W	144	DBV144W	145	DBV145W	146	DBV146W	147	DBV147W

201-205

Volvo B10M-55 — East Lancashire EL2000 — DP51F — 1991

201	J421JBV	202	J422JBV	203	J418JBV	204	J419JBV	205	J420JBV

303	KJF3V	Leyland Leopard PSU3E/4R	Plaxton Supreme IV Express	C53F	1980	Ex Leicester, 1986
304	KBC4V	Leyland Leopard PSU3E/4R	Plaxton Supreme IV Express	C53F	1980	Ex Leicester, 1986
305	CFR489V	Leyland Leopard PSU3E/4R	Plaxton Supreme IV Express	C53F	1979	Ex Leicester, 1986
306	FUT6V	Leyland Leopard PSU3E/4R	Plaxton Supreme IV Express	C53F	1979	Ex Leicester, 1986
307u	LHE254W	Leyland Leopard PSU5E/4R	Plaxton Supreme IV	C53F	1981	Ex National Travel East, 1987
308u	LHE255W	Leyland Leopard PSU5E/4R	Plaxton Supreme IV	C53F	1981	Ex National Travel East, 1987

Representing the Blackburn double-deck fleet is 11, OCW11X, a Leyland Atlantean with locally-built bodywork from East Lancashire Coachbuilders. A folding board on the front and the route number in the 300 series indicate this is working a tendered service for Lancashire County Council.
Paul Wigan

317	B417CMC	Leyland Tiger TRCTL11/3R	Plaxton Paramount 3200	C53F	1985	Ex British Airways, 1987
318	PCB24	Volvo B10M-61	Caetano Algarve	C49FT	1986	Ex Park's, 1988
319	D319NEC	Leyland Tiger TRCTL11/3RH	Plaxton Paramount 3200 III	C53F	1987	
320	D320NEC	Leyland Tiger TRCTL11/3RH	Plaxton Paramount 3200 III	C53F	1987	
321	F984HGE	Volvo B10M-60	Plaxton Paramount 3500 III	C53F	1988	Ex Park's, 1991
322	MIB920	Volvo B10M-61	Caetano Algarve	C49FT	1987	Ex The King's Ferry, 1991
323	G996RKN	Volvo B10M-60	Caetano Algarve	C49FT	1990	Ex The King's Ferry, 1991
324	LIJ749	Volvo B10M-61	Caetano Algarve	C49FT	1988	Ex The King's Ferry, 1992
325	G999RKN	Volvo B10M-60	Caetano Algarve	C49FT	1990	Ex The King's Ferry, 1992
326	H174EJU	Volvo B10M-60	Plaxton Paramount 3500 III	C53F	1991	Ex Ambassador Travel, 1994
327	H724VWU	Volvo B10M-60	Plaxton Paramount 3500 III	C53F	1991	Ex Dodsworth, Boroughbridge, 1995
410	PUS158W	Leyland Leopard PSU3F/4R	Alexander AYS	B53F	1981	Ex Kelvin Scottish, 1987
411	TSU639W	Leyland Leopard PSU3G/4R	Alexander AYS	B53F	1981	Ex Kelvin Scottish, 1987
412	TSU640W	Leyland Leopard PSU3G/4R	Alexander AYS	B53F	1981	Ex Kelvin Scottish, 1987
413	TSU641W	Leyland Leopard PSU3G/4R	Alexander AYS	B53F	1981	Ex Kelvin Scottish, 1988
414	WPH134Y	Leyland Tiger TRCTL11/2R	Eastern Coach Works B51	DP51F	1982	Ex Kentish Bus, 1988
415	WPH137Y	Leyland Tiger TRCTL11/2R	Eastern Coach Works B51	DP51F	1982	Ex Kentish Bus, 1988
416	WPH138Y	Leyland Tiger TRCTL11/2R	Eastern Coach Works B51	DP51F	1982	Ex Kentish Bus, 1988
417	WPH141Y	Leyland Tiger TRCTL11/2R	Eastern Coach Works B51	DP51F	1982	Ex Kentish Bus, 1988
423	BVP807V	Leyland National 2 NL116L11/1R	East Lancs Greenway (1993) B49F		1980	Ex North Western, 1992
424	AFM5W	Leyland National 2 NL116AL11/2R	East Lancs Greenway (1993) B49F		1981	Ex North Western, 1992
425	PJT267R	Leyland National 11351A/2R	East Lancs Greenway (1994) B49F		1976	Ex Solent Blue Line, 1994
426	TCW868T	Leyland National 11351A/2R	East Lancs Greenway (1994) B49F		1979	Ex North Devon, 1994
427	TJN505R	Leyland National 11351A/1R(Vo)	East Lancs Greenway (1995) B49F		1977	Ex Eastern National, 1995
428	TOF649S	Leyland National 11351A/1R(Vo)	East Lancs Greenway (1995) B49F		1978	Ex Midland, 1995
429	YEV317S	Leyland National 11351A/1R(Vo)	East Lancs Greenway (1995) B49F		1978	Ex Thamesway, 1995
430	YEV324S	Leyland National 11351A/1R(Vo)	East Lancs Greenway (1995) B49F		1978	Ex Thamesway, 1995
525	BFV861R	Leyland National 10351A/2R	East Lancs Greenway (1993) B41F		1977	Ex London Buses, 1992
526	BYW361V	Leyland National 10351A/2R	East Lancs Greenway (1993) B41F		1979	Ex Evag Cannon, Bolton, 1992
527	LRN552N	Leyland National 10351/2R	East Lancs Greenway (1993) B41F		1975	Ex Isle of Man Road Services, 1992
528	JDT432N	Leyland National 10351/2R	East Lancs Greenway (1993) B41F		1975	Ex Isle of Man Road Services, 1992
529	JWG191P	Leyland National 10351/2R	East Lancs Greenway (1993) B41F		1975	Ex Isle of Man Road Services, 1992
530	HPF313N	Leyland National 10351/1R/SC	East Lancs Greenway (1993) B41F		1975	Ex Birmingham Omnibus, Smethwick, 1992
531	AYR354T	Leyland National 10351A/2R	East Lancs Greenway (1994) B41F		1979	Ex PMT, 1994
532	JJG907P	Leyland National 10351/1R	East Lancs Greenway (1994) B41F		1975	Ex Busylink, Hemel Hempstead, 1994
533	M533RCW	Volvo B6-9.9M	East Lancashire	B41F	1994	
534	M534RCW	Volvo B6-9.9M	East Lancashire	B41F	1994	
535	M535RCW	Volvo B6-9.9M	East Lancashire	B41F	1994	
536	M536RCW	Volvo B6-9.9M	East Lancashire	B41F	1994	

602-611

MCW MetroRider MF151/4   MCW   B23F*   1987   *603/11 are M151/5 and DP23F

602	D602AFR	607	D607AFR	608	D608AFR	609	D609AFR	611	D611AFR
603	D603AFR								

616-626

MCW MetroRider MF159/3   MCW   B33F*   1988   *625/6 are MF159/4 and DP33F

616	F616UBV	619	F619UBV	621	F621UBV	623	F623UBV	625	F625UBV
617	F617UBV	620	F620UBV	622	F622UBV	624	F624UBV	626	F626UBV
618	F617UBV								

627-632

Optare MetroRider MR15   Optare   B31F*   1995   * 631/2 are MR17 and B29F

627	M627WBV	629	M629WBV	630	M630WBV	631	M631WFR	632	M632WFR
628	M628WBV								

Previous Registrations:

BFV861R	OJD880R		LRN552N	JDT437N, 3176MAN
CFR489V	FUT5V		MIB920	E841EUT
JDT432N	JDT432N, 4647MAN		PCB24	C673KDS
JWG191P	JWG191P, 4648MAN		TCW868T	AFJ757T
LIJ749	F870TNH			

Livery: Ivory and green

Opposite, top: **Blackburn have been involved with the Greenway conversions and have taken examples of both lengths of the product for their own fleet. These include several buses with interesting backgrounds. Four examples have the Volvo engine conversion including 430, YEV324S, photographed while heading for Darwen Cemetery.** *Tony Wilson*
Opposite, bottom: **The latest arrivals with Blackburn are a further batch of Optare MetroRiders which have replaced some of the early MCW examples. Pictured at the main rail and bus terminus in the town is 628, M628WBV.** *Paul Wigan*

BLACKPOOL

Blackpool Transport Services Ltd, Blackpool & Fleetwood Tramway, Fylde Transport Ltd,
Rigby Road, Blackpool, Lancashire, FY1 5DD

Blackpool Buses

103-130   DAF SB220LC550   Optare Delta   DP46F   1990-93

103	G103NBV	109	H109YHG	116	H116YHG	121	H121CHG	126	J126GRN
104	G104NBV	110	H110YHG	117	H117YHG	122	H122CHG	127	K127UFV
105	G105NBV	112	H112YHG	118	H118CHG	123	J123GRN	128	K128UFV
106	G106NBV	113	H113YHG	119	H119CHG	124	J124GRN	129	K129UFV
107	G107NBV	114	H114YHG	120	H120CHG	125	J125GRN	130	K130UFV
108	G108NBV	115	H115YHG						

331-340   Leyland Atlantean AN68A/2R   East Lancashire   H50/36F   1979-80

331	AHG331V	333u	AHG333V	336	AHG336V	338	AHG338V	340	AHG340V
332u	AHG332V	334u	AHG334V	337	AHG337V	339	AHG339V		

341-350   Leyland Atlantean AN68C/2R   East Lancashire   H50/36F   1981

341	GHG341W	344	GHG344W	346	GHG346W	348	GHG348W	350	GHG350W
343	GHG343W	345	GHG345W	347	GHG347W	349	GHG349W		

351-362   Leyland Atlantean AN68D/2R   East Lancashire   H49/36F   1982-83

351	UHG351Y	354	UHG354Y	357	A357HHG	359	A359HHG	361	A361HHG
352	UHG352Y	355	A355HHG	358	A358HHG	360	A360HHG	362	A362HHG
353	UHG353Y	356	A356HHG						

363	B363UBV	Leyland Atlantean AN68D/2R	East Lancashire	DPH45/29F	1984
365	UWW5X	Leyland Olympian ONLXB/1R	Roe	H47/29F	1982 Ex West Yorkshire PTE, 1986
366	UWW11X	Leyland Olympian ONLXB/1R	Roe	H47/29F	1982 Ex West Yorkshire PTE, 1986
367	UWW15X	Leyland Olympian ONLXB/1R	Roe	H47/29F	1982 Ex West Yorkshire PTE, 1986

368-373   Leyland Olympian ONCL10/1RZ   East Lancashire   H45/31F   1989

368	F368AFR	370	F370AFR	371	F371AFR	372	F372AFR	373	F373AFR
369	F369AFR								

374-379   Volvo Olympian YN2RC16Z4   Northern Counties Palatine II H43/29F   1994

374	M374SCK	376	M376SCK	377	M377SCK	378	M378SCK	379	M379SCK
375	M375SCK								

507u	HFR507E	Leyland Titan PD3A/1	MCW	H41/30R	1967

521-531   AEC Routemaster 2R2RH*   Park Royal   H36/28R   1961-64 Ex London Buses, 1986-88
*522/6/7/30/1 are R2RH

521	583CLT	524	640DYE	526	735DYE	528	357CLT	530	ALD989B
522	WLT848	525	650DYE	527	WLT879	529	ALD966B	531	ALM71B
523	627DYE								

532	DHC784E	Leyland Titan PD2A/30	East Lancashire	O32/28R	1967	Ex Eastbourne, 1989
533	ALM89B	AEC Routemaster R2RH	Park Royal	H36/28R	1964	Ex London Buses, 1988

Opposite, top: **In 1994 Blackpool took six of the attractive Northern Counties Palatine II bodies for their Volvo Olympians. These are normally found on the 22 service which now operate across the town from Cleveleys in the north to Lytham in the south. Seen at the northern end is 375, M375SCK.** *Paul Wigan*

Opposite, bottom: **Minibus services operated by Blackpool use the black and yellow Handybus colours which are also starting to appear on former Blue Bus minibuses. A recent addition to the fleet is 585, N585GRN seen near Victoria Hospital while heading for Poulton-le-Fylde.** *Paul Wigan*

Still the main attraction of Blackpool for many is the tramway. The long, hot summer of 1995 provided much work for the open boats with several forays north to Fleetwood. Pictured departing from the ferry terminus is 604. *Paul Wigan*

553-568				Volkswagen LT55		Optare City Pacer		B21F*	1987	565/6 Ex Optare demonstrators, 1987
										*565/6 are DP21F
553	E553GFR	556	E556GFR	558	E558GFR	565	D854MUA		567	E567GFR
554	E554GFR	557	E557GFR	559	E559GFR	566	D898NUA		568	E568GFR
555	E555GFR									

569-582				Volkswagen LT55		Optare City Pacer		B21F	1988	
569	E569OCW	572	F572RCW	575	F575RCW	578	F578RCW		581	F581WCW
570	E570OCW	573	F573RCW	576	F576RCW	579	F579WCW		582	F582WCW
571	F571RCW	574	F574RCW	577	F577RCW	580	F580WCW			

583	F934AWW	Volkswagen LT55		Optare City Pacer		DP21F	1988	Ex Optare demonstrator, 1989
584	M924TYG	Optare MetroRider		Optare		B25F	1995	Ex Optare, 1995

585-592				Optare MetroRider MR37		Optare		B25F	1995	
585	N585GRN	587	N587GRN	589	N589GRN	591	N591GRN		592	N592GRN
586	N586GRN	588	N588GRN	590	N590GRN					

Blackpool & Fleetwood Tramway

600-607				English Electric M4d		English Electric		OST56C*	1934-35	*602 is OST52C
600		602		604		605	606		607	

619		English Electric M4d		Blackpool Corporation (1987)	ST52D	1973

621-637				EMB M4d		Brush		ST48C	1937	
621	623	626	630	631	632	633	634		636	637
622	625	627								

Recently restored and now used for specials Coronation car 660 is seen here on Central Promenade, Blackpool. These cars were built by Roberts in Sheffield and formed the main type to operate the full-length service in the 1950s and 1960s. *Paul Wigan*

641-647		Primrose/Brush M4d		East Lancashire		ST52D	1984-88	641 is ST55D	
641	642	643	644	645	646	647			

648		Maley & Taunton/Brush M4d		East Lancashire		ST53D	1985	
660		Maley & Taunton M4d		Roberts		ST56C	1953	

671-677		English Electric 1935 M4s		English Electric		ST53C	1960	
671	672	673	674	675	676	677		

678		English Electric 1935 M4d		English Electric		ST48C	1960	
679		English Electric 1935 M4d		English Electric		ST48C	1960	
680		English Electric 1935 M4d		English Electric		ST48C	1960	

681-687		Maley & Taunton M4d		MCW		ST61C	1960	
681	682	683	684	685	686	687		

700-726			English Electric M4d		English Electric			DT54/40C*	1934/35	*706 is ODT54/40C	
700	703	707u	710	713	716	718	720	722	724
701	704	708	711	715	717	719	721	723	726
702	706	709	712						

732		Dick Kerr M4s		Blackpool Corporation	48-seat	1960	Moon Rocket
733		English Electric M4d		Blackpool Corporation	35-seat	1962	Wild West Loco
734		Dick Kerr B4s		Blackpool Corporation	60-seat	1962	Wild West coach
735		English Electric M4d		Blackpool Corporation	57/42	1963	Hovercraft
736		Dick Kerr M4d		Blackpool Corporation	71-seat	1965	Frigate
761		English Electric (1934) M4d		Blackpool/East Lancs	DT56/44F	1979	
762		English Electric (1934) M4d		Blackpool/East Lancs	DT56/34D	1982	

The first two of Blackpool's Optare Delta buses have been renumbered into the Blue Buses fleet and painted blue and cream. Wearing the livery and new motif is 9, G102NBV, pictured here as it joins the Promenade at Manchester Square. *Paul Wigan*

Blue Buses

1	H1FBT	DAF SB220LC550	Optare Delta	DP48F	1991	
2	H2FBT	DAF SB220LC550	Optare Delta	DP48F	1991	
3	H3FBT	DAF SB220LC550	Optare Delta	DP48F	1991	
4	TKU462K	Leyland Atlantean AT68M/2RF	N Counties Paladin (1992)	DP42F	1971	Ex Kingston-upon-Hull, 1987
5	TKU465K	Leyland Atlantean AT68M/2RFT	N Counties Paladin (1992)	DP42F	1971	Ex Kingston-upon-Hull, 1987
6	TKU466K	Leyland Atlantean AT68M/2RFT	N Counties Paladin (1992)	DP42F	1971	Ex Kingston-upon-Hull, 1987
7	TKU469K	Leyland Atlantean AT68M/2RFT	N Counties Paladin (1992)	DP42F	1971	Ex Kingston-upon-Hull, 1987
8	G101NBV	DAF SB220LC550	Optare Delta	DP46F	1990	
9	G102NBV	DAF SB220LC550	Optare Delta	DP46F	1990	
21	F699ENE	Leyland Tiger TRCL10/3RZA	Plaxton Paramount 3200 III	C53F	1988	Ex Timeline, 1995
22	F700ENE	Leyland Tiger TRCL10/3RZA	Plaxton Paramount 3200 III	C53F	1988	Ex Timeline, 1995
23	F703ENE	Leyland Tiger TRCL10/3RZA	Plaxton Paramount 3200 III	C53F	1988	Ex Timeline, 1995
24	G812RNC	Leyland Tiger TR2R62C21Z5	Plaxton Paramount 3200 III	C53F	1990	Ex Shearings, 1993
25	G813RNC	Leyland Tiger TR2R62C21Z5	Plaxton Paramount 3200 III	C53F	1990	Ex Shearings, 1993
26	J26LRN	DAF SB3000DKV601	Van Hool Alizée	C51FT	1992	
27	MJI7846	Leyland Tiger TRCTL11/3RH	Duple Laser 2	C53F	1985	
28	TRN772	Leyland Leopard PSU3C/4R	Duple 320 (1989)	C53F	1977	
29	YNJ434	Leyland Leopard PSU3C/4R	Duple 320 (1990)	C53F	1975	
30	NUT16W	Leyland Leopard PSU3F/5R	Duple Dominant II	C53F	1981	Ex Wood, Blackpool, 1988
31	SIB4631	Volvo B58-56	Duple Dominant II	C53F	1980	
32w	PJI5632	Leyland Leopard PSU3B/4R	Duple Dominant	C53F	1974	Ex Wood, Blackpool, 1988
33w	OHG33T	Leyland Leopard PSU3E/4R	Duple Dominant I	C53F	1979	
34w	OHG34T	Leyland Leopard PSU3E/4R	Duple Dominant I	C53F	1979	
36	XRN29V	Leyland Leopard PSU3E/4R	Plaxton Supreme IV Express	C53F	1980	
41	HIL5341	Leyland Atlantean AN68C/2R	Northern Counties	DPH43/33F	1981	
42	HIL5342	Leyland Atlantean AN68C/2R	Northern Counties	DPH43/33F	1982	
43	HIL5943	Leyland Atlantean AN68D/2R	Northern Counties (1992)	DPH43/33F	1983	
44	NJI5504	Leyland Atlantean AN68D/2R	Northern Counties	DPH43/33F	1983	
45	NJI5505	Leyland Atlantean AN68D/2R	Northern Counties	DPH43/33F	1984	
47	B364UBV	Leyland Atlantean AN68D/2R	East Lancashire	DPH45/29F	1984	
49	ARH314K	Leyland Atlantean PDR1A/1	Roe	H43/29F	1972	Ex Kingston-upon-Hull, 1988
50	HRN100N	Leyland Atlantean AN68/1R	NCounties/Willowbrook	H43/31F	1975	
51	DBA227C	Leyland Atlantean PDR1/1	MCW	O43/33F	1965	Ex Lancaster, 1986
52	TKH266H	Leyland Atlantean PDR1A/1	Roe	O43/28F	1969	Ex Kingston-upon-Hull, 1987

53	WRH294J	Leyland Atlantean PDR1A/1	Roe	O43/28F	1970	Ex Kingston-upon-Hull, 1987
54	ARH309K	Leyland Atlantean PDR1A/1	Roe	O43/29F	1971	Ex Kingston-upon-Hull, 1987
55	ARH304K	Leyland Atlantean PDR1A/1	Roe	HO39/29F	1971	Ex Kingston-upon-Hull, 1986
56	WRH291J	Leyland Atlantean PDR1A/1	Roe	H43/28F	1970	Ex Kingston-upon-Hull, 1987
57	WRH295J	Leyland Atlantean PDR1A/1	Roe	H43/28F	1970	Ex Kingston-upon-Hull, 1987
58	ATD281J	Leyland Atlantean PDR1A/1	Northern Counties	HO44/33F	1970	
59	ARH301K	Leyland Atlantean PDR1A/1	Roe	H43/29F	1971	Ex Kingston-upon-Hull, 1988
60w	ARH308K	Leyland Atlantean PDR1A/1	Roe	H43/29F	1971	Ex Kingston-upon-Hull, 1988
65	ONF660R	Leyland Atlantean AN68A/1R	Northern Counties	H43/32F	1976	Ex GM Buses, 1989
66	ONF669R	Leyland Atlantean AN68A/1R	Northern Counties	H43/32F	1976	Ex GM Buses, 1989
67	ONF673R	Leyland Atlantean AN68A/1R	Northern Counties	H43/32F	1976	Ex GM Buses, 1989
68	SRJ756R	Leyland Atlantean AN68A/1R	Northern Counties	H43/32F	1977	Ex GM Buses, 1989
69	SRJ757R	Leyland Atlantean AN68A/1R	Northern Counties	H43/32F	1977	Ex GM Buses, 1989
70	TSD571S	Leyland Atlantean AN68A/1R	Northern Counties	H44/34F	1978	Ex Clyde Coast, Ardrossan, 1990
71	OJI4371	Leyland Atlantean AN68A/1R	Northern Counties (1990)	H43/31F	1977	
72	OJI4372	Leyland Atlantean AN68M/1RF	Northern Counties (1991)	H43/31F	1977	
73	OJI4373	Leyland Atlantean AN68M/1RF	Northern Counties (1991)	H43/31F	1977	
74	OJI4374	Leyland Atlantean AN68A/1R	Northern Counties (1992)	H43/31F	1977	
75	SIB8405	Leyland Atlantean AN68M/1RFT	Northern Counties (1993)	H43/31F	1976	
78	HRN98N	Leyland Atlantean AN68/1R	NCounties/Willowbrook	H43/31F	1975	
79	HRN99N	Leyland Atlantean AN68/1R	NCounties/Willowbrook	H43/31F	1975	
81	HRN101N	Leyland Atlantean AN68/1R	NCounties/Willowbrook	H43/31F	1975	
82	HRN102N	Leyland Atlantean AN68/1R	NCounties/Willowbrook	H43/31F	1975	
83	HRN103N	Leyland Atlantean AN68/1R	NCounties/Willowbrook	H43/31F	1975	
86	MIW8186	Leyland Atlantean PDR1A/1	Roe	H43/29F	1971	Ex Kingston-upon-Hull, 1987
87	MIW8187	Leyland Atlantean AN68/1R	Roe	H43/29F	1973	Ex Kingston-upon-Hull, 1992
88	MIW8188	Leyland Atlantean AN68/1R	Roe	H43/29F	1972	Ex Kingston-upon-Hull, 1988
89w	RIB4089	Leyland Atlantean AN68/1R	Roe	H43/29F	1972	Ex Kingston-upon-Hull, 1988
90	RIB6590	Leyland Atlantean PDR1A/1	Roe	H43/29F	1971	Ex Kingston-upon-Hull, 1987
91	IIL4291	Leyland Atlantean PDR1A/1	Roe	H43/29F	1971	Ex Kingston-upon-Hull, 1992
92	NIW6492	Leyland Atlantean AN68/1R	Roe	H43/29F	1972	Ex Kingston-upon-Hull, 1992
93	ARH306K	Leyland Atlantean PDR1A/1	Roe	H43/29F	1971	Ex Kingston-upon-Hull, 1992
95	RHG95T	Leyland Atlantean AN68A/1R	Northern Counties	H43/31F	1979	
96	XHG96V	Leyland Atlantean AN68A/1R	Northern Counties	H43/31F	1980	

101-118

101-118		Renault-Dodge S56	Northern Counties	B25F	1987-88	107 Ex Northern Counties, 1987

*105 is DP20F, 104 is B22F, 117/8 are B23F

104	D104AFV	108	E108LCW	111	E111LCW	113	E113LCW	117	E164CNC
105	D105AFV	110	E110LCW	112	E112LCW	114	E114LCW	118	E165CNC

120-125

120-125		Renault-Dodge S56	Northern Counties	B27F	1988	*120 is DP27F

120	F120UFR	122	F142UFR	123	F143UFR	124	F144UFR	125	F145UFR
121	F141UFR								

134	BTB928	Leyland Lion LT7C	Leyland	B34R	1936	Re-acquired 1988

322-330

322-330		Leyland Atlantean AN68A/2R	East Lancashire	H50/36F	1979	

322	URN322V	324	URN324V	326	URN326V	328	URN328V	330	URN330V
323	URN323V	325	URN325V	327	URN327V	329	URN329V		

Previous Registrations:

HIL5341	HBV97W	NIW6492	DRH327L	RIB4089	DRH329L
HIL5342	PCW98X	NJI5504	A74LHG	RIB6590	ARH311K
HIL5943	ACK99Y	NJI5505	B75URN	SIB4631	XRN28V
IIL4291	ARH298K	OJI4371	EBV85S	SIB8405	OCK84P
MIW8186	ARH309K	OJI4372	EBV86S	TRN772	XRN36R
MIW8187	NAT339M	OJI4373	EBV87S	YNJ434	HRN97N
MIW8188	DRH330L	OJI4374	EBV88S		
MJI7846	C27ECW	PJI5632	YNA400M		

Livery: Cream and green (most full-size Blackpool Buses and trams); red and white 507, 521/3-33, 604; black and yellow (Handybus) most minibuses; blue and white (full-size Fylde buses)

On order: 6 Optare Excel integral low floor buses for the Blue Buses' fleet.

Bluebird provide services in the Middleton area which is situated between Rochdale, Oldham and Manchester. The large Langley Estate nearby also provides much patronage for this expanding fleet. Shown here are 80, G280MWU, an Iveco 49.10 with Reeve Burgess bodywork to the Beaver design and 98, a Dennis Lancet SD505 which was new to Blackpool. This vehicle carries Marshall Camair body style. Both photographs were taken in Middleton's Arndale bus station. *Paul Wigan*

BLUEBIRD

MTG, TA & M Dunstan, Alexander House, Greengate, Middleton, Rochdale, M24 1RT

2	K2BLU	Iveco Daily 49.10	Dormobile Routemaker	B23F	1992	
3	K3BLU	Iveco Daily 49.10	Dormobile Routemaker	B23F	1992	
4	L4BLU	Iveco Turbodaily 59.12	Marshall C31	B27F	1994	
5	M5BLU	Iveco Turbodaily 59.12	Marshall C31	B19F	1995	
6	M6BLU	Iveco Turbodaily 59.12	Marshall C31	B19F	1995	
7	N7BLU	Iveco Turbodaily 59.12	WS Dailybus	B27F	1995	
8	M8BLU	Iveco Turbodaily 59.12	Marshall C31	B19F	1995	
9	M9BLU	Iveco Turbodaily 59.12	Marshall C31	B19F	1995	
10	M10BLU	Iveco Turbodaily 59.12	Marshall C31	B19F	1995	
12	M12BLU	Iveco Turbodaily 59.12	Marshall C31	B19F	1995	
13	N13BLU	Iveco Turbodaily 59.12	Mellor	B27F	1995	
14	N14BLU	Iveco Turbodaily 59.12	Mellor	B27F	1995	
15	YHG15V	Leyland Leopard PSU4E/4R	Alexander AY	DP45F	1980	Ex Burnley & Pendle, 1993
16	LBU607V	Leyland Leopard PSU4E/4R	Alexander AY	DP45F	1980	Ex Burnley & Pendle, 1993
17	N17BLU	Iveco Turbodaily 59.12	WS Dailybus	B27F	1995	
22	N22BLU	Dennis Dart 9.8SDL3054	Marshall C37	B37F	1995	
32	G532VND	Iveco Daily 49.10	Carlyle Dailybus 2	B23F	1989	
33	G533SBA	Iveco Daily 49.10	Carlyle Dailybus 2	DP23F	1989	
35	H835DNE	Iveco Daily 49.10	Phoenix	DP23F	1990	
42	F242FNE	Iveco Daily 49.10	Northern Counties	B22F	1988	
48	G148LRM	Mercedes-Benz 609D	Reeve Burgess Beaver	B20F	1989	Ex North Western, 1994
51	SCH151X	Leyland Leopard PSU3F/4R	Willowbrook 003	C49F	1982	Ex Mayne, Manchester, 1994
52	SCH152X	Leyland Leopard PSU3F/4R	Willowbrook 003	C49F	1982	Ex Trent, 1995
54	VNN54Y	Leyland Leopard PSU3F/4R	Willowbrook 003	C49F	1982	Ex Mayne, Manchester, 1994
60	URA604S	Leyland National 11351A/1R		B49F	1978	Ex Merseybus, 1995
71	SJI1887	Leyland Leopard PSU3B/4R	Plaxton Elite III Express	C53F	1974	Ex Mayne, Manchester, 1994
75	G275MWU	Iveco Daily 49.10	Reeve Burgess Beaver	B25F	1990	Ex Keighley & District, 1995
76	G276MWU	Iveco Daily 49.10	Reeve Burgess Beaver	B25F	1990	Ex Keighley & District, 1995
77	G277MWU	Iveco Daily 49.10	Reeve Burgess Beaver	B25F	1990	Ex Harrogate & District, 1995
78	G278MWU	Iveco Daily 49.10	Reeve Burgess Beaver	B25F	1990	Ex Harrogate & District, 1995
79	G279MWU	Iveco Daily 49.10	Reeve Burgess Beaver	B25F	1990	Ex Keighley & District, 1995
80	G280MWU	Iveco Daily 49.10	Reeve Burgess Beaver	B25F	1990	Ex Harrogate & District, 1995
85	OIB1285	Leyland Tiger TRCTL11/2R	Plaxton Paramount 3200 E	C53F	1983	Ex Rossendale, 1993
86	J886PNC	Iveco Daily 49.10	Carlyle Dailybus 2	B23F	1991	
87	F642NVU	Freight Rover Sherpa	Carlyle Citybus 2	B21F	1988	Ex Daly Bus, Eccles, 1993
88	F288FLG	Iveco Daily 49.10	Northern Counties	B22F	1988	Ex Northern Counties demo, 1990
89	E189CNE	Iveco Daily 49.10	Northern Counties	B22F	1988	Ex GM Buses, 1989
90	VCW598Y	Dennis Lancet SD505	Marshall Camair	B51F	1992	Ex Knotty Bus, Chesterton, 1995
u	PVS830	AEC Routemaster R2RH	Park Royal	H36/28R	1962	Ex London Buses, 1995

Previous Registrations:

F642NVU	F225AKG, SJI1887	OIB1285	A110EPA	SJI1887	PNN771M
LBU607V	YHG16V	PVS830	20CLT		

Livery: Blue and white.

BLUE BUS

Blue Bus and Coach Services Ltd; Yorkshire Blue Bus Company Ltd,
Unit 4a, Locomotion Industrial Estate, Chorley New Road, Horwich, Bolton, BL6 5UE

Depots: Chorley New Road, Horwich and Canal Street, Huddersfield.

1	K1BLU	Dennis Dart 9.8SDL3017	East Lancashire	B40F	1993	
2	M2BLU	Dennis Dart 9.8SDL3043	East Lancashire	B40F	1994	
3	N3BLU	Dennis Dart 9.8SDL3054	Plaxton Pointer	B40F	1995	
4	N4BLU	Dennis Dart 9.8SDL3054	Alexander Dash	B40F	1995	
5	N5BLU	Dennis Dart 9.8SDL3054	Alexander Dash	B40F	1996	
7	OSJ607R	Leyland Leopard PSU3C/3R	Alexander AY	B53F	1976	Ex Leigh HGV Trainig, 1993
9	OEX799W	Leyland Leopard PSU3E/4R	Willowbrook 003	C49F	1980	Ex C & H, Fleetwood, 1991
10	DDM30X	Leyland Leopard PSU3E/4R	Willowbrook 003	C48F	1982	Ex Reynolds, Gwespyr, 1993
11	PRA115R	Leyland Leopard PSU3D/4R	Alexander AT	DP49F	1976	Ex South Lancs, St Helens, 1991
12	LHL246P	Leyland Leopard PSU3C/4R	Alexander AT	DP51F	1976	Ex Graham's, Stoke, 1993
14	PRA114R	Leyland Leopard PSU3D/4R	Alexander AT	DP49F	1976	Ex Vale, Cheetham, 1994
15	YSF99S	Leyland Leopard PSU3E/4R	Alexander AYS	B53F	1977	Ex Fife Scottish, 1993
16	ULS316T	Leyland Leopard PSU3E/4R	Alexander AYS	B53F	1979	Ex Rossendale, 1993
17	YSF97S	Leyland Leopard PSU3D/4R	Alexander AYS	B53F	1977	Ex Fife Scottish, 1992
18	ULS318T	Leyland Leopard PSU3E/4R	Alexander AYS	B53F	1979	Ex Rossendale, 1993
19	ULS329T	Leyland Leopard PSU3E/4R	Alexander AYS	B53F	1979	Ex OK Travel, 1994
20	SCS360M	Leyland Leopard PSU3/3R	Alexander AY	DP49F	1974	Ex Meredith, Malpas, 1993
21	GMS291S	Leyland Leopard PSU3E/4R	Alexander AYS	B53F	1978	Ex OK Travel, 1994
22	ULS322T	Leyland Leopard PSU3E/4R	Alexander AYS	B53F	1979	Ex Rossendale, 1993
24	ULS334T	Leyland Leopard PSU3E/4R	Alexander AYS	B53F	1979	Ex Rossendale, 1993
25	GMS294S	Leyland Leopard PSU3E/4R	Alexander AYS	B53F	1978	Ex Moffat & Williamson, Gauldry, 1994
26	GMS276S	Leyland Leopard PSU3E/4R	Alexander AYS	B53F	1978	Ex Moffat & Williamson, Gauldry, 1994
27	GMS277S	Leyland Leopard PSU3E/4R	Alexander AYS	B53F	1978	Ex Moffat & Williamson, Gauldry, 1994
28	GMS278S	Leyland Leopard PSU3E/4R	Alexander AYS	B53F	1978	Ex OK Travel, 1994
29	GMS299S	Leyland Leopard PSU3E/4R	Alexander AYS	B53F	1978	Ex Moffat & Williamson, Gauldry, 1994
30	GMS310S	Leyland Leopard PSU3E/4R	Alexander AYS	B53F	1978	Ex OK Travel, 1994
31	CWG691V	Leyland Atlantean AN68A/1RSp	Alexander AL	H45/29D	1979	Ex South Yorkshire's Transport, 1991
32	CWG683V	Leyland Atlantean AN68A/1RSp	Alexander AL	H45/29D	1979	Ex South Yorkshire's Transport, 1991
33	JFV313S	Leyland Atlantean AN68A/2R	East Lancashire	H50/36F	1978	Ex Blackpool, 1991
35	EGB51T	Leyland Leopard PSU3E/3R	Alexander AYS	B53F	1979	Ex Kelvin Central, 1995
36	EGB60T	Leyland Leopard PSU3E/3R	Alexander AYS	B53F	1979	Ex Kelvin Central, 1995
37	TSJ57S	Leyland Leopard PSU3D/4R	Alexander AY	B53F	1978	Ex Clydeside, 1995
39	OIB9379	Leyland Atlantean AN68/1R	Alexander AL	H45/36F	1973	Ex Lancaster, 1991
41	VUP514V	Leyland Leopard PSU3E/4R	Duple Dominant	B55F	1980	Ex Vale of Manchester, 1995
42	GLS267S	Leyland Leopard PSU3E/4R	Alexander AT	DP49F	1978	Ex Timeline, 1994
44	OWO234Y	Leyland Leopard PSU3G/2R	Duple Dominant	DP49F	1982	Ex Mayne, Manchester, 1993
45	GLS275S	Leyland Leopard PSU3E/4R	Alexander AT	DP49F	1978	Ex Timeline, 1994
46	M646RCP	DAF DB250RS505	Northern Counties Palatine II	H47/30F	1995	Ex Metrobus, Orpington, 1996
47	M647RCP	DAF DB250RS505	Northern Counties Palatine II	H47/30F	1995	Ex Capital Citybus, 1996
51	LDZ2951	Leyland Leopard PSU3F/4R	East Lancs EL2000 (1992)	B51F	1980	Ex Trent, 1992
52	HIL9152	Leyland Leopard PSU3F/4R	East Lancs EL2000 (1992)	B51F	1982	Ex Trent, 1992
53	WIB4053	Leyland Leopard PSU3F/4R	East Lancs EL2000 (1994)	B51F	1982	Ex National Welsh, 1993
54	WIB4054	Leyland Leopard PSU3F/4R	East Lancs EL2000 (1995)	B51F	1982	Ex United, 1995
61	RJI2161	Volvo B58-56	East Lancs EL2000 (1995)	DP49F	1979	Ex Pride of the Road, 1994
71	LBZ4071	Leyland Tiger TRCTL11/2R	East Lancs EL2000 (1994)	B51F	1981	Ex Burman, Dordon 1994
72	A72VTX	Leyland Tiger TRBTL11/2RP	East Lancashire	B47F	1983	Ex Rhondda, 1994
73	A73VTX	Leyland Tiger TRBTL11/2RP	East Lancashire	B47F	1983	Ex Rhondda, 1994
75	B25ADW	Leyland Tiger TRBTL11/2RP	East Lancashire	DP47F	1984	Ex Rhondda, 1995
81	ASD31T	Leyland Atlantean AN68A/1R	Alexander AL	H45/33F	1979	Ex Western Scottish, 1995
85	KSU851P	Leyland Atlantean AN68A/1R	Alexander AL	H45/31F	1975	Ex ABC Travel, Ainsdale, 1992
89	KSA189P	Leyland Atlantean AN68A/1R	Alexander AL	H45/29D	1976	Ex G & M, Cefn Cribwr, 1992
100	K100BLU	DAF SB3000DKVF601	Van Hool Alizée	C55F	1993	
101	F701ENE	Leyland Tiger TRCL10/3ARZA	Plaxton Paramount 3200 III	C53F	1989	Ex Shearings, 1992
102	F702ENE	Leyland Tiger TRCL10/3ARZA	Plaxton Paramount 3200 III	C53F	1989	Ex Shearings, 1992

Previous Registrations:

HIL9152	SCH150X	LDZ2951	KVO143W	WIB4053	KWO563
K100BLU	K109TCP	OIB9379	NRG162M	WIB4054	LPY460W
LBZ4071	ESU157X, 403EXH, RDV903, HGD802X			XRJI2161	PYD984V

Livery: Blue and cream

Blue Bus of Horwich also operate from a depot in Huddersfield that takes around sixteen buses. One of these is number 1, K1BLU which is a Dennis Dart with East Lancashire bodywork, seen here on service 331. *Roy Marshall*

Pictured in Blackpool on express service X14 is 61, RJI2161, a Volvo B58 which was rebodied by East Lancashire during 1995 and features high-back seating.Two DAF double-deck buses with the latest Northern Counties Palatine II bodywork will enter service from Howrich during February, though for the time being they will retain white liveries. *Paul Wigan*

BORDER

P Cartmell, Heasandford Villa, Queen Victoria Road, Burnley, BB10 2AH

Depots: Bancroft Road, Burnley

5	SKN905R	Leyland National 11351A/1R		DP48F	1977	Ex Maidstone & District, 1995
6	NLG926T	Leyland Leopard PSU5C/4R	Duple Dominant II	C53F	1979	Ex Huxley, Threapwood, 1995
9	VVU229S	Leyland Leopard PSU5A/4R	Duple Dominant II	C55F	1978	Ex Davies, Slough, 1995
15	PTD415S	Leyland Atlantean AN68A/1R	East Lancashire	H43/32F	1977	Ex Rossendale, 1994
16	PTD416S	Leyland Atlantean AN68A/1R	East Lancashire	H43/32F	1977	Ex Rossendale, 1994
21	ABN721V	Leyland Atlantean AN68A/1R	East Lancashire	H43/32F	1979	Ex Rossendale, 1995
31	KSU857P	Leyland Atlantean AN68/1R	Alexander AL	H45/31F	1976	Ex Rossendale, 1993
39	PRJ485R	Daimler Fleetline CRG6LXB	Northern Counties	H43/32F	1976	Ex Rossendale, 1995
40	KSJ940P	Leyland Leopard PSU3C/4R	Alexander AYS	B53F	1976	Ex Western Scottish, 1993
44	SRJ744R	Leyland Atlantean AN68A/1R	Northern Counties	H43/32F	1977	Ex Yorkshire Rider, 1993
74	RRC485R	Leyland Leopard PSU3C/4R	Plaxton Supreme III Express	C53F	1976	Ex Hyndburn, 1991
81	YCD81T	Leyland National 11351A/1R		B48F	1978	Ex Sovereign, 1995
113	CAU113T	Leyland Fleetline FE30ALR	Northern Counties	H44/31F	1979	Ex Nottingham, 1994
155	NRG155M	Leyland Atlantean AN68/1R	Alexander AL	H45/36F	1974	Ex Shaw Hadwin, 1995
160	NRG160M	Leyland Atlantean AN68/1R	Alexander AL	H45/36F	1974	Ex Shaw Hadwin, 1995
161	NRG161M	Leyland Atlantean AN68/1R	Alexander AL	H45/36F	1974	Ex Blue Bus, Horwich, 1993
165	NRG165M	Leyland Atlantean AN68/1R	Alexander AL	H45/36F	1974	Ex Blue Bus, Horwich, 1993
167	NRG167M	Leyland Atlantean AN68/1R	Alexander AL	H45/36F	1974	Ex Blue Bus, Horwich, 1993
172	PJI9172	Leyland Leopard PSU3G/4R	Eastern Coach Works B51	DP53F	1982	Ex Rossendale, 1995
173	PJI9173	Leyland Leopard PSU3G/4R	Eastern Coach Works B51	DP53F	1982	Ex Rossendale, 1994
174	PJI9174	Leyland Leopard PSU3G/4R	Eastern Coach Works B51	DP53F	1982	Ex Rossendale, 1994
178	UDT178S	Leyland Atlantean AN68A/1R	East Lancashire	H45/31F	1978	Ex Mancunian, Manchester, 1994
182	VOY182X	Leyland Tiger TRCTL11/2R	Plaxton Viewmaster IV Exp	C53F	1981	Ex British Airways, 1995
309	CFS264S	Leyland Leopard PSU5B/4R	Plaxton Supreme III	C53F	1978	Ex Rossendale, 1994
311	LCB652P	Leyland Leopard PSU5A/4RT	Plaxton Supreme III	C53F	1976	Ex Rossendale, 1993
1788	OEM788S	Leyland Atlantean AN68/1R	MCW	H43/32F	1978	Ex Merseybus, 1993
1811	PKA725S	Leyland Atlantean AN68/1R	MCW	H43/32F	1978	Ex Merseybus, 1993

Previous Registrations:

NLG926T	BWE197T, HIL3932	PJI9173	WEX827X
PJI9172	JNH183Y, PJI9175, WEC504Y	PJI9174	XPW876X

Livery: Red and white

Border is, as the name suggests, an operation established on the Yorkshire-Lancashire border with many vehicles acquired from the Rossendale fleet. Latterly from the Yorkshire side of the border is 44, SRJ744R, although this Northern Counties-bodied Atlantean was new to Greater Manchester in 1977.
Roy Marshall

BORDERBUS

GD, PB & AG Palmer, Borderbus Garage, Church Street, Caldewgate, Carlisle, CA2 5TJ

FTV10L	Volvo B58-56	Duple Dominant	C51F	1973	Ex Escourt Coaches, Enfield, 1988
GAS656N	Volvo B58-56	Duple Dominant	C53F	1974	Ex Watson's Tours, Annfield Plain, 1988
OFJ870	Volvo B58-56	Duple Dominant II	C53F	1979	Ex Grant's Coaches, Balloch, 1992
YDN921V	Volvo B58-56	Duple Dominant II	C55FT	1980	Ex K&B, Clifton, 1992
USU641	Volvo B58-61	Plaxton Supreme	C57F	1980	Ex Cumbria Coaches, 1993
USU643	Volvo B58-61	Duple Dominant II	C53F	1981	Ex Cumbria Coaches, 1993
SMK828	Volvo B10M-61	Duple Dominant IV	C57F	1981	Ex Scottish Citylink, 1995
USU642	Volvo B10M-61	Duple Dominant II	C57F	1983	Ex Brown, Crawley, 1993
CGV159	Van Hool T813	Van Hool Alicron	C40FT	1983	Ex K-Line, Kirkburton, 1994
513ERH	Volvo B10M-61	Berkhof Everset 365	C49FT	1983	Ex Waddon, Bedwas, 1994
ESK978	Hestair Duple 425	Duple 425	C55FT	1985	Ex Cumbria Coaches, 1993

Previous Registrations:

513ERH	BDV863Y, 4384VT, 467VT, PMB61Y, 467VT, XUJ427Y, ESK985, USK373Y (9 index marks)		
CGV159	FDU5Y	USU641	MDS238V
ESK978	JPY606, C326VNP	USU642	MSU594Y, YDL435, CYJ365Y
OFJ870	MSF359T	USU643	ASM377W
SMK828	NCS115W, VLT154, WGB816W		

Border operate a Leyland Tiger with uncommon Plaxton Viewmaster Express bodywork as its 182, VOY182X. This was previously with British Airways and it is seen here in their colours shortly after its acquisition. *Paul Wigan*

BROWNRIGGS

S H Brownrigg Ltd, 53 Main Street, Egremont, Cumbria, CA22 2DB

UTF736M	Leyland Leopard PSU3B/4R	Duple Dominant	C49F	1974	Ex Cumberland, 1989
XBF63S	Leyland Leopard PSU3E/4R	Duple Dominant	C53F	1978	Ex Mayne, Manchester, 1987
AHN394T	Leyland Leopard PSU3E/4R	Plaxton Supreme IV Express	DP55F	1979	Ex East Midland, 1995
KRN104T	Leyland Leopard PSU3E/4R	Duple Dominant II Express	C47F	1978	Ex Cumberland, 1993
KGF306T	Leyland Leopard PSU5C/4R	Plaxton Supreme IV	C55F	1979	Ex Cumberland, 1992
JND259V	Leyland Leopard PSU5C/4R	Duple Dominant II	C53F	1980	Ex Ribble, 1991
JND264V	Leyland Leopard PSU5C/4R	Duple Dominant II	C53F	1980	Ex Ribble, 1991
GRM623V	Leyland Leopard PSU3E/4R	Duple Dominant II Express	C49F	1980	Ex Cumberland, 1992
PWK7W	Leyland Leopard PSU3F/5R	Duple Dominant II	C53F	1981	Ex Robinsons, Gt Harwood, 1986
WIB1366	Volvo B10M-61	Van Hool Alizée	C48F	1981	Ex Cumberland, 1995
WIB1364	Volvo B10M-61	Van Hool Alizée	C48F	1982	Ex Cumberland, 1995
318EVO	Leyland Tiger TRCTL11/3R	Plaxton Paramount 3500	C49FT	1984	Ex Moxon, Oldcotes, 1989
563UM	Leyland Royal Tiger RTC	Leyland Doyen	C49FT	1986	Ex East Midland, 1995
D405FRV	Iveco Daily 49.10	Robin Hood City Nippy	B19F	1987	Ex Ribble, 1993
E71XKW	Mercedes-Benz 609D	Reeve Burgess	C19F	1988	Ex East Midland, 1995
E632VBA	Freight Rover Sherpa	Freight Rover	M11	1988	Ex private owner, 1994
E754CHH	MCW MetroRider MF150/29	MCW	C25F	1988	
G915KWF	Iveco Daily 49.10	Reeve Burgess Beaver	B25F	1989	Ex East Midland, 1995
H282WHH	Ford Transit VE6	Ford	M12	1991	
H142SAO	Ford Transit VE6	Ford	M8	1991	Ex Lakeland Self Drive, 1995
H149SAO	Ford Transit VE6	Ford	M12	1991	Ex Lakeland Self Drive, 1995

Livery: White and green

Previous Registrations:

318EVO	A443DTO, 5711MT, A992ERB	WIB1264	RUT842
563UM	RUT842	WIB1366	TGD766W, VLF578

Two Leyland Leopards with Duple Dominant II bodywork are seen at Whitehaven on school duty for Brownriggs. These are KRN104T and GRM623V being new to Ribble and Cumberland respectively. The latest arrivals have also come from a Stagecoach operator, this time East Midland. Three of the coaches were taken into East Midland stock following its acquisition of other operators in the area.
Brian Pritchard

R BULLOCK

R Bullock & Co (Transport) Ltd, Commercial Garage, Stockport Road,
Cheadle, SK8 2AG.

	Reg	Type	Body	Seating	Year	Notes
	KJA299G	Bristol RESL6G	Marshall	B45F	1969	Ex Greater Manchester, 1984
	YNA354M	Daimler Fleetline CRG6LXB	Northern Counties	H43/32F	1973	Ex Finglands, Manchester, 1994
u	BNE736N	Daimler Fleetline CRG6LXB	Northern Counties	H43/32F	1974	Ex G M Buses, 1987
	HFM804N	Leyland Leopard PSU5/4R	Plaxton Elite III	C57F	1978	
u	GFJ660N	Leyland National 11351/2R		B..D	1975	Ex Manchester Handling, Wythenshaw, 1994
	JIL8214	Daimler Fleetline CRL6	Park Royal	H44/27D	1976	Ex Grimsby-Cleethorpes, 1991
	JIL8204	Leyland Fleetline FE30ALR	MCW	H44/24D	1976	Ex Network Express, Maidenhead, 1993
	JIL8205	Leyland Fleetline FE30AGR	Roe	H43/30F	1976	Ex Derby, 1990
	JIL8202	Leyland Fleetline FE30AGR	Northern Counties	H43/31F	1977	Ex Yorkshire Rider, 1990
	JIL8303	Leyland Fleetline FE30AGR	Eastern Coach Works	H43/31F	1977	Ex Wealden, Five Oak Green, 1991
	JIL8206	Leyland Fleetline FE30ALR	Park Royal	H44/27F	1977	Ex London Buses, 1991
	JIL8207	Leyland Fleetline FE30ALR	MCW	H44/29F	1978	Ex London Buses, 1991
	JIL8208	Leyland Fleetline FE30ALR	Park Royal	H44/32F	1978	Ex London Buses, 1991
	JIL8209	Leyland Fleetline FE30AGR	Northern Counties	H44/33F	1978	Ex PMT, 1989
	JIL8210	Leyland Fleetline FE30AGR	Roe	H43/33F	1978	Ex Yorkshire Rider, 1990
	OJD457R	Leyland Fleetline FE30ALR Sp	MCW	H44/24D	1979	Ex Network Express, Maidenhead, 1993
	JIL8212	Leyland National 10351A/2R		B36D	1978	Ex London Buses, 1990
	SWH271T	AEC Reliance 6U2R	Duple Dominant II Express	C53F	1979	Ex Bibby, Ingleton, 1994
	JIL8211	Leyland Fleetline FE30AGR	Eastern Coach Works	H43/32F	1979	Ex Clydeside 2000, 1993
	JIL8213	Leyland Fleetline FE30AGR	Northern Counties	H44/33F	1980	Ex PMT, 1989
	BYW362V	Leyland National 10351A/2R		B44F	1980	Ex Rose Hill, Marple, 1994
	BUI1675	Leyland Leopard PSU3F/4R	East Lancashire (1993)	B51F	1981	Ex Go-Ahead Northern, 1990
	JIL8215	MCW Metrobus DR102/28	Alexander RL	H45/33F	1982	Ex BTS, Borehamwood, 1992
	JIL8216	MCW Metrobus DR102/28	Alexander RL	H45/33F	1982	Ex BTS, Borehamwood, 1992
	JIL8217	MCW Metrobus DR102/24	Alexander RL	H45/33F	1982	Ex BTS, Borehamwood, 1992
	JFT413X	Scania BR112DH	Alexander RH	H47/31F	1982	Ex Busways, 1995
	JFT414X	Scania BR112DH	Alexander RH	H47/31F	1982	Ex Busways, 1995
	BUI1424	Dennis Dorchester SDA805	Berkhof Esprite 350	C53F	1983	Ex Berkhof demonstrator, 1984
	BUI1610	Dennis Dorchester SDA805	Plaxton Paramount 3200	C57F	1984	
	A301JFA	Leyland National 2 NL116HLXCT/1R		DP47F	1984	Ex Victoria Travel, Haydock, 1994
	A303JFA	Leyland National 2 NL116HLXCT/1R		DP47F	1984	Ex Victoria Travel, Haydock, 1994
	BUI1133	Dennis Dorchester SDA805	Plaxton Paramount 3200	C57F	1985	
	BUI1484	Leyland Tiger TRCLXCT/3RZ	Plaxton P'mount 3500(1983)	C51FT	1986	
	C281BBP	Dennis Dominator DDA1008	East Lancashire	H45/31F	1986	Ex Southampton Citybus, 1991
	C282BBP	Dennis Dominator DDA1008	East Lancashire	H45/31F	1986	Ex Southampton Citybus, 1991
	C283BBP	Dennis Dominator DDA1008	East Lancashire	H45/31F	1986	Ex Southampton Citybus, 1991
	C284BBP	Dennis Dominator DDA1008	East Lancashire	H45/31F	1986	Ex Southampton Citybus, 1991
	C285BBP	Leyland Olympian ONLXB/1R	East Lancashire	DPH43/27F	1986	Ex Southampton Citybus, 1992

R Bullock operates three MCW Metrobuses with Alexander bodywork new to Midland Scottish in 1982. These were taken into stock from BTS of Borehamwood and have since been re-registered in the JIL series. Pictured passing the Arndale centre in Manchester is ULS616X, now JIL8215.
Ralph Stevens

Busways sold its two examples of the Scania BR112DH chassis during 1995, both being purchased by R Bullock. Now in full livery, and seen heading out of Manchester along Princess Street is JFT414X. Only 37 BR112DHs were imported into the UK and of these 29 went to Newport Transport. *Paul Wigan*

D52RJA	Iveco Daily 49.10	Robin Hood City Nippy	B19F	1987	Ex Manchester Airport, 1995
D53RJA	Iveco Daily 49.10	Robin Hood City Nippy	B19F	1987	Ex Manchester Airport, 1995
D54RJA	Iveco Daily 49.10	Robin Hood City Nippy	B19F	1987	Ex Manchester Airport, 1995
BUI1300	Ford R1014	Plaxton Paramount 3200 II	C35FT	1987	
E419YLG	Mercedes-Benz 609D	Made-to-Measure (1991)	C26F	1987	Ex van, 1991
E758OWY	Mercedes-Benz 709D	Made-to-Measure (1993)	B20F	1988	Ex van, 1993
E393SWX	Mercedes-Benz 811D	Olympus (1994)	B21F	1988	Ex van, 1994
F452FDB	Leyland Tiger TRBTL11/2RP	Duple 300	DP55F	1989	
F926HAL	Ford Transit VE6	Steedrive	M8	1989	Ex private owner, 1995
G481HNP	Mercedes-Benz 811D	Olympus (1994)	B23F	1990	Ex van, 1994
G423SNF	Leyland Tiger TRBTL11/2RP	Duple 300	DP55F	1990	
H10BUL	Volvo B10M-60	Plaxton Paramount 3500 III	C53F	1991	Ex Park's, 1992
J6GFM	Mercedes-Benz 609D	Olympus	DP24F	1992	Ex van, 1994
J200BUL	Leyland Tiger TRCL10/3ARZA	Plaxton Paramount 3200 III	C57F	1991	
J400BUL	Volvo B10M-60	Plaxton Paramount 3500 III	C53F	1992	
K600BUL	Volvo B10M-60	Plaxton Paramount 3200 III	C53F	1993	
K700BUL	Dennis Javelin 11SDA1906	Duple 320	C53F	1993	
L10BUL	Leyland Olympian ON2R50C13Z4	East Lancashire	H45/31F	1993	
L20BUL	Leyland Olympian ON2R50C13Z4	East Lancashire	H45/31F	1993	
L800BUL	Volvo B10M-60	Van Hool Alizée	C51FT	1994	
M781NBA	Volvo B10M-62	Caetano Algarve II	C53F	1994	
M782NBA	Dennis Javelin 12SDA2131	Plaxton Premiére 320	C57F	1995	
M783NBA	Dennis Javelin 12SDA2131	Plaxton Premiére 320	C53F	1995	
M784NBA	Dennis Javelin 12SDA2131	Plaxton Premiére 320	C57F	1995	
M785NBA	Dennis Javelin 12SDA2131	Plaxton Premiére 320	C57F	1995	
M788NBA	Volvo Olympian YN2RV18Z4	East Lancashire	H45/30F	1995	
M789NBA	Volvo Olympian YN2RV18Z4	East Lancashire	H45/30F	1995	
M790NBA	Volvo Olympian YN2RC16Z5	East Lancashire	H45/31F	1994	
N620XBU	Volvo B10M-62	Caetano Algarve II	C53FT	1995	
N630XBU	Scania L113CRL	Wright Axcess-Ultralow	B43F	1996	
N631XBU	Scania L113CRL	Wright Axcess-Ultralow	B42F	1996	
N632XBU	Scania L113CRL	Wright Axcess-Ultralow	B42F	1996	
N633XBU	Scania L113CRL	Wright Axcess-Ultralow	B42F	1996	

Once one of six Leyland National 2s in the PMT fleet, A301JFA is now one of two now operating with R Bullock. Both are fitted with high-back seating and are the only full-length single-deck buses in the fleet though they have recently been joined by four Scania L113s with Wrights Axcess-Ultralow bodywork.
Richard Godfrey

The latest double-deck buses with R Bullock are three Volvo Olympians with East Lancashire bodywork. Shown here is M790NBA.
Richard Godfrey

Previous Registrations:

BUI1133	B593SNC	JIL8203	OHR182R	JIL8212	AYR347T
BUI1300	D391BNR	JIL8204	OJD249R	JIL8213	LVT699V
BUI1424	KNO224Y	JIL8205	RCH282R	JIL8214	KUC216P
BUI1484	C33EVM	JIL8206	THX539S	JIL8215	ULS616X
BUI1610	A530OBU	JIL8207	THX272S	JIL8216	ULS617X
BUI1675	FNL687W	JIL8208	THX563S	JIL8217	CKS385X
H10BUL	H838AHS	JIL8209	AFA489S	K600BUL	K433ANE
J400BUL	J729KBC	JIL8210	WUM107S	K700BUL	K326ANC
JIL8202	SUA9R	JIL8211	ULS665T	SWH271T	YPL88T, BIB7667

Livery: Red (buses); white, red and gold (coaches)

BURNLEY & PENDLE

Burnley & Pendle Transport Co Ltd; Vicount Central Ltd,
Queensgate, Colne Road, Burnley, Lancashire, BB10 1HH

1	OIJ201	Aüwaerter Neoplan N116/3	Aüwaerter Cityliner	C48FT	1991	Ex Parry, Cheslyn Hay, 1994
2	GSU552	Volvo B10M-61	Jonckheere Jubilee P50	C49F	1986	
3	GSU553	Volvo B10M-61	Jonckheere Jubilee P50	C49F	1986	
7	XSU907	Volvo C10M-70	Ramseier & Jenzer	C49FT	1985	Ex Park's, 1990
8	XSU908	Volvo C10M-70	Ramseier & Jenzer	C49FT	1985	Ex Park's, 1990
9	XSU909	Volvo B10M-61	Jonckheere Jubilee P50	C51FT	1986	Ex Parry, Cheslyn Hay, 1990
10	XSU910	Volvo B10M-61	Jonckheere Jubilee P50	C49FT	1987	Ex Parry, Cheslyn Hay, 1990
11	HXI311	Volvo B10M-61	Jonckheere Jubilee P50	C49FT	1988	Ex Parry, Cheslyn Hay, 1991
12	NXI812	Volvo B10MT-53	Van Hool Alizée	C48FT	1989	Ex Rothwell, Heywood, 1991
13	GXI613	Volvo B10MT-50	Plaxton Paramount 4000RS	CH53/12DT	1989	Ex Flight's, 1992
14	NXI414	Volvo B10MT-53	Jonckheere Jubilee P95	CH54/13DT	1985	Ex Flight's, 1988
15	K815TJU	Toyota HDB30R	Caetano Optimo	C21F	1992	
16	F94AEL	Volvo B10MT-53	Van Hool Astral	C52/13FT	1989	Ex Excelsior, 1995

17-23		Volvo Citybus B10M-55		Alexander PS		B51F	1991

17	H617ACK	19	H619ACK	21	H621ACK	22	H622ACK	23	H623ACK
18	H618ACK	20	H620ACK						

24	J24MCW	Volvo Citybus B10M-50	East Lancashire EL2000	B45F	1992
25	J25MCW	Volvo Citybus B10M-50	East Lancashire EL2000	B45F	1992
26	K26WBV	Volvo Citybus B10M-50	East Lancashire EL2000	B45F	1993
27	K27WBV	Volvo Citybus B10M-50	East Lancashire EL2000	B45F	1993

30-43		Leyland Leopard PSU4E/4R		East Lancashire		B47F	1978-80

30	MFV30T	33	MFV33T	36	MFV36T	39	DBV39W	42	DBV42W
31	MFV31T	34	MFV34T	37	MFV37T	40	DBV40W	43	DBV43W
32	MFV32T	35	MFV35T	38	DBV38W	41	DBV41W		

44-50		Leyland National 2 NL116L11/1R				B52F	1980

44	XRN44V	46	XRN46V	48	XRN48V	49	XRN49V	50	XRN50V
45	XRN45V	47	XRN47V						

51	GSU551	Leyland Tiger TRCTL11/3R	Plaxton Paramount 3500	C53F	1983	
54	GSU554	Leyland Tiger TRCTL11/3R	Duple Laser 1	C53F	1983	Ex GM Buses, 1989
55	XSU905	Leyland Tiger TRCTL11/3R	Duple Laser 1	C55F	1983	Ex GM Buses, 1989
56	XSU906	Mercedes-Benz 709D	Reeve Burgess Beaver	C19F	1987	
57	VFV7V	Leyland Leopard PSU3E/4R	Duple Dominant II	C53F	1979	

61-66		Volvo Citybus B10M-55		Alexander P		DP53F*	1988	*61 is B53F

61	E61JFV	63	E63JFV	64	E64JFV	65	E65JFV	66	E66JFV
62	E62JFV								

67	G67PFR	Volvo Citybus B10M-55	East Lancashire EL2000	B51F	1990	
68	G68PFR	Volvo Citybus B10M-55	East Lancashire EL2000	B51F	1990	
69	BUH239V	Leyland National 2 NL106L11/1R		B44F	1980	Ex National Welsh, 1988
70	BUH240V	Leyland National 2 NL106L11/1R		B44F	1980	Ex National Welsh, 1989
71	BUH241V	Leyland National 2 NL106L11/1R		B44F	1980	Ex National Welsh, 1988
72	FUH32V	Leyland National 2 NL116L11/1R		B49F	1980	Ex Taff Ely, 1988
73	FUH33V	Leyland National 2 NL116L11/1R		B49F	1980	Ex Taff Ely, 1988
74	FUH34V	Leyland National 2 NL116L11/1R		B49F	1980	Ex Taff Ely, 1988
78	H78CFV	Mercedes-Benz 811D	Alexander AM	B31F	1991	
79	H79CFV	Mercedes-Benz 811D	Alexander AM	B31F	1991	
80	C80OCW	Mercedes-Benz L608D	Reeve Burgess	B20F	1986	

**Opposite: Two examples of the Volvo B10M with Alexander bodywork in the Burnley & Pendle fleet.
The upper picture shows 64, E64JFV with a P-type single-deck body seen on service 21 to Padiham.
The lower picture shows 101, E101JFV, the first of fifteen double-decks with RV-type bodies. Four
of these have high-back seating and are often used, as seen here, for the longer services such as
The Blackpool Flyer.** *Paul Wigan*

Above: **Minibuses at Burnley & Pendle operate in a livery of red and yellow with Whizzard titles - a name conjured up, no doubt, by the infamous Pendle witch. Seen near Bury interchange is 179, L179KHG.**
Roy Marshall

East Lancashire bodywork was chosen for the latter Volvo B10M buses. Noteworthy is the diagonal radiator bar symbolic of the Volvo product. Pictured midway through a change of destination display is 26, K26WBV.
Mike Fowler

81	D81UFV	Mercedes-Benz L608D	Sparshatts	B20F	1986
82	D82UFV	Mercedes-Benz L608D	Sparshatts	B20F	1986
83	D83UFV	Mercedes-Benz L608D	Sparshatts	B20F	1986
84	E84HRN	Mercedes-Benz 709D	Robin Hood	B29F	1987

85-90
Mercedes-Benz 811D — Robin Hood — B29F — 1987-88

85	E85HRN	87	E87HRN	88	E88HRN	89	E89HRN	90	E90JHG
86	E86HRN								

91	E91LBV	Mercedes-Benz 709D	Alexander AM	B25F	1988
92	E92LHG	Mercedes-Benz 709D	Alexander AM	B25F	1988
93	E93LHG	Mercedes-Benz 709D	Alexander AM	B25F	1988
94	E94LHG	Mercedes-Benz 709D	Alexander AM	B25F	1988
95	XFK305	Mercedes-Benz 709D	Reeve Burgess Beaver	DP25F	1988
96	G96MRN	Mercedes-Benz 811D	Reeve Burgess Beaver	B31F	1990
97	G97MRN	Mercedes-Benz 811D	Reeve Burgess Beaver	B31F	1990
98	G98PCK	Mercedes-Benz 811D	Reeve Burgess Beaver	B31F	1990
99	G99PCK	Mercedes-Benz 709D	Reeve Burgess Beaver	B23F	1990
101	E101JFV	Volvo Citybus B10M-50	Alexander RV	DPH47/35F	1988
102	E102JFV	Volvo Citybus B10M-50	Alexander RV	DPH47/35F	1988

103-112
Volvo Citybus B10M-50 — Alexander RV — H47/37F — 1989

103	F103XCW	105	F105XCW	107	F107XCW	109	F109XCW	111	F111XCW
104	F104XCW	106	F106XCW	108	F108XCW	110	F110XCW	112	F112XCW

113	H113ABV	Volvo Citybus B10M-50	Alexander RV	H47/37F	1991
114	H114ABV	Volvo Citybus B10M-50	Alexander RV	DPH47/35F	1991
115	H115ABV	Volvo Citybus B10M-50	Alexander RV	DPH47/35F	1991

166-174
Bristol VRT/SL3/6LXB — Eastern Coach Works — H43/31F — 1978

166	FFR166S	168	FFR168S	172	FFR172S	173	FFR173S	174	FFR174S
167	FFR167S								

175	K75XCW	Optare MetroRider MR03	Optare	B29F	1993
176	J176MCW	Optare MetroRider MR09	Optare	B23F	1992
177	J177MCW	Optare MetroRider MR09	Optare	B23F	1992
178	L178KHG	Optare MetroRider MR17	Optare	B29F	1994
179	L179KHG	Optare MetroRider MR17	Optare	B29F	1994

193-205
Bristol VRT/LL3/6LXB — Alexander AL — H49/35F — 1977 — Ex Tayside, 1982

193	OSR193R	195	OSR195R	196	OSR196R	197	OSR197R	205	OSR205R

Previous Registrations:

F94AEL	XEL14	HXI311	E508KNV	XSU906	E206FRN
GSU551	A201MFR	NXI414	B708EOF, HHG25	XSU907	C641KDS
GSU552	D202VBV	NXI812	G827UMU	XSU908	C661KDS
GSU553	D203VBV	OIJ201	H166RHE	XSU909	D111BNV
GSU554	ANA52Y	XFK305	F95VBV	XSU910	E507KNV
GXI613	F705COA	XSU905	ANA53Y, XFK305		

Livery: Crimson and cream; white grey and maroon (Viscount Central) 1-3, 7-16, 51/4/5

BU-VAL

M Bull, Unit 5, Paragon Industrial Estate, Smithybridge, Littleborough, OL15 8QF

D699THF	Renault-Dodge S56	Alexander AM	B23F	1987	Ex Merseybus, 1994
D979TKC	Renault-Dodge S56	Alexander AM	B23F	1987	Ex Merseybus, 1994
E181CNE	Iveco Daily 49.10	Northern Counties	B22F	1988	Ex GM Buses, 1989
E186CNE	Iveco Daily 49.10	Northern Counties	B22F	1988	Ex GM Buses, 1989
E187CNE	Iveco Daily 49.10	Northern Counties	B22F	1988	Ex GM Buses, 1989
E238UWR	MCW MetroRider MF150/80	MCW	B23F	1988	Ex Yorkshire Rider, 1995
E245UWR	MCW MetroRider MF150/80	MCW	B23F	1988	Ex Yorkshire Rider, 1995
E253UWR	MCW MetroRider MF150/80	MCW	B23F	1988	Ex Yorkshire Rider, 1995
E254UWR	MCW MetroRider MF150/80	MCW	B23F	1988	Ex Yorkshire Rider, 1995
E255UWR	MCW MetroRider MF150/80	MCW	B23F	1988	Ex Yorkshire Rider, 1995
E256UWR	MCW MetroRider MF150/80	MCW	B23F	1988	Ex Yorkshire Rider, 1995
E257UWR	MCW MetroRider MF150/80	MCW	B23F	1988	Ex Yorkshire Rider, 1995
F226FNE	Iveco Daily 49.10	Northern Counties	B24F	1988	
F241FNE	Iveco Daily 49.10	Northern Counties	B22F	1988	
F243FNE	Iveco Daily 49.10	Northern Counties	B22F	1988	
L803FBA	Iveco TurboDaily 59.12	Mellor	B27F	1994	
L804FBA	Iveco TurboDaily 59.12	Mellor	B27F	1994	

Livery: Red, white and grey.

Bu-Val have recently acquired several MCW Metrobuses from Yorkshire Rider. Shown in Rochdale while heading for the Wardle district is E253UWR.

CITY NIPPY

P V Walsh (J P Executive Travel), Cromer Garage, John Lee Fold,
Middleton, Rochdale, M24

C875JMB	Mercedes-Benz 307D	Mercedes-Benz	M12	1986	Ex Hawkes, Darley Abbey, 1995
D337VBB	Mercedes-Benz 307D	Mercedes-Benz	M12	1987	
LIL2830	Renault-Dodge S56	Northern Counties	B22F	1987	Ex Stagecoach South, 1993
LIL2831	Renault-Dodge S56	Northern Counties	B22F	1987	Ex Stagecoach South, 1993
E216WVM	Iveco Daily 49.10	Northern Counties	B22F	1988	Ex NCounties demonstrator, 1988
E357KPO	Iveco Daily 49.10	Robin Hood City Nippy	B25F	1988	
F726DNB	Iveco Daily 49.10	Robin Hood City Nippy	B25F	1988	
F638HVU	Renault-Dodge S56	Northern Counties	B22F	1988	
F639HVU	Renault-Dodge S56	Northern Counties	B22F	1988	
G888TJA	Mercedes-Benz 709D	Phoenix	B29F	1990	
G889TJA	Mercedes-Benz 709D	Phoenix	B29F	1990	
JIL5229	Mercedes-Benz 609D	Reeve Burgess Beaver	DP19F	1988	Ex North Western, 1994
G139LRM	Mercedes-Benz 609D	Reeve Burgess Beaver	DP19F	1988	Ex North Western, 1994
G140LRM	Mercedes-Benz 609D	Reeve Burgess Beaver	DP19F	1988	Ex North Western, 1995
G143LRM	Mercedes-Benz 609D	Reeve Burgess Beaver	DP19F	1988	Ex North Western, 1994
H147CBU	Mercedes-Benz 709D	Phoenix	B29F	1991	
H691FNB	Mercedes-Benz 709D	Phoenix	B29F	1991	
H84PTG	Mercedes-Benz 811D	Optare StarRider	B33F	1991	Ex Wall's, Sharston, 1995
J685PJA	Mercedes-Benz 609D	Made-to-Measure	B21F	1992	
J686PJA	Mercedes-Benz 609D	Made-to-Measure	B21F	1992	
J9JPT	Mercedes-Benz 609D	Made-to-Measure	B24F	1992	
J20JPT	Mercedes-Benz 609D	Made-to-Measure	B21F	1992	
K84UND	Mercedes-Benz 609D	Made-to-Measure	B21F	1992	
K123AJA	Mercedes-Benz 709D	Wright	B27F	1993	
L196DVM	Mercedes-Benz 709D	Wright	B27F	1993	
L502FVU	Mercedes-Benz 709D	Marshall C19	DP27F	1994	
M2JPT	Mercedes-Benz 709D	Marshall C19	B27F	1994	
M7JPT	Mercedes-Benz 709D	Marshall C19	B27F	1995	
M8JPT	Mercedes-Benz 709D	Marshall C19	B27F	1995	

Previous Registrations:

J19JPT	J9JPT, J614PNE	JIL5229	F120KAO	LIL2831	E408EPE
J20JPT	J615PNE	LIL2830	E406EPE		

Livery: Blue and silver

Middleton bus station is the location of this view of City Nippy M2JPT. Four of the Marshall C19 model are operated, the first being equipped with high-back seating.
Paul Wigan

CUMBERLAND

Cumberland Motor Services, PO Box 17, Tangier Street, Whitehaven,
Cumbria, CA28 7XF

Depots : Walney Road, Barrow; Willowholme Industrial Estate, Carlisle; Station Road, Kendal; and Lillyhall, Workington.
Outstations Ambleside, Appleby, Askam, Grange, Haverthwaite, Millom, Orton, Penrith, Sedbergh and Ulverston.

1-15

| | | | | | | | | B23F | 1995 |

Mercedes-Benz 709D   Alexander Sprint   B23F   1995

1	N201UHH	4	N204UHH	7	N207UHH	10	N210UHH	13	N213UHH
2	N202UHH	5	N205UHH	8	N208UHH	11	N211UHH	14	N214UHH
3	N203UHH	6	N206UHH	9	N209UHH	12	N212UHH	15	N215UHH

35-46

Mercedes-Benz L608D   Reeve Burgess   B20F   1986-87

35	D35UAO	37	D37UAO	39	D39UAO	43	D43UAO	45	D45UAO
36	D36UAO	38	D38UAO	42	D42UAO	44	D44UAO	46	D46UAO

47-53

Mercedes-Benz 709D   Alexander Sprint   B25F   1988   51-53 ex Hampshire Bus, 1989

47	E47CHH	49	E49CHH	51	E510PVV	52	E511PVV	53	E512PVV
48	E48CHH	50	E50CHH						

54-70

Mercedes-Benz 709D   Alexander Sprint   B23F*   1990-91   55-70 ex Magicbus, 1990-91
*57-9/61-4 are B25F

54	G178PAO	58	G268TSL	61	G263TSL	64	G266TSL	67	G295TSL
55	G299TSL	59	G269TSL	62	G264TSL	65	G297TSL	68	G294TSL
56	G300TSL	60	G296TSL	63	G265TSL	66	G298TSL	70	G293TSL
57	G267TSL								

71-78

Mercedes-Benz 709D   Alexander Sprint   B25F   1993

71	K871GHH	73	K873GHH	75	K875GHH	77	K877GHH	78	K878GHH
72	K872GHH	74	K874GHH	76	K876GHH				

79-86

Mercedes-Benz 709D   Alexander Sprint   B25F   1993   Ex Ribble, 1994

79	K626UFR	81	K622UFR	83	K121XHG	85	L123DRN	86	K113XHG
80	K623UFR	82	K114XHG	84	L126DRN				

Cumberland have made a considerable effort to attract the tourist, and in particular the car user as conservationists fight to protect the English Lakeland. Providing a regular service through the main link are Volvo Olympians, typified by 1027, J127XHH seen in Ambleside.
Tony Wilson

Captured on film in St Helens is Cumberland 125, L125NAO. One of eight National Expressliner 2s in the Cumberland fleet these differ from the Plaxton Premiére 350 in having features specifically built for National Express. *Paul Wigan*

101	109DRM	Leyland Tiger TRCTL11/2R	Duple Laser	C50F	1984	
102	A102DAO	Leyland Tiger TRCTL11/2R	Duple Laser	C50F	1984	
103	B103HAO	Leyland Tiger TRCTL11/3RH	Duple Laser 2	C50F	1984	
105	B105HAO	Leyland Tiger TRCTL11/3RH	Duple Laser 2	C53F	1984	
106	B106HAO	Leyland Tiger TRCTL11/3RH	Duple Laser 2	C49FT	1984	
107	TCK841	Leyland Tiger TRCTL11/3RH	Duple Laser 2	C46FT	1984	
109	WLT706	Leyland Tiger TRCTL11/3RH	Plaxton Paramount 3500 II	C48FT	1986	
110	WLT824	Leyland Tiger TRCTL11/3RH	Plaxton Paramount 3500 II	C46FT	1986	
111	VRR447	Leyland Tiger TRCTL11/3RH	Plaxton Paramount 3500 II	C48FT	1985	Ex Hampshire Bus, 1988
114	PSU787	Leyland Tiger TRCTL11/3RZ	Duple Caribbean 2	C49FT	1986	Ex East Midland, 1995
120	J120AHH	Volvo B10M-60	Plaxton Expressliner	C46FT	1991	
121	J121AHH	Volvo B10M-60	Plaxton Expressliner	C46FT	1991	
125	L125NAO	Volvo B10M-62	Plaxton Expressliner 2	C46FT	1994	
126	L126NAO	Volvo B10M-62	Plaxton Expressliner 2	C46FT	1994	
127	L127NAO	Volvo B10M-62	Plaxton Expressliner 2	C46FT	1994	
128	N128VAO	Volvo B10M-62	Plaxton Expressliner 2	C44FT	1995	
129	N129VAO	Volvo B10M-62	Plaxton Expressliner 2	C44FT	1995	
130	N130VAO	Volvo B10M-62	Plaxton Expressliner 2	C44FT	1995	
131	N131VAO	Volvo B10M-62	Plaxton Expressliner 2	C44FT	1995	
132	N132VAO	Volvo B10M-62	Plaxton Expressliner 2	C44FT	1995	
153	LJC800	Volvo B10M-61	Van Hool Alizée	C48F	1982	Ex Magicbus, 1988
156	PCK335	Leyland Tiger TRCTL11/3RH	Duple Laser 2	C53F	1985	Ex Ribble, 1989
158	DSV943	Volvo B10M-61	Plaxton Paramount 3500 III	C48FT	1987	Ex Wallace Arnold, 1990
159	LJY145	Volvo B10M-61	Plaxton Paramount 3500 III	C48FT	1987	Ex Ribble, 1995
160	YDG616	Volvo B10M-61	Plaxton Paramount 3500 III	C48FT	1987	Ex Ribble, 1995
161	JPU817	Volvo B10M-61	Plaxton Paramount 3500 III	C53F	1987	Ex Wallace Arnold, 1990
162	B162WRN	Leyland Tiger TRCTL11/3RH	Duple Laser 2	C53F	1985	Ex Ribble, 1991
251	F251JRM	Leyland Lynx LX112L10ZR1R	Leyland	B51F	1989	
252	F252JRM	Leyland Lynx LX112L10ZR1R	Leyland	B51F	1989	
253	F253KAO	Leyland Lynx LX112L10ZR1R	Leyland	B51F	1989	
254	E709MFV	Leyland Lynx LX112L10ZR1R	Leyland	B51F	1988	Ex Leyland Bus, 1989
255	C544RAO	Leyland Lynx LX112TL11FR1 (Cummins) Leyland		B51F	1986	Ex Ribble, 1991

270-282

Volvo B6-9.9M   Alexander Dash   B40F   1993

270	L270LHH	272	L272LHH	274	L274LHH	276	L276JAO	282	L282JAO
271	L271LHH	273	L273LHH	275	L275JAO				

420-437

Bristol VRT/SL3/6LXB   Eastern Coach Works   H43/31F   1980

420	FAO420V	424	FAO424V	427	FAO427V	432	KRM432W	435	KRM435W
421	FAO421V	425	FAO425V	428	FAO428V	433	KRM433W	436	KRM436W
422	FAO422V	426	FAO426V	431	KRM431W	434	KRM434W	437	KRM437W
423	FAO423V								

505u	LUA273V	Leyland Leopard PSU3F/4R	Plaxton Supreme IV	C51F	1980	Ex Yeowart, Whitehaven, 1988
509	ORY640	DAF SB2305DHTD585	Plaxton Paramount 3200 III	C53F	1988	Ex Yeowart, Whitehaven, 1988
520	D520RCK	Mercedes-Benz L608D	Reeve Burgess	DP19F	1986	Ex Ribble, 1989

525-560

Mercedes-Benz L608D   Reeve Burgess   B20F   1986   Ex Ribble, 1989

525	D525RCK	529	D529RCK	531	D531RCK	534	D534RCK	559	D559RCK
528	D528RCK	530	D530RCK	533	D533RCK	558u	D558RCK	560	D560RCK

569u	LUA275V	Leyland Leopard PSU3E/4R	Plaxton Supreme IV	C51F	1980	Ex Kirkpatrick, Brigham, 1988
625u	GRM625V	Leyland Leopard PSU3F/4R	Duple Dominant II	C49F	1980	

699-788

Volvo B10M-55   Alexander PS   B49F*   1992-93   *772-788 are DP48F

699	K699ERM	717	K717DAO	735	K735DAO	754	K754DAO	771	K771DAO
700	K700DAO	718	K718DAO	736	K736DAO	755	K755DAO	772	K772DAO
701	K701DAO	719	K719DAO	737	K737DAO	756	K756DAO	773	K773DAO
702	K702DAO	720	K720DAO	738	K738DAO	757	K757DAO	774	K774DAO
703	K703DAO	721	K721DAO	739	K739DAO	758	K758DAO	775	K775DAO
704	K704ERM	722	K722DAO	740	K740DAO	759	K759DAO	776	K776DAO
705	K705DAO	723	K723DAO	741	K741DAO	760	K760DAO	777	K777DAO
706	K706DAO	724	K724DAO	742	K742DAO	761	K761DAO	778	K778DAO
707	K707DAO	725	K725DAO	743	K743DAO	762	K762DAO	779	K779DAO
708	K708DAO	726	K726DAO	744	K744DAO	763	K763DAO	780	K780DAO
709	K709DAO	727	K727DAO	745	K745DAO	764	K764DAO	781	K781DAO
710	K710DAO	728	K728DAO	746	K746DAO	765	K765DAO	783	K783DAO
711	K711DAO	729	K729DAO	748	K748DAO	766	K766DAO	784	K784DAO
712	K712DAO	730	K730DAO	749	K749DAO	767	K767DAO	785	K785DAO
713	K713DAO	731	K731DAO	750	K750DAO	768	K768DAO	786	K786DAO
714	K714DAO	732	K732DAO	751	K751DAO	769	K769DAO	787	K787DAO
715	K715DAO	733	K733DAO	752	K752DAO	770	K770DAO	788	K788DAO
716	K716DAO	734	K734DAO	753	K753DAO				

789	N789NRM	Volvo B10M-55	Alexander PS	DP48F	1995	
790	N790NRM	Volvo B10M-55	Alexander PS	DP48F	1995	
810	TRN810V	Leyland National 10351B/1R		B44F	1979	Ex Ribble, 1986
1001	URM801Y	Leyland Olympian ONLXB/1R	Eastern Coach Works	DPH45/30F	1982	
1002	URM802Y	Leyland Olympian ONLXB/1R	Eastern Coach Works	H45/32F	1982	

1003-1011

Leyland Olympian ONLXB/2RZ   Alexander RL   H51/36F   1988

1003	F803FAO	1005	F805FAO	1007	F807FAO	1009	F809FAO	1011	F811FAO
1004	F804FAO	1006	F806FAO	1008	F808FAO	1010	F810FAO		

1012-1019

Leyland Olympian ON2R56G13Z4 Alexander RL   H51/34F   1990

1012	H112SAO	1014	H114SAO	1016	H116SAO	1018	H118SAO	1019	H119SAO
1013	H113SAO	1015	H115SAO	1017	H117SAO				

Opposite, top: **The English Lakeland provide the opportunity for many rural shots providing the weather is fine. Working service 505 at the village of Near Sawry is Volvo B6 282, L282JAO.** *Tony Wilson*
Opposite, bottom: **Now the main single-deck vehicle for the Stagecoach group, the first examples of the Volvo B10M/Alexander PS combination were placed in service with Cumberland. Representing the type is 714, K714DAO pictured in Carlisle while working one of the city services.** *Richard Godfrey*

1020-1027

Leyland Olympian ON2R56G13Z4 Alexander RL   DPH47/27F 1991

1020	J120AAO	**1022**	J122AAO	**1024**	J124XHH	**1026**	J126XHH	**1027** J127XHH
1021	J121AAO	**1023**	J123XHH	**1025**	J125XHH			

1028-1035

Leyland Olympian ON2R50G13Z4 Alexander RL   DPH43/27F 1992

1028	K128DAO	**1030**	K130DAO	**1032**	K132DAO	**1034**	K134DAO	**1035** K135DAO
1029	K129DAO	**1031**	K131DAO	**1033**	K133DAO			

1090	C382SAO	Leyland Olympian ONLXB/1RV	Alexander RL	H47/30F	1986	Ex Bluebird, 1991
1091	C383SAO	Leyland Olympian ONLXB/1RV	Alexander RL	H47/30F	1986	Ex Bluebird, 1991
1092	D384XAO	Leyland Olympian ONLXB/1RV	Alexander RL	H47/30F	1987	Ex Bluebird, 1991
1093	D380XRS	Leyland Olympian ONLXB/1RV	Alexander RL	H47/30F	1987	Ex Bluebird, 1992
1094	D381XRS	Leyland Olympian ONLXB/1RV	Alexander RL	H47/30F	1987	Ex Bluebird, 1992
1103	KRN103T	Leyland Leopard PSU3E/4R	Duple Dominant II	C47F	1978	Ex Ribble, 1989
1105	KRN105T	Leyland Leopard PSU3E/4R	Duple Dominant II	C47F	1978	Ex Ribble, 1989
1113	KRN113T	Leyland Leopard PSU3E/4R	Duple Dominant II	C47F	1979	Ex Ribble, 1989
1119	KRN119T	Leyland Leopard PSU3E/4R	Duple Dominant II	C47F	1979	Ex Ribble, 1986
1151	B151WRN	Leyland Tiger TRCTL11/2RH	Duple Laser 2	C49F	1985	Ex Ribble, 1991
1153	B153WRN	Leyland Tiger TRCTL11/2RH	Duple Laser 2	C49F	1985	Ex Ribble, 1991
1154	B154WRN	Leyland Tiger TRCTL11/2RH	Duple Laser 2	C49F	1985	Ex Ribble, 1991
1155	B43MAO	Leyland Tiger TRCTL11/3RH	Duple Laser 2	C53F	1985	Ex Ribble, 1991
1162	WLT980	Volvo B10M-61	Plaxton Paramount 3500 II	C48F	1986	Ex Ribble, 1994
1175	MRJ275W	Leyland Leopard PSU5D/4R	Plaxton Supreme IV	C50F	1981	Ex Ribble, 1989
1199	FDV799V	Leyland Leopard PSU3E/4R	Plaxton Supreme IV Express	C49F	1980	Ex Ribble, 1989
1201	F201FHH	Leyland Olympian ONLXCT/3RZ	Alexander RL	DPH55/41F	1989	
1202	F202FHH	Leyland Olympian ONLXCT/3RZ	Alexander RL	DPH55/41F	1989	
1253	HNE253V	Leyland Leopard PSU5C/4R	Duple Dominant II	C53F	1980	Ex Ribble, 1989
1928	ERV251D	Leyland Atlantean PDR1/1 MkII	Metro Cammell	O43/31F	1966	Ex Southdown, 1991
2002	CBV2S	Bristol VRT/SL3/6LXB	Eastern Coach Works	O43/31F	1977	Ex Ribble, 1986
2024	DBV24W	Bristol VRT/SL3/6LXB	Eastern Coach Works	H43/31F	1980	Ex Ribble, 1986
2032	DBV32W	Bristol VRT/SL3/6LXB	Eastern Coach Works	H43/31F	1980	Ex Ribble, 1986
2035	UWV610S	Bristol VRT/SL3/6LXB	Eastern Coach Works	O43/31F	1977	Ex Southdown, 1990
2036	UWV612S	Bristol VRT/SL3/6LXB	Eastern Coach Works	O43/31F	1977	Ex Southdown, 1990
2037	UWV618S	Bristol VRT/SL3/6LXB	Eastern Coach Works	O43/31F	1978	Ex Southdown, 1990
2038	UWV620S	Bristol VRT/SL3/6LXB	Eastern Coach Works	O43/31F	1978	Ex Southdown, 1990
2075	XRR175S	Bristol VRT/SL3/6LXB	Eastern Coach Works	O43/27F	1980	Ex Ribble, 1995
2076	UWV622S	Bristol VRT/SL3/6LXB	Eastern Coach Works	O43/31F	1980	Ex Ribble, 1996
2134	DBV134Y	Leyland Olympian ONLXB/1R	Eastern Coach Works	H45/32F	1983	Ex Ribble, 1989
2175	C175ECK	Leyland Olympian ONLXB/1R	Eastern Coach Works	DPH42/30F	1985	Ex Ribble, 1989
2176	C176ECK	Leyland Olympian ONLXB/1R	Eastern Coach Works	DPH42/30F	1985	Ex Ribble, 1989
2177	C177ECK	Leyland Olympian ONLXB/1R	Eastern Coach Works	DPH42/30F	1986	Ex Ribble, 1989

Previous Registrations:

109DRM	A101DAO	LJY145	D205LWX
B43MAO	B155WRN, PCK335	ORY640	E986AHH
C382SAO	C473SSO, GSO3V	PCK335	B156WRN
C383SAO	C474SSO, GSO4V	PSU787	C495LJV
D384XAO	D375XRS, GSO5V	TCK841	B107HAO
D560RCK	D561RCK	VRR447	B180RLJ
DSV943	D203LWX	WLT980	C105DWR
E709MFV	E709MFV, BMN88G	WLT706	C109OHH
JPU817	D207LWX	WLT824	C110OHH
LJC800	From new	YDG616	D206LWX

Livery variations:

Coachline:	109/11/4, 153/8/60/1, 1153.
Lakeland Experience:	276/82, 520/58/60, 810, 1928, 2002/35-8/75/6.
National Express:	120/1/5-32.

Named vehicles: 520 *William Wordsworth*, 558 *John Ruskin*, 560 *Beatrix Potter*.

DARWEN COACH SERVICES

D R Russell, 5 West View, Chapels, Darwen, Lancashire, BB3 0NP

B931YCW	Mercedes-Benz L307D	Rovanne	M12	1985	Ex ?, 1987
D711HUA	Freight Rover Sherpa	Optare	B16F	1986	Ex Fishwick, 1989
D117NON	Freight Rover Sherpa	Carlyle	B18F	1986	Ex RoadCar, 1994
D181NON	Freight Rover Sherpa	Carlyle	B20F	1987	Ex Bee Line Buzz, 1992
D447NNA	Renault-Dodge S56	Northern Counties	B22F	1987	Ex South Lancashire, St Helens, 1995
D159RAK	Renault-Dodge S56	Reeve Burgess Beaver	B25F	1987	Ex Mainline, 1995
E177UWF	Renault-Dodge S56	Reeve Burgess Beaver	B25F	1987	Ex Mainline, 1995
E144RAX	Freight Rover Sherpa	Carlyle	B20F	1987	Ex Powercrafts, Blackburn, 1995
F217AKG	Freight Rover Sherpa	Carlyle Citybus 2	B20F	1988	Ex National Welsh, 1989
F948CUA	Freight Rover Sherpa	Carlyle Citybus 2	B20F	1988	Ex Dixon, Blackburn, 1993

Livery: Green

The dark green livery of Darwen Coaches owes much to two minibuses acquired in 1989 from Fishwick. Others now display these colours including D181NON, one of three Carlyle-bodied examples of the Sherpa in the fleet to have been new to the Bee Line Buzz operation. *Roy Marshall*

DARWEN MINIBUS SERVICE

Whitehead, 1 Glencarron Close, Hoddlesden, Darwen, Lancashire, BB3 3RF

Depot: St James Crescent, Darwen

WL9475	Ford R1014	Duple Dominant II	C24DLT	1981	Ex Blackburn Health Authority, 1993
C664BEX	Freight Rover Sherpa	Dormobile	B16F	1986	Ex Stagecoach South, 1994
C515DYM	Iveco Daily 49.10	Robin Hood City Nippy	B21F	1986	Ex The Shires, 1995
D831RYS	Renault-Dodge S56	Alexander AM	B25F	1987	Ex Fife Scottish, 1994
E815JSX	Renault-Dodge S56	Alexander AM	DP25F	1987	Ex Fife Scottish, 1994
E919HHG	Mercedes-Benz 609D	Reeve Burgess Beaver	DP19F	1987	
F956WCK	Mercedes-Benz 609D	Reeve Burgess Beaver	DP23F	1988	
F378UCP	Mercedes-Benz 609D	Reeve Burgess Beaver	B24F	1988	Ex Starline, Knutsford 1995
H380XHG	Mercedes-Benz 811D	Reeve Burgess Beaver	C33F	1990	
L76ATA	Mercedes-Benz 410D	Devon Conversions	M15L	1993	

Previous Registrations:
WL9475　　　ECW549W

Livery: White, orange and yellow.

Darwen Minibus Service operate four Reeve Burgess Beaver minibuses. Shown on school duties passing through Whitehead the earliest is E919HHG with high-back seating. *Roy Marshall*

DENNIS'S

R & M Cooper, Unit 4, Charles Street, Dukinfield,
Tameside, SK16 4SD

NFN62M	Leyland National 1151/1R/2402		B52F	1973	Ex Isle of Man RS, 1994
JBN948N	Leyland National 11351/1R		B52F	1975	Ex Isle of Man RS, 1994
UPB336S	Leyland National 10351A/1R		B41F	1977	Ex Victoria Travel, Earlestown, 1995
YPF771T	Leyland National 10351A/1R		B41F	1977	Ex Victoria Travel, Earlestown, 1995
D93VCC	Mercedes-Benz L608D	Reeve Burgess	B20F	1987	Ex Crosville Wales, 1995
D95VCC	Mercedes-Benz L608D	Reeve Burgess	B20F	1987	Ex Crosville Wales, 1995
D97VCC	Mercedes-Benz L608D	Reeve Burgess	B20F	1987	Ex Crosville Wales, 1995
D535XBC	Mercedes-Benz 709D	Advanced Vehicle Builders	DP25F	1987	
E996VYS	Mercedes-Benz 609D	Reeve Burgess Beaver	C19F	1987	Ex Henderson, Hamilton, 1993
F220JBB	Mercedes-Benz 609D	Reeve Burgess Beaver	C21F	1988	
G506PFM	Mercedes-Benz 811D	PMT	B29F	1989	
G507PFM	Mercedes-Benz 811D	PMT	B29F	1989	
H210CVU	Mercedes-Benz 811D	Reeve Burgess Beaver	B33F	1990	
H933DBU	Mercedes-Benz 811D	Reeve Burgess Beaver	B33F	1990	
J23GCX	DAF SB220LC550	Optare Delta	B49F	1991	
K286ESF	Mercedes-Benz 709D	Dormobile Routemaker	B27F	1993	
K287ESF	Mercedes-Benz 709D	Dormobile Routemaker	B27F	1993	
K289ESF	Mercedes-Benz 709D	Dormobile Routemaker	B27F	1993	
K290ESF	Mercedes-Benz 709D	Dormobile Routemaker	B27F	1993	
	Mercedes-Benz 709D	Plaxton Beaver	B27F	1994-95	

L680GNA	L683GNA	M729MBU	N321YNC	N258DUR
L681GNA	L510JND	M730MBU	N322YNC	N259DUR
L682GNA	M728MBU	N320YNC	N257DUR	

Livery: Red and grey

Previous Registrations:

JBN948N	MAN17D		
NFN62M	NFN62M, MAN19D		

Mercedes-Benz
709Ds with Plaxton
Beaver bodywork
are now the
preferred model for
the Dennis's fleet.
Seen entering
Manchester
Piccadilly on route
216 from Stalybridge
is L683GNA.
Bill Potter

FINGLANDS

Finglands Coachways Ltd, 261 Wilmslow Road, Rusholme, Manchester, M14 5LJ

234	SIB6614	Leyland Leopard PSU3F/4R	East Lancs EL2000 (1992)	DP49F	1981	Ex East Yorkshire, 1995
235	SIB6615	Leyland Leopard PSU5B/4R	East Lancs EL2000 (1992)	DP51F	1977	Ex East Yorkshire, 1995
237	KGE74T	Leyland Leopard PSU5C/4R	Plaxton Derwent II	B57F	1979	Ex Loch Lomond Coaches, Milngavie, 1995
301	F301JNC	Leyland Tiger TRBTL11/2RZ	Duple 300	B55F	1989	
302	F302JNC	Leyland Tiger TRBTL11/2RZ	Duple 300	B55F	1989	
343	F303JNC	Mercedes-Benz 609D	PMT	DP24F	1989	Ex Fieldsend, Rusholme, 1992
344	HIL7748	Mercedes-Benz 609D	Reeve Burgess Beaver	DP19F	1990	
351	JNB151N	Leyland Leopard PSU3C/4R	Plaxton Elite III Express	C53F	1975	
352	CIB3202	Leyland Tiger TRCTL11/3R	Plaxton Paramount 3200	C57F	1984	
355	HIL7747	Leyland Tiger TRCTL11/3RZ	Plaxton Paramount 3200 II	C57F	1985	
356	HIL7923	Leyland Tiger TRCTL11/3RZ	Plaxton Paramount 3200 II	C57F	1985	Ex Fieldsend, Rusholme, 1992
357	RYV77	Volvo B10M-61	Caetano Algarve	C53F	1986	
358	HIL7745	Volvo B10M-61	Plaxton Paramount 3500 III	C28FT	1986	
359	HIL7746	Volvo B10M-61	Plaxton Paramount 3500 III	C53FT	1989	
360	10RU	Mercedes-Benz 0303/15R	Mercedes-Benz	C49FT	1990	
361	SIA6180	Mercedes-Benz 0303/15R	Mercedes-Benz	C53FT	1990	
362	647JOE	Leyland Tiger TRCL10/3ARZM	Plaxton Paramount 3500 III	C49FT	1991	
363	H907AHS	Volvo B10M-60	Plaxton Paramount 3500 III	C53F	1991	Ex Park's, 1993
364	M364SNB	Volvo B10M-62	Berkhof Excellence	C49FT	1995	
903	UNA844S	Leyland Atlantean AN68A/1R	Park Royal	H43/32F	1974	Ex East Yorkshire, 1993
904	LJA611P	Leyland Atlantean AN68/1R	Northern Counties	H43/32F	1974	Ex East Yorkshire, 1993
934	SRJ734R	Leyland Atlantean AN68A/1R	Northern Counties	H41/32F	1977	Ex East Yorkshire, 1993
937	BNC947T	Leyland Atlantean AN68A/1R	Park Royal	H43/32F	1979	Ex East Yorkshire, 1993
938	UNA848S	Leyland Atlantean AN68A/1R	Park Royal	H43/32F	1978	Ex East Yorkshire, 1993
939	UNA819S	Leyland Atlantean AN68A/1R	Park Royal	H43/32F	1978	Ex East Yorkshire, 1993

1415-1427

		Volvo B10M-55	Alexander PS	DP48F	1994	Ex Ribble, 1995

1415	M415RRN	1418	M418RRN	1421	M421RRN	1424	M424RRN	1426	M426RRN
1416	M416RRN	1419	M419RRN	1422	M422RRN	1425	M425RRN	1427	M427RRN
1417	M417RRN	1420	M420RRN	1423	M423RRN				

1710	F242MBA	Volvo Citybus B10M-50	Alexander RV	DPH43/35F	1989	
1720w	ONF695R	Leyland Atlantean AN68A/1R	Northern Counties	H43/32F	1977	Ex East Kent, 1991
1721	ONF653R	Leyland Atlantean AN68A/1R	Northern Counties	H43/32F	1977	Ex East Kent, 1991
1722	ONF663R	Leyland Atlantean AN68A/1R	Northern Counties	H43/32F	1977	Ex East Kent, 1991
1723	RJA703R	Leyland Atlantean AN68A/1R	Northern Counties	H43/32F	1977	Ex East Kent, 1991
1726	E473SON	MCW Metrobus DR102/63	MCW	H45/30F	1987	Ex London Buses, 1992
1727	E474SON	MCW Metrobus DR102/63	MCW	H45/30F	1987	Ex London Buses, 1992
1728	E476SON	MCW Metrobus DR102/63	MCW	H45/30F	1987	Ex London Buses, 1992
1729	E477SON	MCW Metrobus DR102/63	MCW	H45/30F	1987	Ex London Buses, 1992
1730	E480UOF	MCW Metrobus DR102/65	MCW	H45/30F	1987	Ex London Buses, 1992
1731	LTK91R	Leyland Atlantean AN68A/1R	Roe	H43/30F	1977	Ex Hyndburn, 1992
1732	LTK93R	Leyland Atlantean AN68A/1R	Roe	H43/30F	1977	Ex Hyndburn, 1992
1733	LTK94R	Leyland Atlantean AN68A/1R	Roe	H43/30F	1977	Ex Hyndburn, 1992
1734w	LTK96R	Leyland Atlantean AN68A/1R	Roe	H43/30F	1977	Ex Hyndburn, 1992
1735	NRN397P	Leyland Atlantean AN68/1R	Park Royal	H43/30F	1976	Ex East Yorkshire, 1993
1736w	JDB121N	Leyland Atlantean AN68A/1R	Northern Counties	H43/32F	1975	Ex Ribble, 1993
1737w	KBU912P	Leyland Atlantean AN68A/1R	Northern Counties	H43/32F	1975	Ex Ribble, 1993
1738w	KDB686P	Leyland Atlantean AN68A/1R	Northern Counties	H43/32F	1975	Ex Ribble, 1993
1739	M832HVC	Volvo Olympian YN2RV18Z4	Alexander Royale	H45/29F	1994	Ex Volvo demonstrator, 1995
1740	N740VBA	Volvo Olympian YN2RV18Z4	Alexander Royale	H45/29F	1995	
1741	N741VBA	Volvo Olympian YN2RV18Z4	Alexander Royale	H45/29F	1995	
1742	N742VBA	Volvo Olympian YN2RV18Z4	Alexander Royale	H45/29F	1995	
1743	N743VBA	Volvo Olympian YN2RV18Z4	Alexander Royale	H45/29F	1995	
1744	N744ANE	Volvo Olympian YN2RV18Z4	Northern Counties Palatine	H45/29F	1996	
1745	N745ANE	Volvo Olympian YN2RV18Z4	Northern Counties Palatine	H45/29F	1996	
1746	N746ANE	Volvo Olympian YN2RV18Z4	Northern Counties Palatine	H45/29F	1996	
1747	N47ANE	Volvo Olympian YN2RV18Z4	Northern Counties Palatine	H45/29F	1996	
1748	N748ANE	Volvo Olympian YN2RV18Z4	Northern Counties Palatine	H45/29F	1996	

Previous Registrations:

10RU	From new	HIL7746	F300JNC	RYV77		C666DJA	
647JOE	From new	HIL7747	B88WRJ	SIA6180		From new	
CIB3202	A402HRJ	HIL7748	G880VVR	SIB6614		XAG206X	
HIL7745	D400MND	HIL7923	B106WRJ	SIB6615		UGR501R	
		KGE74T	Q652WWJ, SBS6791				

JOHN FISHWICK & SONS

John Fishwick & Sons, Golden Hill Garage, Golden Hill Lane, Leyland,
Lancashire, PR5 2LE

1	NFR558T	Leyland National 11351A/1R		B49F	1979	
2	A462LFV	Leyland Atlantean AN69/2L	Eastern Coach Works	H47/35F	1983	
3	J7JFS	Leyland Lynx LX2R11C15Z4R	Leyland Lynx 2	B51F	1991	
4	H64CCK	Leyland Lynx LX2R11C15Z4R	Leyland Lynx 2	B47F	1991	
5	H65CCK	Leyland Lynx LX2R11C15Z4R	Leyland Lynx 2	B51F	1991	
6	NFR559T	Leyland National 11351A/1R		B49F	1979	
7	GCK428W	Leyland National 2 NL116AL11/1R		B49F	1981	
8	GCK429W	Leyland National 2 NL116AL11/1R		B49F	1981	
9	WRN412V	Leyland National 2 NL116L11/1R		B49F	1980	
10	WRN413V	Leyland National 2 NL116L11/1R		B49F	1980	
11w	NFR560T	Leyland National 11351A/1R		B49F	1979	
12	GCK430W	Leyland National 2 NL116AL11/1R		B49F	1981	
14	J14JFS	Leyland Lynx LX2R11C15Z4R	Leyland Lynx 2	B51F	1992	
15	UMR194T	Leyland Fleetline FE30AGR	Eastern Coach Works	H43/31F	1979	Ex Thamesdown, 1993
16	OFV620X	Leyland National 2 NL116AL11/1R		B49F	1981	
17	UMR196T	Leyland Fleetline FE30AGR	Eastern Coach Works	H43/31F	1979	Ex Thamesdown, 1994
18	XTB728N	Leyland Atlantean AN68/1R	East Lancashire	H43/31F	1974	
19	XTB729N	Leyland Atlantean AN68/1R	East Lancashire	H43/31F	1974	
20	LUA714V	Bristol VRT/SL3/6LXB	Eastern Coach Works	H43/31F	1979	Ex Northern Bus, Anston, 1994
21	DWU295T	Bristol VRT/SL3/6LXB	Eastern Coach Works	H43/31F	1979	Ex Northern Bus, Anston, 1994
22	SRN103P	Leyland Atlantean AN68A/1R	East Lancashire	H43/32F	1976	
23	GRN895W	Leyland Atlantean AN69/1L	Eastern Coach Works	H43/31F	1981	
24	XCW955R	Leyland National 11351A/1R		B49F	1977	
25	D25VCW	Leyland Lynx LX112TL11ZR1	Leyland	B47F	1986	
26	OFV621X	Leyland National 2 NL116AL11/1R		B49F	1981	
27	ABV939Y	Leyland National 2 NL116TL11/1R		B49F	1982	
28	FBV524S	Leyland National 11351A/1R		B49F	1978	
31	FBV525S	Leyland National 11351A/1R		B49F	1978	Ex MTL, 1995
30	D30VCW	Leyland Lynx LX112TL11ZR1	Leyland	B47F	1986	
32	D32YCW	Leyland Lynx LX112TL11ZR1S	Leyland	B47F	1987	
33	D33YCW	Leyland Lynx LX112TL11ZR1S	Leyland	B47F	1987	
34w	XCW957R	Leyland National 11351A/1R		B49F	1977	
	L1JFS	EOS E180Z	EOS 90	C49FT	1994	
	K3JFS	DAF SB3000WS601	Van Hool Alizée	C51FT	1995	
	M664WCK	Volvo B10M-62	Plaxton Excalibur	C49FT	1995	
	M665WCK	Volvo B10M-62	Plaxton Excalibur	C49FT	1995	
	J158OHG	DAF SB3000DKV601	Van Hool Alizée	C49FT	1991	
	J9JFS	EOS E180Z	EOS 90	C48FT	1995	
M1	F705WFV	Mercedes-Benz 609D	Reeve Burgess Beaver	C19F	1989	
M2	F706WFV	Mercedes-Benz 609D	Reeve Burgess Beaver	C19F	1989	
M5	E45HBV	Mercedes-Benz 609D	Reeve Burgess Beaver	B20F	1987	
M6	E46HBV	Mercedes-Benz 609D	Reeve Burgess Beaver	B20F	1987	
M7	E47HBV	Mercedes-Benz 609D	Reeve Burgess Beaver	B20F	1987	
M8	D84BLF	Mercedes-Benz 609D	Reeve Burgess Beaver	DP19F	1987	Ex Mercedes-Benz demonstrator, 1987
M9	D210OKY	Mercedes-Benz 709D	Reeve Burgess	B20F	1986	Ex Reeve Burgess demonstrator, 1988
M10	E100MFV	Mercedes-Benz 609D	Reeve Burgess Beaver	DP19F	1988	
M11	K5JFS	Mercedes-Benz 814D	Autobus Classique 2	C29F	1993	

Livery: Two-tone green.

Previous Registrations:

J9JFS	M823RCP	J158OHG	J9JFS	K5JFS	K721GBE

Overleaf: **Finglands is a subsidiary of EYMS Group Ltd and have expanded and modernised their Wilmslow Road services of late, as well as operating the former Stagecoach Manchester service on the Stockport corridor. Shown here are Park Royal-bodied Atlantean 903, UNA844S which came from East Yorkshire, and MCW Metrobus 1730, E480UOF, both of which are seen in fleet livery of white, orange and brown.** *Cliff Beeton*

Opposite: **Representing the John Fishwick fleet are one of the latest EOS coaches and one of the minibuses which operate the Leyland town services. The EOS, opposite top, carries L1JFS plates and is seen in Stockport at the start of a tour. Pictured operating town service 2 to Springfield Estate is M8, D84BLF. This Reeve Burgess Beaver-bodied 709 was originally a demonstrator for Mercedes-Benz.** *Paul Wigan/Bill Potter*

GLOSSOPDALE

D Whyatt, 5 Railway Street, Glossop, Derbyshire, SK13 9AG

E84OUH	Freight Rover Sherpa	Carlyle Citybus 2	B20F	1987	Ex Fen Travel, Syston, 1993
E107OUH	Freight Rover Sherpa	Carlyle Citybus 2	B20F	1988	Ex Dalybus, Eccles, 1995
E157RNY	Freight Rover Sherpa	Carlyle Citybus 2	B20F	1988	Ex Red & White, 1994
E176TWO	Freight Rover Sherpa	Carlyle Citybus 2	B20F	1988	Ex West London, Tylers Green, 1994
F229BAX	Freight Rover Sherpa	Carlyle Citybus 2	B20F	1989	Ex Dalybus, Eccles, 1995
M634FJF	Mercedes-Benz 811D	Marshall C16	B31F	1994	
M635FJF	Mercedes-Benz 711D	Marshall C19	B27F	1994	
M636FJF	Mercedes-Benz 711D	Marshall C19	B27F	1994	
M85DEW	Dennis Dart 9.8SDL3054	Marshall C37	B40F	1994	
M86DEW	Dennis Dart 9.8SDL3054	Marshall C37	B40F	1994	
N746YVR	Mercedes-Benz 711D	Marshall C19	B27F	1995	
N748YVR	Mercedes-Benz 711D	Marshall C19	B27F	1995	

Livery: Two-tone green

Marshall bodied Mercedes-Benz 711s feature in the Glossopdale fleet with two new additions during 1995. Seen in Stockport bus station about to return home on service 361 through Hazel Grove and New Mills is M636FJF. In September 1995 Glossopdale took over the commercial services previously operated by Tame Valley. *Roy Marshall*

GMN

Greater Manchester Buses North Ltd, Wallshaw Place, Oldham, Greater Manchester, OL1 3UY

Depots : Howe Bridge, Atherton; Crook Street, Bolton; Rochdale Road, Bury; Boyle Street, Manchester; Queens Road, Manchester; Mumps Bridge, Oldham; Southport and Melverley Street, Wigan.

Fleet	Reg	Type	Body	Year	Notes
101	FWA474V	Leyland National 2 NL106L11/1R	B44F	1980	Ex Citybus, Middleton, 1995
102	PNW606W	Leyland National 2 NL116L11/1R	B52F	1980	Ex Citybus, Middleton, 1995
103	XLV163W	Leyland National 2 NL116AL11/1R	B49F	1981	Ex MTL, 1995
104	XTJ4W	Leyland National 2 NL116AL11/1R	DP44F	1981	Ex MTL, 1995
105	XTJ5W	Leyland National 2 NL116AL11/1R	B49F	1981	Ex MTL, 1995
106	WWM905W	Leyland National 2 NL116AL11/1R	B49F	1981	Ex MTL, 1995
107	XTJ7W	Leyland National 2 NL116AL11/1R	B49F	1981	Ex MTL, 1995
108	SKF8T	Leyland National 11351A/1R	B49F	1979	Ex MTL, 1995
109	SKF9T	Leyland National 11351A/1R	B49F	1979	Ex MTL, 1995
161	CKB161X	Leyland National 2 NL116AL11/1R	B49F	1981	
162	CKB162X	Leyland National 2 NL116AL11/1R	B49F	1981	
163	CKB163X	Leyland National 2 NL116AL11/1R	B49F	1981	
164	CKB164X	Leyland National 2 NL116AL11/1R	B49F	1981	
179	RBU179R	Leyland National 11351A/1R	B49F	1977	
180	VBG80V	Leyland National 2 NL116L11/1R	B49F	1980	Ex MTL, 1995
181	VBG81V	Leyland National 2 NL116L11/1R	B49F	1980	Ex MTL, 1995
182	VBG82V	Leyland National 2 NL116L11/1R	B49F	1980	Ex MTL, 1995
183	VBG83V	Leyland National 2 NL116L11/1R	B49F	1980	Ex MTL, 1995
185	VBG85V	Leyland National 2 NL116L11/1R	B49F	1980	Ex MTL, 1995
186	VBG86V	Leyland National 2 NL116L11/1R	B49F	1980	Ex MTL, 1995
187	VBG97V	Leyland National 2 NL116L11/1R	B49F	1980	Ex MTL, 1995
195	VBG95V	Leyland National 2 NL116L11/1R	B49F	1980	Ex MTL, 1995
197w	ABA22T	Leyland National 11351A/1R	B49F	1977	
198	VBG98V	Leyland National 2 NL116L11/1R	B49F	1980	Ex MTL, 1995
199	VBG99V	Leyland National 2 NL116L11/1R	B49F	1980	Ex MTL, 1995
201	ABA26T	Leyland National 11351A/1R	B49F	1977	
202w	ABA27T	Leyland National 11351A/1R	B49F	1977	
203w	ABA28T	Leyland National 11351A/1R	B49F	1977	

436-463

		Type			Body	Year
		Leyland Leopard PSU3D/2R	Plaxton Derwent		B48F	1976

436w	LTE487P	440w	LTE491P	454w	MTE22R	455w	MTE23R	463w	MTE31R
439w	LTE490P	444w	LTE495P						

Still unique in the GMN fleet is 701, J461OVU, the Volvo B10M with the original Northern Counties Paladin bodywork. Currently, this is allocated to Wigan where the initial three Volvo Citybus double-deckers are also based.
Richard Godfrey

GMN are currently taking delivery of fifty-five Volvo B10Bs with Wright Endurance bodywork, and these are to be followed by five Volvo B10Ls with the new Wright Liberator design. Seen operating service 135 out of Queens Road depot is 516, M516PNA. *Richard Godfrey*

501-555

Volvo B10B — Wright Endurance — DP50F — 1995-96

501	M501PNA	512	M512PNA	523	N523WVR	534	N534WVR	545	N545WVR
502	M502PNA	513	M513PNA	524	N524WVR	535	N535WVR	546	N546WVR
503	M503PNA	514	M514PNA	525	N525WVR	536	N536WVR	547	N547WVR
504	M504PNA	515	M515PNA	526	N526WVR	537	N537WVR	548	N548WVR
505	M505PNA	516	M516PNA	527	N527WVR	538	N538WVR	549	N549WVR
506	M506PNA	517	M517PNA	528	N528WVR	539	N539WVR	550	N550WVR
507	M507PNA	518	M518PNA	529	N529WVR	540	N540WVR	551	N551WVR
508	M508PNA	519	M519PNA	530	N530WVR	541	N541WVR	552	N552WVR
509	M509PNA	520	M520PNA	531	N531WVR	542	N542WVR	553	N553WVR
510	M510PNA	521	N521WVR	532	N532WVR	543	N543WVR	554	N554WVR
511	M511PNA	522	N522WVR	533	N533WVR	544	N544WVR	555	N

608-618

Dennis Dart 9.8SDL3054 — Northern Counties Paladin 2 B39F — 1995

608	M608SBA	611	M611SBA	613	M613SBA	615	M615SBA	617	M617SBA
609	M609SBA	612	M612SBA	614	M614SBA	616	M616SBA	618	M618SBA
610	M610SBA							

701	J461OVU	Volvo B10M-55	Northern Counties Paladin	B49F	1991

1051-1070

Volvo B6-50 — Northern Counties Paladin 2 B40F — 1994

1051	M251NVM	1055	M255NVM	1059	M259NVM	1063	M263SVU	1067	M267SVU
1052	M252NVM	1056	M256NVM	1060	M260NVM	1064	M264SVU	1068	M268SVU
1053	M253NVM	1057	M257NVM	1061	M261SVU	1065	M265SVU	1069	M269SVU
1054	M254NVM	1058	M258NVM	1062	M262SVU	1066	M266SVU	1070	M270SVU

1071	N71YNF	Volvo B6LE	Wright Crusader	B37F	1995

Opposite, top: New buses are now being delivered to GMN in an attempt to replace elderly vehicles acquired with the management buy-out. Ten Volvo B6s were placed in service during 1994 with a further ten, and a low floor version in 1995. These are based at Bolton and Bury. Shown in Oldham Street, Manchester, working service 65 is 1067, M267SVU, an example displaying BE depot codes. *Lee Whitehead*
Opposite, bottom: Carrying the new GMN livery scheme is Metrobus 5015, GBU15V, pictured heading for the Langley estate. *Tony Wilson*

The only four Leyland Lynx with GMN are all now at Bolton where 1403, D503LNA, is seen in Thyne Street as the bus arrived in the town. *John Robinson*

1101-1107

Dennis Dart 9.8SDL3054 — Northern Counties Paladin 2 B39F — 1995

1101	M101RRJ	1103	M103RRJ	1105	M105RRJ	1106	M106RRJ	1107	M107RRJ
1102	M102RRJ	1104	M104RRJ						

1401	D501LNA	Leyland Lynx LX563.6LXCTZR1	Leyland	B48F	1986
1402	D502LNA	Leyland Lynx LX112LXCTZR1	Leyland	B48F	1986
1403	D503LNA	Leyland Lynx LX112LXCTZR1	Leyland	B48F	1986
1404	D504LNA	Leyland Lynx LX112LXCTZR1	Leyland	B48F	1986

1410-1416

Iveco TurboDaily 59.12 — Marshall C 31 — B18F — 1995 — Ex Citybus, Middleton, 1995

1410	M410RND	1412	M412RND	1414	M414RND	1415	M415RND	1416	M416RND
1411	M411RND	1413	M413RND						

1441	D266OOJ	Freight Rover Sherpa	Carlyle	B20F	1987	Ex MTL 1995
1448	M248NNF	Iveco TurboDaily 59.12	Marshall C 31	B18F	1995	Ex Citybus, Middleton, 1995
1449	M249NNF	Iveco TurboDaily 59.12	Marshall C 31	B18F	1995	Ex Citybus, Middleton, 1995
1481	C481CBU	Volvo Citybus B10M-50	Northern Counties	H46/33F	1986	
1482	C482CBU	Volvo Citybus B10M-50	Northern Counties	H46/33F	1986	
1483	C483CBU	Volvo Citybus B10M-50	Northern Counties	H46/33F	1986	

1572-1580

MCW MetroRider MF150/30 — MCW — B23F — 1987 — Ex Cardiff, 1994

1572	E126RDW	1574	E128RDW	1576	E121RDW	1578w	E123RDW	1580	E125RDW
1573	E127RDW	1575	E120RDW	1577	E122RDW	1579w	E124RDW		

1581-1599

MCW MetroRider MF150/16 — MCW — B25F — 1987 — Ex SWT, 1994

1581	E254REP	1585	E259REP	1589w	E265REP	1593	E271REP	1597	E275REP
1582	E255REP	1586w	D260PEP	1590	E266REP	1594	E272REP	1598w	E276REP
1583w	D256PEP	1587w	E263REP	1591	E267REP	1595	E273REP	1599	E277REP
1584	E258REP	1588w	E264REP	1592	E268REP	1596	E274REP		

The majority of GM Buses' MetroRiders stayed with the southern fleet though several other MetroRiders have been acquired from a number of sources. Shown here is 1691, E241UWR which came from Yorkshire Rider and is seen here with Lancashire Gem titles for the Liverpool operation which has since ceased. *Lee Whitehead*

1616	D616MDB	MCW MetroRider MF151/3	MCW	B23F	1987	
1622	D622MDB	MCW MetroRider MF151/3	MCW	B23F	1987	
1625	D625MDB	MCW MetroRider MF151/3	MCW	B23F	1987	
1631	D631MDB	MCW MetroRider MF151/3	MCW	B23F	1987	
1681w	D474PON	MCW MetroRider MF150/14	MCW	B23F	1987	Ex London Buses, 1993
1682w	E148KYW	MCW MetroRider MF150/38	MCW	B25F	1987	Ex London Buses, 1993
1683	E150KYW	MCW MetroRider MF150/38	MCW	B25F	1987	Ex London Buses, 1993
1684	E638KYW	MCW MetroRider MF150/46	MCW	B25F	1988	Ex London Buses, 1993
1685	E637KYW	MCW MetroRider MF150/46	MCW	B25F	1988	Ex London Buses, 1993
1686	E636KYW	MCW MetroRider MF150/46	MCW	B25F	1988	Ex London Buses, 1993
1687w	E929KYR	MCW MetroRider MF150/46	MCW	B25F	1988	Ex London Buses, 1993

1688-1698

		MCW MetroRider MF150/80	MCW	B23F	1988	Ex Yorkshire Rider, 1994

1688w	E237UWR	1691	E241UWR	1693w	E243UWR	1695	E246UWR	1697	E250UWR
1689w	E239UWR	1692	E242UWR	1694	E244UWR	1696	E247UWR	1698	E251UWR
1690	E240UWR							

1701	K881UDB	Mercedes-Benz 709D	Plaxton Beaver	B27F	1993	Ex Merseybus, 1995
1702	K883UDB	Mercedes-Benz 709D	Plaxton Beaver	B27F	1993	Ex Merseybus, 1995

1703-1714

		Mercedes-Benz 811D	Plaxton Beaver	B28F	1992	Ex Citybus, Middleton, 1995

1703	J603HMF	1706	J606HMF	1708	J608HMF	1709	J609HMF	1714	J614HMF
1704	J604HMF	1707	J607HMF					

1717	F597FAM	Mercedes-Benz 811D	Optare StarRider	DP31F	1989	Ex Merseybus, 1995
1718	F598FAM	Mercedes-Benz 811D	Optare StarRider	DP31F	1989	Ex Merseybus, 1995
1719	J619HMF	Mercedes-Benz 811D	Plaxton Beaver	B28F	1992	Ex Citybus, Middleton, 1995
1722	H722CNC	Renault S75	Northern Counties	B17FL	1990	
1723	H723CNC	Renault S75	Northern Counties	B17FL	1990	
1725	H725CNC	Renault S75	Northern Counties	B17FL	1990	
1730	E949GFV	Renault-Dodge S56	Northern Counties	B20F	1987	Ex Merseybus, 1995
1731	D693SEM	Renault-Dodge S56	Alexander AM	B23F	1987	Ex Merseybus, 1995
1732	D137OWG	Renault-Dodge S56	Reeve Burgess	DP25F	1987	Ex Merseybus, 1995
1733	E178UWF	Renault-Dodge S56	Reeve Burgess Beaver	B25F	1987	Ex Merseybus, 1995

The 1988-89 delivery of Leyland Olympians have a different grille arrangement from the earlier examples. Showing this arrangement is 3279, F279DRJ seen near Manchester Arndale centre while working service 60 from Queens Road depot.

GMN operate several double-decks with high-back seating for express work. These are both Metrobuses and Olympians, all with Northern Counties bodywork. Pictured passing through Liverpool in the latest variant of the Express livery is 3256, D256JVR. *Malc McDonald*

1845-1899

Renault-Dodge S56 — Northern Counties — B20F — 1986-87

1845	D845LND	1857	D857LND	1875	D875MDB	1885	D885MDB	1897	D897MDB
1846	D846LND	1864	D864LND	1876	D876MDB	1889	D889MDB	1899	D899MDB
1852	D852LND	1874	D874MDB	1879	D879MDB	1894w	D894MDB		

1904-1997

Renault-Dodge S56 — Northern Counties — B20F — 1987

1904	D904MDB	1930	D930NDB	1948	D948NDB	1970	D970PJA	1985	E985SJA
1906w	D906NDB	1932	D932NDB	1949	D949NDB	1973	D973PJA	1987	E987SJA
1908	D908NDB	1933	D933NDB	1952	D952NDB	1977	D977PJA	1994	E994SJA
1909w	D909NDB	1941w	D941NDB	1954	D954NDB	1979	D979PJA	1996	E996SJA
1916	D916NDB	1945w	D945NDB	1956	D956PJA	1983	E983SJA	1997	E997SJA
1920	D920NDB	1947	D947NDB	1958	D958PJA	1984	E984SJA		

3011-3015

Leyland Olympian ONTL11/1R — Northern Counties — H43/30F — 1983

3011	A576HDB	3012	A577HDB	3013	A578HDB	3014	A579HDB	3015	A580HDB

3037-3238

Leyland Olympian ONLXB/1R — Northern Counties — H43/30F — 1984-86

3037	B37PJA	3073	B73PJA	3108	B108SJA	3152	B152XNA	3202	C202CBU
3038	B38PJA	3075	B75PJA	3109	B109SJA	3157	C157YBA	3203	C203CBU
3040	B40PJA	3076	B76PJA	3111	B111SJA	3159	C159YBA	3204	C204CBU
3041	B41PJA	3078	B78PJA	3112	B112SJA	3160	C160YBA	3206	C206CBU
3042	B42PJA	3079	B79PJA	3113	B113SJA	3161	C161YBA	3209	C209CBU
3043	B43PJA	3081	B81PJA	3115	B115SJA	3162	C162YBA	3211	C211CBU
3044	B44PJA	3083	B83PJA	3116	B116TVU	3163	C163YBA	3217	C217CBU
3045	B45PJA	3085	B85PJA	3120	B120TVU	3168	C168YBA	3218	C218CBU
3046	B46PJA	3090	B90SJA	3123	B123TVU	3171	C171YBA	3219	C219CBU
3047	B47PJA	3092	B92SJA	3127	B127WNB	3177	C177YBA	3220	C220CBU
3048	B48PJA	3093	B93SJA	3128	B128WNB	3180	C180YBA	3222	C222CBU
3050	B350PJA	3096	B96SJA	3129	B129WNB	3182	C182YBA	3223	C223CBU
3051	B351PJA	3097	B97SJA	3130	B130WNB	3183	C183YBA	3225	C225CBU
3052	B52PJA	3098	B98SJA	3131	B131WNB	3186	C186YBA	3227	C227ENE
3054	B54PJA	3099	B99SJA	3134	B134WNB	3187	C187YBA	3228	C228ENE
3059	B59PJA	3100	B100SJA	3136	B136WNB	3188	C188YBA	3229	C229ENE
3061	B61PJA	3101	B101SJA	3140	B140WNB	3189	C189YBA	3231	C231ENE
3062	B62PJA	3102	B102SJA	3141	B141WNB	3190	C190YBA	3232	C232ENE
3063	B63PJA	3103	B103SJA	3142	B142WNB	3192	C192YBA	3233	C233ENE
3064	B64PJA	3104	B104SJA	3144	B144WNB	3194	C194YBA	3235	C235ENE
3066	B66PJA	3105	B105SJA	3148	B148XNA	3200	C200YBA	3237	C237EVU
3068	B68PJA	3106	B106SJA	3151	B151XNA	3201	C201CBU	3238	C238EVU
3071	B71PJA	3107	B107SJA						

3239-3276

Leyland Olympian ONLXB/1R — Northern Counties — DPH43/26F — 1986-87

3239	C239EVU	3246	C246FRJ	3253	C253FRJ	3262	D262JVR	3270	D270JVR
3240	C240EVU	3247	C247FRJ	3254	C254FRJ	3263	D263JVR	3271	D271JVR
3241	C241EVU	3248	C248FRJ	3256	D256JVR	3264	D264JVR	3273	D273JVR
3242	C242EVU	3249	C249FRJ	3257	D257JVR	3265	D265JVR	3274	D274JVR
3243	C243EVU	3250	C250FRJ	3258	D258JVR	3266	D266JVR	3275	D275JVR
3244	C244EVU	3251	C251FRJ	3259	D259JVR	3267	D267JVR	3276	D276JVR
3245	C245EVU	3252	C252FRJ	3261	D261JVR				

3278-3305

Leyland Olympian ONLXB/1RZ — Northern Counties — H43/30F — 1988-89

3278	F278DRJ	3281	F281DRJ	3287	F287DRJ	3292	F292DRJ	3302	F302DRJ
3279	F279DRJ	3284	F284DRJ	3288	F288DRJ	3293	F293DRJ	3303	F303DRJ
3280	F280DRJ	3286	F286DRJ	3290	F290DRJ	3299	F299DRJ	3305	F305DRJ

4003-4018

Leyland Fleetline FE30AGR — Northern Counties — H43/32F — 1978 — Ex Yorkshire Rider, 1994

4003w	XBU3S	4007	XBU7S	4013	XBU13S	4016	XBU16S	4018	XBU18S
4004	XBU4S	4012w	XBU12S						

4026-4096   Leyland Fleetline FE30AGR   Northern Counties   H43/32F   1978-79   4026 ex Yorkshire Rider, 1994

4026	ANA26T	4057	BVR57T	4072	BVR72T	4079	BVR79T	4090	BVR90T
4039	ANA39T	4058w	BVR58T	4073	BVR73T	4081	BVR81T	4091	BVR91T
4050	ANA50T	4060	BVR60T	4074	BVR74T	4084	BVR84T	4093	BVR93T
4051	BVR51T	4062w	BVR62T	4075w	BVR75T	4086	BVR86T	4095	BVR95T
4054	BVR54T	4063	BVR63T	4077	BVR77T	4088	BVR88T	4096	BVR96T
4056w	BVR56T	4064	BVR64T	4078	BVR78T				

4102-4150   Leyland Fleetline FE30AGR   Northern Counties   H43/32F   1979-80

4102	HDB102V	4113	HDB113V	4122	HDB122V	4131	KDB131V	4142	GNF17V
4104	HDB104V	4114	HDB114V	4123	HDB123V	4132	KDB132V	4143	MNC486W
4105	HDB105V	4115	HDB115V	4125	HDB125V	4133	KDB133V	4146	MNC489W
4106	HDB106V	4117	HDB117V	4126	KDB126V	4136	KDB136V	4147	MNC490W
4108	HDB108V	4118	HDB118V	4127	KDB127V	4139	KDB139V	4148	MNC491W
4109	HDB109V	4119	HDB119V	4128	KDB128V	4140	KDB140V	4149	MNC492W
4110	HDB110V	4120	HDB120V	4129	KDB129V	4141	GNF16V	4150	MNC493W
4111	HDB111V	4121	HDB121V						

4151-4198   Leyland Atlantean AN68A/1R   Northern Counties   H43/32F   1978-79

4151	VBA151S	4163	VBA163S	4179	VBA179S	4184	VBA184S	4194	VBA194S
4155	VBA155S	4165	VBA165S	4180	VBA180S	4189	VBA189S	4196	VBA196S
4158	VBA158S	4167	VBA167S	4181	VBA181S	4191	VBA191S	4197	VBA197S
4159	VBA159S	4171w	VBA171S	4183	VBA183S	4192	VBA192S	4198	VBA198S
4160	VBA160S	4177	VBA177S						

4201-4300   Leyland Atlantean AN68A/1R   Northern Counties   H43/32F   1979-80

4201	XRJ201S	4226	ANA226T	4255	FVR255V	4272	FVR272V	4286	FVR286V
4202w	XRJ202S	4228	ANA228T	4256	FVR256V	4273	FVR273V	4287	FVR287V
4205	XRJ205S	4229	ANA229T	4257w	FVR257V	4274	FVR274V	4288	FVR288V
4206w	XRJ206S	4232	ANA232T	4258	FVR258V	4275w	FVR275V	4289w	FVR289V
4207	ANA207T	4233	ANA233T	4260	FVR260V	4276	FVR276V	4292	FVR292V
4208w	ANA208T	4238w	ANA238T	4261w	FVR261V	4277	FVR277V	4293	FVR293V
4209	ANA209T	4239	ANA239T	4263	FVR263V	4278	FVR278V	4296	FVR296V
4213	ANA213T	4240	FVR240V	4265	FVR265V	4279	FVR279V	4297	FVR297V
4216	ANA216T	4243	FVR243V	4266	FVR266V	4282	FVR282V	4298	FVR298V
4221	ANA221T	4244	FVR244V	4268	FVR268V	4284	FVR284V	4299	FVR299V
4223	ANA223T	4251	FVR251V	4269	FVR269V	4285	FVR285V	4300	FVR300V
4224w	ANA224T	4254	FVR254V	4271	FVR271V				

4303-4350   Leyland Atlantean AN68A/1R   Northern Counties   H43/32F   1980-81

4303	KDB303V	4315	MNC515W	4326	MNC526W	4336	MNC536W	4344	MNC544W
4305	MNC505W	4316	MNC516W	4330	MNC530W	4337	MNC537W	4345	MNC545W
4306	MNC506W	4318	MNC518W	4331	MNC531W	4338	MNC538W	4346	MNC546W
4308	MNC508W	4320	MNC520W	4333	MNC533W	4340	MNC540W	4347	MNC547W
4310	MNC510W	4322	MNC522W	4334	MNC534W	4341	MNC541W	4349	MNC549W
4311	MNC511W	4323	MNC523W	4335	MNC535W	4342	MNC542W	4350	MNC550W
4313	MNC513W	4324	MNC524W						

4351-4400   Leyland Atlantean AN68A/1R   Northern Counties   H43/32F   1981

4351	ORJ351W	4360	ORJ360W	4371	ORJ371W	4383	ORJ383W	4390	ORJ390W
4353w	ORJ353W	4361	ORJ361W	4372	ORJ372W	4384	ORJ384W	4391	ORJ391W
4354	ORJ354W	4363	ORJ363W	4373	ORJ373W	4385	ORJ385W	4392	ORJ392W
4355	ORJ355W	4364	ORJ364W	4374	ORJ374W	4386	ORJ386W	4394	ORJ394W
4356	ORJ356W	4366	ORJ366W	4378	ORJ378W	4387	ORJ387W	4398	ORJ398W
4357	ORJ357W	4367	ORJ367W	4379	ORJ379W	4388	ORJ388W	4399	ORJ399W
4358	ORJ358W	4369	ORJ369W	4382	ORJ382W	4389	ORJ389W	4400	ORJ400W
4359	ORJ359W	4370	ORJ370W						

4401-4525

Leyland Atlantean AN68A/1R* *4448/56/60-81/5/90/3/4/502-25 are AN68B/1R   Northern Counties   H43/32F   1981-82

4401	MRJ401W	4426	SND426X	4448	SND448X	4478	SND478X	4503	SND503X
4403	MRJ403W	4427	SND427X	4456	SND456X	4481	SND481X	4504	SND504X
4405	MRJ405W	4428	SND428X	4457	SND457X	4482	SND482X	4507	SND507X
4407	MRJ407W	4431	SND431X	4458	SND458X	4485	SND485X	4508	SND508X
4408	MRJ408W	4433	SND433X	4459	SND459X	4486	SND486X	4509	SND509X
4410	MRJ410W	4434	SND434X	4460	SND460X	4490	SND490X	4510	SND510X
4411	MRJ411W	4436	SND436X	4461	SND461X	4491	SND491X	4511	SND511X
4413	SND413X	4438	SND438X	4463	SND463X	4492	SND492X	4515	SND515X
4414	SND414X	4439	SND439X	4464	SND464X	4493	SND493X	4516	SND516X
4415	SND415X	4441	SND441X	4466	SND466X	4494	SND494X	4517	SND517X
4416	SND416X	4442	SND442X	4469	SND469X	4497	SND497X	4520	SND520X
4417	SND417X	4443	SND443X	4470	SND470X	4498	SND498X	4522	SND522X
4419	SND419X	4444	SND444X	4471	SND471X	4499	SND499X	4523	SND523X
4420w	SND420X	4445	SND445X	4474	SND474X	4500	SND500X	4524	SND524X
4423	SND423X	4446	SND446X	4475	SND475X	4502	SND502X	4525	SND525X
4424	SND424X	4447	SND447X						

4528-4599

Leyland Atlantean AN68D/1R   Northern Counties   H43/32F   1982

4528	SND528X	4542	ANA542Y	4557	ANA557Y	4571	ANA571Y	4584	ANA584Y
4529	SND529X	4544	ANA544Y	4558	ANA558Y	4573	ANA573Y	4587	ANA587Y
4531	ANA531Y	4547	ANA547Y	4560	ANA560Y	4574	ANA574Y	4588	ANA588Y
4532	ANA532Y	4548	ANA548Y	4561	ANA561Y	4575	ANA575Y	4590	ANA590Y
4534	ANA534Y	4549	ANA549Y	4562	ANA562Y	4576	ANA576Y	4591	ANA591Y
4535	ANA535Y	4551	ANA551Y	4563	ANA563Y	4578	ANA578Y	4594	ANA594Y
4536	ANA536Y	4554	ANA554Y	4566	ANA566Y	4580	ANA580Y	4595	ANA595Y
4539	ANA539Y	4555	ANA555Y	4567	ANA567Y	4581	ANA581Y	4598	ANA598Y
4540	ANA540Y	4556	ANA556Y	4570	ANA570Y	4583	ANA583Y	4599	ANA599Y
4541	ANA541Y								

4602-4697

Leyland Atlantean AN68D/1R   Northern Counties   H43/32F   1982-84

4602	ANA602Y	4619	ANA619Y	4638	ANA638Y	4655	ANA655Y	4676	A676HNB
4603	ANA603Y	4621	ANA621Y	4640	ANA640Y	4656	A656HNB	4677	A677HNB
4606	ANA606Y	4622	ANA622Y	4641	ANA641Y	4658	A658HNB	4681	A681HNB
4607	ANA607Y	4623	ANA623Y	4642	ANA642Y	4659	A659HNB	4682	A682HNB
4610	ANA610Y	4626	ANA626Y	4643	ANA643Y	4662	A662HNB	4685	A685HNB
4611	ANA611Y	4628	ANA628Y	4645	ANA645Y	4663	A663HNB	4686	A686HNB
4614	ANA614Y	4629	ANA629Y	4648	ANA648Y	4666	A666HNB	4689	A689HNB
4615	ANA615Y	4633	ANA633Y	4649	ANA649Y	4667	A667HNB	4691	A691HNB
4616	ANA616Y	4634	ANA634Y	4650	ANA650Y	4670	A670HNB	4692	A692HNB
4617	ANA617Y	4635	ANA635Y	4652	ANA652Y	4672	A672HNB	4697	A697HNB
4618	ANA618Y	4636	ANA636Y	4654	ANA654Y	4673	A673HNB		

Typical of the Greater Manchester standard double-deck is Atlantean 4431, SND431X seen at the bus station in Manchester Piccadilly shortly before rebuilding commenced. This model, with Northern Counties bodywork, still forms the main type of double-deck bus in the fleet.

4701-4765 Leyland Atlantean AN68D/1R Northern Counties H43/32F 1984

4701 A701LNC	4717 A717LNC	4728 A728LNC	4738 A738NNA	4755 A755NNA
4703 A703LNC	4718 A718LNC	4729 A729LNC	4739 A739NNA	4756 A756NNA
4707 A707LNC	4720 A720LNC	4731 A731NNA	4740 A740NNA	4758 A758NNA
4709 A709LNC	4721 A721LNC	4732 A732NNA	4742 A742NNA	4760 A760NNA
4712 A712LNC	4723 A723LNC	4733 A733NNA	4746 A746NNA	4763 A763NNA
4713 A713LNC	4724 A724LNC	4736 A736NNA	4753 A753NNA	4765 A765NNA
4716 A716LNC	4727 A727LNC	4737 A737NNA		

4914	PTD642S	Leyland Fleetline FE30AGR	Northern Counties	H41/32F	1977	Ex Yorkshire Rider, 1994
4920	PTD648S	Leyland Fleetline FE30AGR	Northern Counties	H43/32F	1977	Ex Yorkshire Rider, 1994
4922w	PTD650S	Leyland Fleetline FE30AGR	Northern Counties	H43/32F	1977	Ex Yorkshire Rider, 1994
4926w	PTD654S	Leyland Fleetline FE30AGR	Northern Counties	H43/32F	1977	Ex Yorkshire Rider, 1994

4942-4990 Leyland Fleetline FE30AGR Northern Counties H43/32F 1979-81

4942 TWH701T	4953 YTE590V	4967 DWH683W	4975 DWH691W	4985 DWH701W
4943 TWH702T	4955 YTE592V	4970 DWH686W	4976 DWH692W	4986 DWH702W
4946 WWH94T	4956 YTE593V	4971 DWH687W	4977 DWH693W	4987 DWH703W
4947 YTE584V	4961 BCB614V	4972 DWH688W	4979 DWH695W	4988 DWH704W
4948w YTE585V	4962 BCB615V	4973 DWH689W	4981 DWH697W	4989 DWH705W
4949 YTE586V	4963 BCB616V	4974 DWH690W	4982 DWH698W	4990 DWH706W
4952 YTE589V				

5011-5015 MCW Metrobus DR102/10 MCW H43/30F 1980

5011 GBU11V	5012 GBU12V	5013 GBU13V	5014 GBU14V	5015 GBU15V

5031-5105 MCW Metrobus DR102/21 MCW H43/30F 1981

5031 MRJ31W	5057 MRJ57W	5064 MRJ64W	5085 ORJ85W	5097 ORJ97W
5032 MRJ32W	5058 MRJ58W	5068 MRJ68W	5086 ORJ86W	5099 ORJ99W
5033 MRJ33W	5059 MRJ59W	5069 MRJ69W	5087 ORJ87W	5101 SND101X
5034 MRJ34W	5060 MRJ60W	5070 MRJ70W	5088 ORJ88W	5102 SND102X
5035 MRJ35W	5061 MRJ61W	5082 ORJ82W	5089 ORJ89W	5103 SND103X
5039 MRJ39W	5062 MRJ62W	5083 ORJ83W	5090 ORJ90W	5104 SND104X
5050 MRJ50W	5063 MRJ63W	5084 ORJ84W	5096 ORJ96W	5105 SND105X
5056 MRJ56W				

5112-5189 MCW Metrobus DR102/23 MCW H43/30F 1981-83

5112 SND112X	5131 SND131X	5147 SND147X	5168 ANA168Y	5181 ANA181Y
5113 SND113X	5133 SND133X	5148 SND148X	5169 ANA169Y	5182 ANA182Y
5114 SND114X	5134 SND134X	5149 SND149X	5171 ANA171Y	5183 ANA183Y
5115 SND115X	5135 SND135X	5150 SND150X	5172 ANA172Y	5184 ANA184Y
5122 SND122X	5136 SND136X	5151 ANA151Y	5174 ANA174Y	5185 ANA185Y
5126 SND126X	5137 SND137X	5152 ANA152Y	5175 ANA175Y	5186 ANA186Y
5127 SND127X	5138 SND138X	5156 ANA156Y	5176 ANA176Y	5187 ANA187Y
5128 SND128X	5139 SND139X	5166 ANA166Y	5177 ANA177Y	5188 ANA188Y
5129 SND129X	5140 SND140X	5167 ANA167Y	5178 ANA178Y	5189 ANA189Y
5130 SND130X	5146 SND146X			

5201-5210 MCW Metrobus DR132/8 Northern Counties DPH43/29F 1986

5201 C201FVU	5203 C203FVU	5205 C205FVU	5207 C207FVU	5209 C209FVU
5202 C202FVU	5204 C204FVU	5206 C206FVU	5208 C208FVU	5210 C210FVU

5301-5320 MCW Metrobus DR102/51 Northern Counties DPH43/29F 1986-87

5301 D301JVR	5305 D305JVR	5309 D309JVR	5313 D313LNB	5317 D317LNB
5302 D302JVR	5306 D306JVR	5310 D310JVR	5314 D314LNB	5318 D318LNB
5303 D303JVR	5307 D307JVR	5311 D311LNB	5315 D315LNB	5319 D319LNB
5304 D304JVR	5308 D308JVR	5312 D312LNB	5316 D316LNB	5320 D320LNB

The 1992 delivery of Volvo Citybuses all went to GMN when the fleet was divided and can now be found working from Oldham and Wigan. While pictured on the 170 route in Oldham centre, the bus is liveried for the Trans-Lancs Express service 400 where it is normally found. *Paul Wigan*

7001-7008

Volvo Citybus B10M-50   Northern Counties   H41/35F   1991

7001	H701GVM	7003	H703GVM	7005	H705GVM	7007	H707GVM	7008	H708GVM
7002	H702GVM	7004	H704GVM	7006	H706GVM				

7009	J709ONF	Volvo Citybus B10M-50	Northern Counties	H45/25FL	1992
7010	J710ONF	Volvo Citybus B10M-50	Northern Counties	H45/25FL	1992
7077	WBN955L	Leyland Atlantean AN68/1R	Park Royal	O43/32F	1972
7685w	ONF685R	Leyland Atlantean AN68A/1R	Northern Counties	H43/32F	1976	Ex Yorkshire Rider, 1994
7691	ONF691R	Leyland Atlantean AN68A/1R	Northern Counties	H43/32F	1976	Ex Yorkshire Rider, 1994
7698w	ONF698R	Leyland Atlantean AN68A/1R	Northern Counties	H43/32F	1977	Ex Yorkshire Rider, 1994

7706-7797

Leyland Atlantean AN68A/1R   Northern Counties   H43/32F   1977   7706/8/25/62/73/97 ex Yorkshire Rider, 1994

7706	RJA706R	7724	RJA724R	7767w	UNA767S	7779w	UNA779S	7785	UNA785S
7708	RJA708R	7725	RJA725R	7769	UNA769S	7782	UNA782S	7787w	UNA787S
7719w	RJA719R	7726	RJA726R	7771	UNA771S	7783w	UNA783S	7797	UNA797S
7721w	RJA721R	7762w	UNA762S	7773w	UNA773S				

7802-7886

Leyland Atlantean AN68A/1R   Park Royal   H43/32F   1977-78

7802	RJA802R	7809	RJA809R	7828	UNA828S	7834	UNA834S	7852w	UNA852S
7803	RJA803R	7821	UNA821S	7829w	UNA829S	7839	UNA839S	7866w	UNA866S
7805	RJA805R	7822w	UNA822S	7833	UNA833S	7847	UNA847S	7886	WVM886S

7904-7951

Leyland Atlantean AN68A/1R   Park Royal   H43/32F   1978-79

7904	ANC904T	7911	ANC911T	7928w	ANC928T	7937w	BNC937T	7951	BNC951T

Livery: Orange, white and black; pink, orange, red, brown and white (Express) 3239-3277; 5201-5210; 5301-5320

GMS BUSES

Greater Manchester Buses South Ltd, Charterplan House, 151 Charles Street,
Stockport, Greater Manchester, SK1 3JU

Depots : Bennett Street, Manchester; Charles Street, Stockport; Hyde Road, Manchester; York Street, Glossop; Princess
Road, Manchester and Daw Bank, Stockport.

1	OJI9451	Leyland Tiger TRCTL11/3R	Plaxton Paramount 3200 II	C53F	1985	
2	OJI9452	Leyland Tiger TRCTL11/3R	Plaxton Paramount 3200 II	C53F	1985	
3	NIW1673	Leyland Tiger TRCTL11/3RH	Plaxton Paramount 3200 II	C53F	1985	
4	TPX884	Leyland Tiger TRCTL11/3RH	Plaxton Paramount 3500 II	C49FT	1985	
5	OJI9455	Volvo B10M-61	Plaxton Paramount 3200 II	C53F	1985	
6	NIW1676	Volvo B10M-61	Plaxton Paramount 3200 II	C53F	1986	
7	IIL1047	Volvo B10M-61	Plaxton Paramount 3200 II	C53F	1986	
8	OIW1608	Leyland Tiger TRCTL11/3RH	Duple 320	C57F	1986	
9	NIW2399	Leyland Tiger TRCTL11/3RH	Duple 320	C57F	1986	
10	C310ENA	Leyland Tiger TRCTL11/3RH	Duple 320	C57F	1986	
11	SIB1361	Leyland Tiger TRCTL11/3RH	Duple 320	C57F	1986	
12	SIB1832	Leyland Tiger TRCTL11/3RH	Duple 320	C57F	1986	
14	SIB2014	Volvo B10M-61	Plaxton Paramount 3500 II	C49F	1986	Ex Excelsior, 1989
15	PXI7915	Volvo B10M-61	Plaxton Paramount 3500 III	C53F	1988	Ex Park's, 1989
16	PXI8916	Volvo B10M-61	Plaxton Paramount 3500 III	C53F	1988	Ex Park's, 1989
17	OIW1317	Leyland Tiger TRCTL11/3RH	Plaxton Paramount 3500 III	C49FT	1989	
18	OIW1318	Volvo B10M-61	Plaxton Paramount 3500 III	C53F	1989	Ex Park's, 1990
19	OIW1319	Volvo B10M-61	Plaxton Paramount 3500 III	C53F	1989	Ex Park's, 1990
20	583TD	Kässbohrer Setra S215HD	Kässbohrer Tornado	C49F	1990	
22	WIA4122	Kässbohrer Setra S215HD	Kässbohrer Tornado	C49F	1989	Ex Craiggs, Radcliffe, 1991
23	G715TTY	Kässbohrer Setra S215HD	Kässbohrer Tornado	C49F	1989	Ex Craiggs, Radcliffe, 1991
24	J73VTG	Kässbohrer Setra S215HD	Kässbohrer Tornado	C49F	1994	
25	L543YUS	Volvo B10M-60	Van Hool Alizée	C30FT	1989	Ex Park's, 1994
26	SDZ9026	Volvo B10M-60	Jonckheere Deauville P599	C53F	1989	Ex Redwing, Camberwell, 1994
30	515VTB	Kässbohrer Setra S215HD	Kässbohrer Tornado	C49F	1983	
32	OTK802	Kässbohrer Setra S215HD	Kässbohrer Tornado	C49F	1983	
33	OXK373	Kässbohrer Setra S215HD	Kässbohrer Tornado	C49F	1983	
64	RIW3364	Leyland Tiger TRCTL11/3R	Plaxton Paramount 3200	C53F	1983	Ex The Londoners, Nunhead, 1985
65	KGS493Y	Leyland Tiger TRCTL11/3R	Plaxton Paramount 3200	C53F	1983	Ex The Londoners, Nunhead, 1985
82	SND82X	Leyland Leopard PSU3B/4R	Duple Dominant IV (1981)	C51F	1975	
86	SND86X	Leyland Leopard PSU3B/4R	Duple Dominant IV (1982)	C51F	1975	
100	476CEL	Leyland Leopard PSU3B/4R	Duple Dominant IV (1984)	C42FTL	1975	

190-240

									B49F*	1977/79 *190 is DP42F

Leyland National 11351A/1R

190	ABA15T	**194**	ABA19T	**205**	ABA30T	**232**	WBN466T	**240**	WBN474T
192	ABA17T	**199**	ABA24T						

251	RUF41R	Leyland National 11351A/2R	DP52F	1977	Ex Hogg, Glasgow, 1994
252	JIL8374	Leyland National 1151/1R/0401	B49F	1973	Ex Munro, Uddington, 1994
253	JIL7610	Leyland National 1151/1R/0402	B49F	1973	Ex R & I, Milton Keynes, 1994
255	LIL3317	Leyland National 11351A/1R	B49F	1979	Ex Amberley, Pudsey, 1994
256	SJI2054	Leyland National 11351A/1R	B49F	1978	Ex Amberley, Pudsey, 1994
257	SJI4558	Leyland National 11351A/1R	B49F	1978	Ex Amberley, Pudsey, 1994
258	SJI4559	Leyland National 11351/1R	B48F	1975	Ex Amberley, Pudsey, 1994
259	SJI4560	Leyland National 1151/1R/SC	DP45F	1975	Ex Amberley, Pudsey, 1994
260	JIL5279	Leyland National 1151/1R/0403	B49F	1973	Ex Amberley, Pudsey, 1994
261	TJI2488	Leyland National 11351/1R/SC	DP45F	1975	Ex Golden Coaches, Llantwit Major, 1994
267	LIL4612	Leyland National 1151/2R/0403	B44D	1972	Ex Gatwick Handling, 1994
269	JIL7609	Leyland National 1151/2R/0403	B44D	1972	Ex Gatwick Handling, 1994
271	JIL7608	Leyland National 1151/2R/0403	B44D	1973	Ex Gatwick Handling, 1994
272	JIL7607	Leyland National 1151/2R/0403	B44D	1973	Ex Gatwick Handling, 1994
273	JIL7606	Leyland National 11351/2R	B46D	1974	Ex Gatwick Handling, 1994

Opposite: **GMS Buses has recently taken its first new vehicles into stock in the form of thirty Mercedes-Benz 811s with Alexander Sprint bodies. These have followed some twenty Volvo B6s that have been leased to GMS Buses from Stagecoach in a commercial venture. The examples of each type seen here are 319, M459VHE at Manchester's Piccadilly and 401, N401WVR seen at Stockport bus station.** *Paul Wigan/Tony Wilson*

301-310   Volvo B6-9.9M   Alexander Dash   B40F   1994   Ex Busways, 1995

301	M741PRS	303	M743PRS	305	M745PRS	307	M847PRS	309	M749PRS
302	M742PRS	304	M744PRS	306	M746PRS	308	M748PRS	310	M750PRS

311-320   Volvo B6-9.9M   Alexander Dash   B40F   1994   Ex East Midland, 1995

311	M461VHE	313	M846HDF	315	M455VHE	317	M457VHE	319	M459VHE
312	M462VHE	314	M454VHE	316	M456VHE	318	M458VHE	320	M460VHE

401-430   Mercedes-Benz 811D   Alexander Sprint   B31F   1995-96

401	N401WVR	407	N407WVR	413	N413WVR	419	N419WVR	425	N425WVR
402	N402WVR	408	N408WVR	414	N414WVR	420	N420WVR	426	N426WVR
403	N403WVR	409	N409WVR	415	N415WVR	421	N421WVR	427	N427WVR
404	N404WVR	410	.N410WVR	416	N416WVR	422	N422WVR	428	N428WVR
405	N405WVR	411	N411WVR	417	N417WVR	423	N423WVR	429	N429WVR
406	N406WVR	412	N412WVR	418	N418WVR	424	N424WVR	430	N430WVR

1451	NJA568W	Leyland Olympian B45/TL11/1R	Northern Counties	H43/30F	1980	
1461	FWH461Y	Scania BR112DH	Northern Counties	H43/32F	1983	
1462	FWH462Y	Scania BR112DH	Northern Counties	H43/32F	1983	

1463-1467   Scania N113DRB   Northern Counties   H47/28F   1991

1463	H463GVM	1464	H464GVM	1465	H465GVM	1466	H466GVM	1467	H467GVM

1471	A471HNC	Dennis Falcon V	Northern Counties	H47/37F	1984
1472	A472HNC	Dennis Falcon V	Northern Counties	H47/37F	1984
1473	A473HNC	Dennis Falcon V	Northern Counties	H47/37F	1984

1601-1680   MCW Metrorider MF151/3   MCW   B23F*   1987   *1639 is DP19F

1601	D601MDB	1618	D618MDB	1636	D636MDB	1651	D651NNE	1666	D666NNE
1602	D602MDB	1619	D619MDB	1638	D638MDB	1652	D652NNE	1667	D667NNE
1603	D603MDB	1620	D620MDB	1639	D639MDB	1653	D653NNE	1668	D668NNE
1604	D604MDB	1621	D621MDB	1640	D640MDB	1654	D654NNE	1670	D670NNE
1605	D605MDB	1623	D623MDB	1641	D641MDB	1655	D655NNE	1671	D671NNE
1606	D606MDB	1624	D624MDB	1642	D642MDB	1656	D656NNE	1672	D672NNE
1607	D607MDB	1626	D626MDB	1643	D643MDB	1657	D657NNE	1673	D673NNE
1608	D608MDB	1627	D627MDB	1644	D644MDB	1658	D658NNE	1674	D674NNE
1609	D609MDB	1628	D628MDB	1645	D645MDB	1659	D659NNE	1675	D675NNE
1610	D610MDB	1629	D629MDB	1646	D646MDB	1661	D661NNE	1676	D676NNE
1611	D611MDB	1630	D630MDB	1647	D647MDB	1662	D662NNE	1677	D677NNE
1612	D612MDB	1632	D632MDB	1648	D648MDB	1663	D663NNE	1678	D678NNE
1613	D613MDB	1633	D633MDB	1649	D649MDB	1664	D664NNE	1679	D679NNE
1614	D614MDB	1634	D634MDB	1650	D650MDB	1665	D665NNE	1680	D680NNE
1617	D617MDB	1635	D635MDB						

1721-1728   Renault-Dodge S75   Northern Counties   B17FL   1990-91

1721	H721CNC	1724	H724CNC	1726	H726CNC	1727	H727FNC	1728	H728FNC

1751-1770   Dennis Domino SDA1201   Northern Counties   B24F   1985-86

1751	C751YBA	1755	C755YBA	1760	C760YBA	1763	C763YBA	1766	C766YBA
1752	C752YBA	1756	C756YBA	1761	C761YBA	1764	C764YBA	1768	C768YBA
1753	C753YBA	1757	C757YBA	1762	C762YBA	1765	C765YBA	1769	C769YBA
1754	C754YBA	1758	C758YBA						

1772-1892   Renault-Dodge S56   Northern Counties   B20F   1986-87

1772	D772RBU	1776	D776RBU	1791	E791SJA	1797	E797SJA	1891	D891MDB
1773	D773RBU	1781	D781RBU	1792	E792SJA	1843	D843LND	1892	D892MDB
1774	D774RBU	1782	D783RBU	1793	E793SJA				

1917-2000   Renault-Dodge S56   Northern Counties   B20F   1987

1917	D917NDB	1922	D922NDB	1963	D963PJA	1981	E981SJA	1999	E999SJA
1921	D921NDB	1944	D944NDB	1971	D971PJA	1990	E990SJA	2000	E200SVR

Dennis supplied trial Dominators to Greater Manchester in 1980 and 1981, though this trio was sold some years ago. A batch of 30 in 1985 were followed by a further ten in 1991. Illustrated here is 2037, H137GVM. *Richard Godfrey*

2001-2030

Dennis Dominator DDA1003 — Northern Counties — H43/32F — 1985

2001	B901TVR	2007	B907TVR	2013	B913TVR	2019	B919TVR	2025	B25TVU
2002	B902TVR	2008	B908TVR	2014	B914TVR	2020	B920TVR	2026	B26TVU
2003	B903TVR	2009	B909TVR	2015	B915TVR	2021	B21TVU	2027	B27TVU
2004	B904TVR	2010	B910TVR	2016	B916TVR	2022	B22TVU	2028	B28TVU
2005	B905TVR	2011	B911TVR	2017	B917TVR	2023	B23TVU	2029	B29TVU
2006	B906TVR	2012	B912TVR	2018	B918TVR	2024	B24TVU	2030	B30TVU

2031-2040

Dennis Dominator DDA2033 — Northern Counties — H43/29F* — 1991 — *2032 is H42/29F

2031	H131GVM	2033	H133GVM	2035	H135GVM	2037	H137GVM	2039	H139GVM
2032	H132GVM	2034	H134GVM	2036	H136GVM	2038	H138GVM	2040	H140GVM

3001-3010

Leyland Olympian ONTL11/1R — Northern Counties — H43/30F — 1982

3001	ANA1Y	3003	ANA3Y	3005	ANA5Y	3007	ANA7Y	3009	ANA9Y
3002	ANA2Y	3004	ANA4Y	3006	ANA6Y	3008	ANA8Y	3010	ANA10Y

3016-3025

Leyland Olympian ONLXCT/1R — Northern Counties — H43/30F — 1983-84

3016	A581HDB	3018	A583HDB	3020	A585HDB	3022	A22HNC	3024	A24HNC
3017	A582HDB	3019	A584HDB	3021	A21HNC	3023	A23HNC	3025	A25HNC

3026-3035

Leyland Olympian ONLXB/1R — Northern Counties — H43/30F — 1984

3026	A26ORJ	3028	A28ORJ	3030	A30ORJ	3032	A32ORJ	3034	B34PJA
3027	A27ORJ	3029	A29ORJ	3031	A31ORJ	3033	A33ORJ	3035	B35PJA

Large fleet numbers have been applied to the top off-side corner of the double-deck buses to enable their identification on monitors. This feature is shown on Leyland Olympian 3122, B122TVU based at Hyde Road. It is seen turning out of Oldham Street into Piccadilly, Manchester.

3036-3236 — Leyland Olympian ONLXB/1R — Northern Counties — H43/30F* 1984-86 *3139 is DPH43/15F

3198 and 3213 are DPH43/26F; 3214 is DPH43/18F

3036	B36PJA	3084	B84PJA	3132	B132WNB	3165	C165YBA	3196	C196YBA
3039	B39PJA	3086	B86SJA	3133	B133WNB	3166	C166YBA	3197	C197YBA
3049	B49PJA	3087	B87SJA	3135	B135WNB	3167	C167YBA	3198	C198YBA
3053	B53PJA	3088	B88SJA	3137	B137WNB	3169	C169YBA	3205	C205CBU
3055	B55PJA	3089	B89SJA	3138	B138WNB	3170	C170YBA	3207	C207CBU
3056	B56PJA	3091	B91SJA	3139	B139WNB	3172	C172YBA	3208	C208CBU
3057	B57PJA	3094	B94SJA	3143	B143WNB	3173	C173YBA	3210	C210CBU
3058	B58PJA	3095	B95SJA	3145	B145WNB	3174	C174YBA	3212	C212CBU
3060	B60PJA	3110	B110SJA	3146	B146XNA	3175	C175YBA	3213	C213CBU
3065	B65PJA	3114	B114SJA	3147	B147XNA	3176	C176YBA	3214	C214CBU
3067	B67PJA	3117	B117TVU	3149	B149XNA	3178	C178YBA	3215	C215CBU
3069	B69PJA	3118	B118TVU	3150	B150XNA	3179	C179YBA	3216	C216CBU
3070	B70PJA	3119	B119TVU	3153	B153XNA	3181	C181YBA	3221	C221CBU
3072	B72PJA	3121	B121TVU	3154	B154XNA	3184	C184YBA	3224	C224CBU
3074	B74PJA	3122	B122TVU	3155	B155XNA	3185	C185YBA	3226	C226ENE
3077	B77PJA	3124	B124TVU	3156	C156YBA	3191	C191YBA	3230	C230ENE
3080	B80PJA	3125	B125TVU	3158	C158YBA	3193	C193YBA	3234	C234ENE
3082	B82PJA	3126	B126WNB	3164	C164YBA	3195	C195YBA	3236	C236EVU

3255-3277 — Leyland Olympian ONLXB/1R — Northern Counties — DPH43/26F 1986-87

3255	C255FRJ	3268	D268JVR	3269	D269JVR	3272	D272JVR	3277	D277JVR
3260	D260JVR						

3282-3304 — Leyland Olympian ONLXB/1RZ — Northern Counties — H43/30F* 1988-89 *3291 is DPH43/25F

3282	F282DRJ	3289	F289DRJ	3295	F295DRJ	3298	F298DRJ	3301	F301DRJ
3283	F283DRJ	3291	F291DRJ	3296	F296DRJ	3300	F300DRJ	3304	F304DRJ
3285	F285DRJ	3294	F294DRJ	3297	F297DRJ			

4152-4200
Leyland Atlantean AN68A/1R Northern Counties H43/32F 1978

4152	VBA152S	4164	VBA164S	4170	VBA170S	4182	VBA182S	4190	VBA190S
4153	VBA153S	4166	VBA166S	4174	VBA174S	4186	VBA186S	4193	VBA193S
4156	VBA156S	4168	VBA168S	4175	VBA175S	4187	VBA187S	4195	VBA195S
4157	VBA157S	4169	VBA169S	4178	VBA178S	4188	VBA188S	4200	VBA200S
4162	VBA162S								

4203-4295
Leyland Atlantean AN68A/1R Northern Counties H43/32F 1978-80

4203	XRJ203S	4218	ANA218T	4234	ANA234T	4246	FVR246V	4280	FVR280V
4204	XRJ204S	4220	ANA220T	4235	ANA235T	4247	FVR247V	4281	FVR281V
4210	ANA210T	4222w	ANA222T	4236	ANA236T	4249	FVR249V	4283w	FVR283V
4212	ANA212T	4225	ANA225T	4237	ANA237T	4250	FVR250V	4290	FVR290V
4214	ANA214T	4227	ANA227T	4241	ANA241T	4252	FVR252V	4291	FVR291V
4215	ANA215T	4230	ANA230T	4242	FVR242V	4259	FVR259V	4294	FVR294V
4217	ANA217T	4231	ANA231T	4245	FVR245V	4264	FVR264V	4295	FVR295V

4301-4348
Leyland Atlantean AN68A/1R Northern Counties H43/32F 1980-81

4301	KDB301V	4309	MNC509W	4319	MNC519W	4328	MNC528W	4339	MNC539W
4302	KDB302V	4312	MNC512W	4321	MNC521W	4329	MNC529W	4343	MNC543W
4304	MNC504W	4314	MNC514W	4325	MNC525W	4332	MNC523W	4348	MNC548W
4307	MNC507W	4317	MNC517W	4327	MNC527W				

4352-4396
Leyland Atlantean AN68A/1R Northern Counties H43/32F 1981

4352	ORJ352W	4368	ORJ368W	4377	ORJ377W	4381	ORJ381W	4395	ORJ395W
4362	ORJ362W	4375	ORJ375W	4380	ORJ380W	4393	ORJ393W	4396	ORJ396W
4365	ORJ365W	4376	ORJ376W						

4402-4521
Leyland Atlantean AN68A/1R* Northern Counties H43/32F 1981-82
*4425/49/55-72/6/7/80-4, 501-21 are AN68B/1R

4402	MRJ402W	4430	SND430X	4454	SND454X	4479	SND479X	4501	SND501X
4404	MRJ404W	4432	SND434X	4455	SND455X	4480	SND480X	4505	SND505X
4406	MRJ406W	4435	SND435X	4462	SND452X	4483	SND483X	4506	SND506X
4409	MRJ409W	4437	SND437X	4465	SND465X	4484	SND484X	4512	SND512X
4412	SND412X	4440	SND440X	4468	SND468X	4487	SND487X	4513	SND513X
4418	SND418X	4449	SND449X	4472	SND472X	4488	SND488X	4514	SND514X
4421	SND421X	4450	SND450X	4473	SND473X	4489	SND489X	4518	SND518X
4422	SND422X	4451	SND451X	4476	SND476X	4495	SND495X	4519	SND519X
4425	SND425X	4452	SND452X	4477	SND477X	4496	SND496X	4521	SND521X
4429	SND429X	4453	SND453X						

4526-4600
Leyland Atlantean AN68D/1R Northern Counties H43/32F 1982

4526	SND526X	4543	ANA543Y	4559	ANA559Y	4579	ANA579Y	4592	ANA592Y
4527	SND527X	4545	ANA544Y	4564	ANA564Y	4582	ANA582Y	4593	ANA593Y
4530	SND530X	4546	ANA546Y	4568	ANA568Y	4585	ANA585Y	4596	ANA596Y
4533	ANA533Y	4550	ANA550Y	4569	ANA569Y	4586	ANA586Y	4597	ANA597Y
4537	ANA537Y	4552	ANA552Y	4572	ANA572Y	4589	ANA589Y	4600	ANA600Y
4538	ANA538Y	4553	ANA553Y	4577	ANA577Y				

4601-4700
Leyland Atlantean AN68D/1R Northern Counties H43/32F 1983-84

4601	ANA601Y	4627	ANA627Y	4651	ANA651Y	4671	A671HNB	4688	A688HNB
4604	ANA604Y	4630	ANA630Y	4653	ANA653Y	4674	A674HNB	4690	A690HNB
4605	ANA605Y	4631	ANA631Y	4657	A657HNB	4675	A675HNB	4693	A693HNB
4608	ANA608Y	4632	ANA633Y	4660	A660HNB	4678	A678HNB	4694	A694HNB
4609	ANA609Y	4637	ANA637Y	4661	A661HNB	4679	A679HNB	4695	A695HNB
4612	ANA612Y	4639	ANA639Y	4664	A664HNB	4680	A680HNB	4696	A696HNB
4613	ANA613Y	4644	ANA644Y	4665	A665HNB	4683	A683HNB	4698	A698HNB
4620	ANA620Y	4646	ANA646Y	4668	A668HNB	4684	A684HNB	4699	A699HNB
4624	ANA624Y	4647	ANA647Y	4669	A669HNB	4687	A687HNB	4700	A700HNB
4625	ANA625Y								

4702-4764

			Leyland Atlantean AN68D/1R		Northern Counties		H43/32F		1984	

4702	A702LNC	**4714**	A714LNC	**4734**	A734NNA	**4747**	A747NNA	**4754**	A754NNA
4704	A704LNC	**4715**	A715LNC	**4735**	A735NNA	**4748**	A748NNA	**4757**	A757NNA
4705	A705LNC	**4719**	A719LNC	**4741**	A741NNA	**4749**	A749NNA	**4759**	A759NNA
4706	A706LNC	**4722**	A722LNC	**4743**	A743NNA	**4750**	A750NNA	**4761**	A761NNA
4708	A708LNC	**4725**	A725LNC	**4744**	A744NNA	**4751**	A751NNA	**4762**	A762NNA
4710	A710LNC	**4726**	A726LNC	**4745**	A745NNA	**4752**	A752NNA	**4764**	A764NNA
4711	A711LNC	**4730**	A730LNC						

5017-5030

MCW Metrobus DR102/10   MCW   H43/30F   1980

5017	GBU17V	**5020**	GBU20V	**5023**	MNC497W	**5027**	GBU27V	**5029**	GBU29V
5018	MNC494W	**5021**	MNC496W	**5024**	GBU24V	**5028**	GBU28V	**5030**	MNC499W
5019	MNC495W	**5022**	GBU22V	**5026**	MNC498W				

5036-5110

MCW Metrobus DR102/21   MCW   H43/30F   1981

5036	MRJ36W	**5046**	MRJ46W	**5066**	MRJ66W	**5078**	ORJ78W	**5095**	ORJ95W
5037	MRJ37W	**5047**	MRJ47W	**5067**	MRJ67W	**5079**	ORJ79W	**5098**	ORJ98W
5038	MRJ38W	**5048**	MRJ48W	**5071**	MRJ71W	**5080**	ORJ80W	**5100**	ORJ100W
5040	MRJ40W	**5049**	MRJ49W	**5072**	ORJ72W	**5081**	ORJ81W	**5106**	SND106X
5041	MRJ41W	**5051**	MRJ51W	**5073**	ORJ73W	**5091**	ORJ91W	**5107**	SND107X
5042	MRJ42W	**5052**	MRJ52W	**5074**	ORJ74W	**5092**	ORJ92W	**5108**	SND108X
5043	MRJ43W	**5053**	MRJ53W	**5075**	ORJ75W	**5093**	ORJ93W	**5109**	SND109X
5044	MRJ44W	**5054**	MRJ54W	**5076**	ORJ76W	**5094**	ORJ94W	**5110**	SND110X
5045	MRJ45W	**5055**	MRJ55W	**5077**	ORJ77W				

5111-5190

MCW Metrobus DR102/23   MCW   H43/30F   1981-83

5111	SND111X	**5123**	SND123X	**5144**	SND144X	**5159**	ANA159Y	**5165**	ANA165Y
5116	SND116X	**5124**	SND124X	**5145**	SND145X	**5160**	ANA160Y	**5170**	ANA170Y
5117	SND117X	**5125**	SND125X	**5153**	ANA153Y	**5161**	ANA161Y	**5173**	ANA173Y
5118	SND118X	**5132**	SND132X	**5154**	ANA154Y	**5162**	ANA162Y	**5179**	ANA179Y
5119	SND119X	**5141**	SND141X	**5155**	ANA155Y	**5163**	ANA163Y	**5180**	ANA180Y
5120	SND120X	**5142**	SND142X	**5157**	ANA157Y	**5164**	ANA164Y	**5190**	ANA190Y
5121	SND121X	**5143**	SND143X	**5158**	ANA158Y				

7032	VNB132L	Leyland Atlantean AN68/1R	Park Royal	O43/32F	1972
7701	RJA701R	Leyland Atlantean AN68A/1R	Northern Counties	H43/32F	1977
7729	RJA729R	Leyland Atlantean AN68A/1R	Northern Counties	H43/32F	1977
7759	SRJ759R	Leyland Atlantean AN68A/1R	Northern Counties	H43/32F	1977
7766	UNA766S	Leyland Atlantean AN68A/1R	Northern Counties	H43/32F	1977

7815-7960

Leyland Atlantean AN68A/1R   Park Royal   H43/32F   1977-79

7815	RJA815R	**7860**	UNA860S	**7885**	WVM885S	**7912**	ANC912T	**7944**	BNC944T
7820	UNA820S	**7862**	UNA862S	**7891**	WVM891S	**7913**	ANC913T	**7954**	BNC954T
7831	UNA831S	**7870**	WVM870S	**7895**	WVM895S	**7929**	BNC929T	**7956**	BNC956T
7838	UNA838S	**7872**	WVM872S	**7896**	WVM896S	**7941**	BNC941T	**7959**	BNC959T
7843	UNA843S	**7879**	WVM879S						

Previous Registrations:

476CEL	HNE642N	NIW1673	B370VBA	RIW3364	KGS491Y, 583TD
515VTB	From new	NIW1676	C706END	SDZ9026	G174RBD
583TD	H170DVL	NIW2399	C309ENA	SIB1361	C311ENA
IIL1047	C707END	OIW1317	F853JVR	SIB1832	C312ENA
JIL5279	JHU861L	OIW1318	F33HGG	SIB2014	C106AFX
JIL7606	GFJ663N	OIW1319	F35HGG	SJI2054	FNS161T
JIL7607	JHU868L	OIW1608	C308ENA	SJI4558	CFM352S
JIL7608	XRB416L	OJI9451	B368VBA	SJI4559	LPR937P
JIL7609	WFM817L	OJI9452	B369VBA	SJI4560	HMA657N
JIL7610	DBY717M	OJI9455	C167ANA	TJI2488	KDW347P
JIL8374	DBY718M	OTK802	A32KBA	TPX884	B371VBA
L543YUS	XIA257, KSK954	OXK373	A33KBA	WIA4122	G181VBB
LIL3317	EUM900T	PXI7915	E574UHS		
LIL4612	WFM806L	PXI8916	E578UHS		

Livery: Orange, white and brown

Two Scania double-deck buses joined the Greater Manchester Transport fleet in 1983 as 1461 and 1462 and these passed to GMS Buses when the fleet was divided. Shown working the Wilmslow Road services is 1461, FWH461Y with a large Scania badge affixed to the front. *Richard Godfrey*

While the last of the Fleetlines have now been withdrawn from the GMS Buses fleet - these were the ones based on the Wirral in blue livery - similarly aged Leyland Atlanteans remain, though their numbers are diminishing. Photographed in Stockport is 7954, BNC954T one of the type bodied by Park Royal to the then GMT Standard design. *Tony Wilson*

HOLMESWOOD

Holmeswood Coaches Ltd, Fallowfields, Sandy Way, Holmeswood, Rufford, Lancashire

BHF291A	AEC Reliance 2MU3RV	Plaxton Elite III(1973)	C41F	1960	Ex Wimpey, 1973
ECK865E	Leyland Leopard PSU3/4R	Plaxton Supreme(1980)	C49F	1967	Ex Hants & Dorset, 1980
A914RRN	Leyland Tiger B43	Plaxton P 3200(1984)	C49F	1979	Ex Mercers, Longridge, 1984
LCW411W	Leyland Tiger TRCTL11/3R	Duple Dominant II	C57F	1981	Ex Mercers, Preston, 1993
201SC	Leyland Tiger TRCTL11/3R	Plaxton Paramount 3500	C53F	1983	Ex London & Country, 1990
AAX300A	Leyland Tiger TRCTL11/3R	Berkhof Exc. 1000L(1995)	C55F	1984	Ex Tellings-Golden Miller, 1992
466YMG	AEH Puma IV	Wright Condor	C35F	1985	Ex Cooke, Chichester, 1992
B845SEC	Dennis Dorchester SDA810	Plaxton Paramount 3500 II	C46FT	1985	Ex Clydeside 2000, 1994
5AAX	Dennis Dorchester SDA810	Plaxton Paramount 3500 II	C57F	1985	Ex Clydeside 2000, 1994
A4HWD	Dennis Dorchester SDA810	Plaxton Paramount 3500 II	C57F	1985	Ex Clydeside 2000, 1994
F626OHD	DAF SB3000DKZ570	Van Hool Astrobel	CH57/15CT	1988	Ex Birmingham Coach Co, Tividale, 1995
YSU991	AEC Puma IV	Plaxton Paramount 3200 II	C39F	1988	Ex The Londoners, Nunhead, 1993
YTY887	Volvo B10M-60	Plaxton Paramount 3200 II	C57F	1989	Ex Woodstocks, Kidderminster, 1995
H812RWJ	Scania K93CRB	Van Hool Alizée	C53F	1991	
H927DRJ	Scania K93CRB	Plaxton Paramount 3200 III	C55F	1991	Ex Shearings, 1995
H929DRJ	Scania K93CRB	Plaxton Paramount 3200 III	C55F	1991	Ex Shearings, 1995
J710CWT	Volvo B10M-60	Plaxton Paramount 3500 III	C48FT	1992	Ex Wallace Arnold, 1995
L18HWD	Toyota Coaster HZB50R	Caetano Optimo III	C18F	1994	
L8HWD	Dennis Javelin 10SDA2139	Berkhof Excellence 1000L	C41F	1994	
L5HWD	Scania K113CRB	Irizar Century	C49FT	1994	
L749NEO	Scania K113CRB	Van Hool Alizée	C53F	1994	Ex Abbeyways, Halifax, 1995
M4HWD	Scania K113CRB	Berkhof Excellence 2000HL	C51F	1994	
M5HWD	Scania K113CRB	Berkhof Excellence 1000L	C51F	1994	
M6HWD	Scania K113CRB	Van Hool Alizée	C53F	1994	

Previous Registrations:

5AAX	B408OSB, WLT878, B980EGG	BHF291A	466YMG
201SC	ANA106Y	L749NEO	L839KHD, L4HWD
466YMG	B938BVH	LCW411W	KHG184W, 1958PH
A4HWD	B406OSB, VLT166, B982EGG	YSU991	E923LCP
AAX300A	A257VWO	YTY867	F460WFX
B845SEC	B404OSB, FSU661, B984EGG, YTY867		

HULME HALL

Hulme Hall Coaches Ltd, 75 Hulme Hall Road, Cheadle Hulme, Stockport, SK8 6JZ

	PEC345V	Ford R1114	Plaxton Supreme IV	C53F	1980	Ex Bibby, Ingleton, 1987
	RMA432V	Bristol VRT/SL3/501	Eastern Coach Works	H43/31F	1980	Ex Crosville Wales, 1991
	PFC514W	Bristol VRT/SL3/6LXB	Eastern Coach Works	H43/27D	1981	Ex Oxford Bus Company, 1993
	PFC515W	Bristol VRT/SL3/6LXB	Eastern Coach Works	H43/27D	1981	Ex Oxford Bus Company, 1993
	WTU490W	Bristol VRT/SL3/501	Eastern Coach Works	H43/31F	1981	Ex PMT, 1990
	VUA472X	Bristol VRT/SL3/6LXB	Eastern Coach Works	H43/31F	1981	Ex West Riding, 1994
	SND288X	Leyland Leopard PSU5D/4R	Duple Dominant IV	C53F	1982	Ex North Western, 1990
w	RJI4082	MCW Metroliner DR130/3	MCW	CH57/25FT	1984	Ex Happy Days, Woodseaves, 1991
	C360BRJ	Freight Rover Sherpa	Dixon Lomas	C16F	1985	
	HUI4575	Iveco Daily 49.10	Robin Hood City Nippy	DP19F	1986	Ex Stagecoach Midland Red, 1995
	RJI8918	Leyland Tiger TRCTL11/3R	Duple 340	C49FT	1986	Ex ?, 1994
	RJI4083	MCW Metroliner DR130/23	MCW	CH57/18FT	1986	Ex Happy Days, Woodseaves, 1991
	CSU917	MCW Hiliner HR131/11	MCW	C48FT	1987	Ex Central Coachways, 1992

Previous Registrations:

CSU917	D905POF	RJI4082	A762VAF	RJI8918	C75KLG
HUI4575	D882CKV	RJI4083	C647FTT		

HYNDBURN

Hyndburn Transport Ltd, Ellison Street, Accrington, Lancashire, BB5 1RB

Depots: Ellison Street, Accrington; Bradley Fold and Patricroft

001	RJI8613	Bedford YMP	Plaxton Paramount 3200	C31F	1984	Ex Sanders, Holt, 1995
002	MIW9048	Bova EL26/581	Bova Europa	C47F	1982	Ex Crescent, North Walsham, 1992
004	SJI5407	Volvo B10M-61	Van Hool Alizée	C46FT	1983	Ex Fraser, Accrington, 1993
003	EYN165	Leyland Tiger TRCTL11/3R	Duple Laser	C50F	1983	Ex Turner, Bury, 1993
005	HFB845X	Volvo B58-61	Duple Dominant IV	C53F	1981	Ex Rigby, Patricroft, 1993
007	SWH127T	Volvo B58-61	Plaxton Supreme IV	C49FT	1979	Ex Rigby, Patricroft, 1993
008	FIL7287	Bova EL26/581	Bova Europa	C49F	1983	Ex Crescent, North Walsham, 1992
009	SND289X	Leyland Leopard PSU5D/4R	Duple Dominant IV	C53F	1981	Ex Ribble, 1990
3	J263KRN	Leyland Swift ST2R44C97A4	Reeve Burgess Harrier	B39F	1991	
4	J264KRN	Leyland Swift ST2R44C97A4	Reeve Burgess Harrier	B39F	1991	
19	L448FFR	Iveco TurboDaily 59.12	Mellor	B27F	1994	
20	L447FFR	Iveco TurboDaily 59.12	Mellor	B27F	1994	
21	L445FFR	Iveco TurboDaily 59.12	Mellor	B27F	1994	
22	L446FFR	Iveco TurboDaily 59.12	Mellor	B27F	1994	
23	D860FOT	Iveco Daily 49.10	Robin Hood City Nippy	B19F	1987	Ex Ribble, 1993
24	E24GCK	MCW MetroRider MF151/6	MCW	B23F	1987	
25	E25GCK	MCW MetroRider MF151/6	MCW	B23F	1987	
26	E26GCK	MCW MetroRider MF151/6	MCW	B23F	1987	
27	E27GCK	MCW MetroRider MF151/7	MCW	DP25F	1987	
28	E28GCK	MCW MetroRider MF151/7	MCW	DP25F	1987	
29	E29GCK	MCW MetroRider MF151/7	MCW	DP25F	1987	
30	F913HTU	Iveco Daily 49-10	Robin Hood City Nippy	B25F	1989	
31	F914HTU	Iveco Daily 49-10	Robin Hood City Nippy	B25F	1989	
32	F882CJC	Iveco Daily 49-10	Robin Hood City Nippy	B25F	1989	Ex Alpine, Llandudno, 1989
33	F883CJC	Iveco Daily 49-10	Robin Hood City Nippy	B25F	1989	Ex Alpine, Llandudno, 1989
34	G41XBK	Iveco Daily 49-10	Phoenix	B25F	1990	
35	G767CDU	Leyland Swift LBM6T/2RA	Reeve Burgess Harrier	B39F	1990	Ex Volvo demonstrator, 1990
36	H36YCW	Leyland Swift ST2R44C97A4	Reeve Burgess Harrier	B39F	1990	
37	H37YCW	Leyland Swift ST2R44C97A4	Reeve Burgess Harrier	B39F	1990	
38	H38YCW	Leyland Swift ST2R44C97A4	Reeve Burgess Harrier	B39F	1990	
39	H39YCW	Leyland Swift ST2R44C97A4	Reeve Burgess Harrier	B39F	1990	
41	JFV294N	Leyland Leopard PSU3B/4R	East Lancashire(1983)	B52F	1975	Ex Halton, 1988
42	JFV295N	Leyland Leopard PSU3B/4R	East Lancashire(1983)	B52F	1975	Ex Halton, 1988

43-48

		Leyland Leopard PSU4E/2R	East Lancashire	DP43F	1977-78	

43	EHG43S	45	EHG45S	46	EHG46S	47	NFR747T	48	NFR748T
44	EHG44S								

49	GCK49W	Leyland Leopard PSU4E/2R	East Lancashire	DP43F	1981	
50	A50LHG	Dennis Falcon H SDA413	East Lancashire	DP43F	1984	
51	B51XFV	Dennis Falcon H SDA413	East Lancashire	DP40F	1985	
52	AFM1W	Leyland National 2 NL116AL11/2R	East Lancs Greenway(1992)	B48F	1981	Ex North Western, 1992
54 w	KIB7257	Leyland Leopard PSU3E/4R	Duple Dominant II	C49F	1978	Ex PG Travel, Middlewich, 1978
55	VNH157W	Leyland Leopard PSU3F/4R	Duple Dominant IV Express	C49F	1981	Ex Milton Keynes, 1987
56	YKA8W	Leyland Leopard PSU3E/4R	Duple Dominant II Express	C49F	1981	Ex Merseybus, 1988
57	WWM576W	Leyland Leopard PSU3F/4R	Duple Dominant II Express	C49F	1980	Ex Merseybus, 1988
66 w	YFR496R	Leyland Leopard PSU3E/4R	Duple Dominant I	C47F	1977	Ex Ribble, 1988
70 w	BKJ150T	Leyland Leopard PSU3E/4R	Duple Dominant I	C47F	1979	Ex Maidstone & District, 1990
125	CWR525Y	Leyland Olympian ONLXB/1R	Eastern Coach Works	H45/32F	1983	Ex West Riding, 1994
126	CWR526Y	Leyland Olympian ONLXB/1R	Eastern Coach Works	H45/32F	1983	Ex West Riding, 1994
134	JKW286W	Leyland Atlantean AN68B/1R	Alexander AL	H45/32F	1981	Ex Lodge, High Easter, 1992

135-139

		Leyland Atlantean AN68C/1R	East Lancashire	H46/30F	1980-81	Ex Ipswich, 1991

135	RGV40W	136	RBJ36W	137	RGV37W	138	RGV38W	139	RGV39W

Hyndburn 138, RGV38W is one of five similar vehicles to have been purchased from Ipswich during 1991. These Leyland Atlanteans carry similar East Lancashire bodies to Hyndburn's own product though the Ipswich models were fitted with dual-door layout at that time. *Roy Marshall.*

140-144

		Leyland Atlantean AN68B/1R	Willowbrook	H45/33F	1980-81 Ex Merseybus, 1989		
140	WWM920W	**141**	AFY191X	**142**	WWM922W	**143**	WWM933W	**144**	AFY181X

194	KHG194T	Leyland Atlantean AN68A/1R	East Lancashire	H45/33F	1978	
196	VCW196V	Leyland Atlantean AN68A/1R	East Lancashire	H45/33F	1979	
197	VCW197V	Leyland Atlantean AN68A/1R	East Lancashire	H45/33F	1979	
199	DBV199W	Leyland Atlantean AN68B/1R	East Lancashire	H45/33F	1980	
208w	NRN383P	Leyland Atlantean AN68/1R	Park Royal	H43/30F	1976	Ex Ribble, 1990
209	GBV109N	Leyland Atlantean AN68/2R	Alexander AL	H49/35F	1975	Ex Preston, 1990
210	GBV110N	Leyland Atlantean AN68/2R	Alexander AL	H49/35F	1975	Ex Preston, 1990
211	GBV101N	Leyland Atlantean AN68/2R	Alexander AL	H49/35F	1974	Ex Preston, 1990
212	GBV108N	Leyland Atlantean AN68/2R	Alexander AL	H49/35F	1975	Ex Preston, 1990
214	NRN390P	Leyland Atlantean AN68/1R	Park Royal	H43/30F	1976	Ex Ribble, 1990
215w	NRN402P	Leyland Atlantean AN68/1R	Park Royal	H43/30F	1976	Ex Ribble, 1990
216	NRN404P	Leyland Atlantean AN68/1R	Park Royal	H43/30F	1976	Ex Ribble, 1990

Previous Registrations:

EYN165	BPR105Y	RJI8613	A953FNJ, WSV503
FIL7287	CDC879Y	SJI5407	PGC522Y, 3402FM
KIB7257	LWL5S	SWH127T	CJF7T, 9874ND
MIW9048	YUR828X, 3253VU, XBC272X	WPC316X	SCA9X, 292CLT

Livery: Blue, red and grey; green and white (Rigbys) - 75/6/8, 301-3, 381-7/90/5

Opposite: Hyndburn's area of operation has expanded significantly since deregulation. The upper picture shows 19, L448FFR, an Iveco 59.12 with Mellor bodywork built in near-by Rochdale. The lower picture shows 126, CWR526Y, a Leyland Olympian with Eastern Coach Works body previously with West Riding. One of a pair, they are now the newest double-decks in the fleet. *Paul Wigan*

KEN ROUTLEDGE TRAVEL

K J Routledge, 1A St Helens Street, Cockermouth, Cumbria, CA13 9HX

G690ORM	Mercedes-Benz 609D	Coachcraft	C21F	1990
J712BAO	Mercedes-Benz 811D	Autobus Classique	C33F	1991
K831FEE	Mercedes-Benz 410D	Autobus Classique	M16	1993
L435KHH	Mercedes-Benz 711D	Plaxton Beaver	C25F	1983
L743MAO	Ford Transit VE6	Deansgate	M12	1994
M792RHH	Ford Transit VE6	Ford	M9	1995

KIRKBY LONSDALE MINI COACHES

S J Sutton, Twenty Acres, Moor End, Hutton Roof, Kirkby Lonsdale, Cumbria, LA6 2PF

Depots : Scotland Road, Carnforth and Whittington

DUI4760	Leyland Leopard PSU5/4R	Plaxton Supreme III	C57F	1978	Ex M&C Travel, Forrest Gate, 1993
B909BGA	Mercedes-Benz L608D	PMT Hanbridge	C21F	1984	Ex Cunningham, Carlisle, 1993
B512PRF	Ford Transit 190	Dormobile	B16F	1985	Ex Midland Red, 1995
D140NUS	Mercedes-Benz L608D	Alexander AM	B21F	1986	Ex Kelvin Scottish, 1992
E717BSU	Freight Rover Sherpa	Freight Rover Sherpa	M8	1988	Ex private owner, 1994
E430YLG	Mercedes-Benz 609D	PMT	DP26F	1988	Ex Smith, Ledbury, 1994
G344ESC	Mercedes-Benz 811D	PMT Ami	C33F	1989	Ex Liberton Travel, Edinburgh, 1995

Previous Registrations:
DUI4760   BGJ315S

Livery: White, maroon and blue

KNIGHT BUS & COACH

R D Clark, Unit 2, Drydens Foundry, Manchester Road, Preston, PR1 3BT

C801CBU	Renault-Dodge S56	Northern Counties	B18F	1986	Ex Bu-Val, Littleborough, 1994
C810CBU	Renault-Dodge S56	Northern Counties	B18F	1987	Ex Bu-Val, Littleborough, 1994
C813CBU	Renault-Dodge S56	Northern Counties	B18F	1987	Ex Bu-Val, Littleborough, 1994
C828CBU	Renault-Dodge S56	Northern Counties	B18F	1987	Ex Bu-Val, Littleborough, 1994
D37TKA	Freight Rover Sherpa	Dormobile	B16F	1987	Ex Whittakers, Preston, 1993
D308SDS	Renault-Dodge S56	Alexander AM	B25F	1987	Ex Clydeside Buses, 1995

Livery: White and red.

Kirkby Lonsdale Mini Coaches' D140NUS is seen departing Lancaster bus station at the start of a return trip home. The Mercedes-Benz L608D was part of a batch with Kelvin Scottish and carries a body conversion by Alexander. *Paul Wigan*

Lancashire Rose Taxi Bus has recently commenced trading as Knight bus and coach following the introduction of several late evening services. A picture of the former livery is shown here on XRF370X, a Ford Transit with a conversion based on a Dormobile cowl. *Richard Godfrey*

MANCHESTER INTERNATIONAL AIRPORT

Manchester Airport plc, Manchester International Airport, Ringway, Manchester, M22 5PA

N1-N8

		Leyland National 2 NL116AL11/3R					B30T	1981	
N1	NHH358W	N3	Q580GRJ	N5	unreg	N7	unreg	N8	unreg
N2	NHH359W	N4	unreg	N6	unreg				

Fleet	Reg	Chassis	Body	Code	Year	Notes
N9	YCD78T	Leyland National 11351A/2R		B44D	1979	Ex Southdown, 1992
N10	YCD88T	Leyland National 11351A/2R		B44D	1979	Ex Southdown, 1992
N11	WYJ164S	Leyland National 11351A/2R		B44D	1978	Ex Southdown, 1992
N12	UFG62S	Leyland National 11351A/2R		B44D	1978	Ex Southdown, 1992
N13	RUF44R	Leyland National 11351A/2R		B44D	1977	Ex Southdown, 1992
N14	XNK206X	Ford R1014	Plaxton Bustler	B29D	1982	Ex Miller, Foxton, 1992
N15	XNK209X	Ford R1014	Plaxton Bustler	B29D	1982	Ex Miller, Foxton, 1992
N16	XNK212X	Ford R1014	Plaxton Bustler	B29D	1982	Ex Miller, Foxton, 1992
N17	XNK215X	Ford R1014	Plaxton Bustler	B29D	1982	Ex Miller, Foxton, 1992
	H199ENC	Mercedes-Benz 709D	Reeve Burgess Beaver	B20F	1990	
	H201ENC	Mercedes-Benz 709D	Reeve Burgess Beaver	B20F	1990	
	H726LOL	Mercedes-Benz 811D	Carlyle	B27F	1990	
	K125TCP	DAF SB220LC550	Ikarus CitiBus	B26DL	1993	
	K126TCP	DAF SB220LC550	Ikarus CitiBus	B26DL	1993	
	K127TCP	DAF SB220LC550	Ikarus CitiBus	B26DL	1993	
	K977JWW	Optare MetroRider MR39	Optare	B23F	1993	
	K978JWW	Optare MetroRider MR39	Optare	B23F	1993	
	M958VWY	Optare MetroRider MR33	Optare	B23F	1995	
	M359OBU	Dennis Dart 9SDL3053	Plaxton Pointer	B29F	1994	
	M360OBU	Dennis Dart 9SDL3053	Plaxton Pointer	B29F	1994	
	M361OBU	Dennis Dart 9SDL3053	Plaxton Pointer	B29F	1994	
	M362OBU	Dennis Dart 9SDL3053	Plaxton Pointer	B29F	1994	
	N962WJA	Dennis Dart 9SDL3054	Marshall C36	B27F	1995	
	N963WJA	Dennis Dart 9SDL3054	Marshall C36	B27F	1995	
	N964WJA	Dennis Dart 9SDL3054	Marshall C36	B27F	1995	
	N599XRJ	Dennis Dart 9SDL3054	Marshall C36	B25FL	1995	
	N601XRJ	Dennis Dart 9SDL3054	Marshall C36	B25FL	1995	
	N602XRJ	Dennis Dart 9SDL3054	Marshall C36	B25FL	1995	

Livery: Yellow, grey and white

Internal transport at Manchester International Airport has increased significantly since the time of the first triple-doored Leyland Nationals were used air-side to move people between the terminal and aircraft. Services are now operated between the two international terminals and the various car parks. Seen during duty on terminal transfer work is K127TCP, a DAF SB220 with Ikarus dual-door bodywork. *Malc McDonald*

MANCHESTER METROLINK

Greater Manchester Metro Ltd, Metrolink House, Queens Road,
Manchester, M8 7RY

1001-1026		GEC Alsthom		Firema		86-seat	1991-92
1001	1005	1009	1012	1015	1018	1021	1024
1002	1006	1010	1013	1016	1019	1022	1025
1003	1007	1011	1014	1017	1020	1023	1026
1004	1008						

Livery: Ivory and turquoise

Named trams:

1002 *Manchester Arndale Voyager;* 1003 *The Robert Owen;* 1005 *Greater Altrincham Enterprise;* 1007 *The Guiness Record Breaker;* 1009 *Co-operative Insurance;* 1010 *Manchester Champion;* 1014 *Manchester 2000;* 1015 *Sparky;* 1016 *Signal Express;* 1017 *Rosie;* 1019 *The Eric Black;* 1024 *The John Greenwood;* 1025 *Christie Metro Challenger.*

Pictured about to enter the Piccadilly low level terminal is tram 1013 of Manchester Metrolink. Alternate trams reach this terminal while the others run direct between Altrincham and Bury. Another reason for visiting this spot is the Ian Allan transport bookshop, from where the picture was taken.
Bill Potter

MAYNE

A Mayne and Son Ltd, Ashton New Road, Clayton, Manchester, M11 4PD

2	THX515S	Leyland Fleetline FE30ALR Sp	Park Royal	H44/31F	1978	Ex London Buses, 1991
3	OJD163R	Leyland Fleetline FE30AGR	Park Royal	H44/29F	1976	Ex Stevensons, 1985
5	IAZ4775	Leyland Fleetline FE30AGR	Northern Counties	H43/32F	1980	Ex Barry Cooper, 1995
6	IAZ4776	Leyland Fleetline FE30AGR	Northern Counties	H43/32F	1980	Ex Barry Cooper, 1995
7	THX322S	Leyland Fleetline FE30ALR Sp	MCW	H44/31F	1978	Ex London Buses, 1991
9	THX579S	Leyland Fleetline FE30ALR Sp	Park Royal	H44/27F	1978	Ex London Buses, 1991
10	M210NDB	Scania N113DRB	East Lancashire	H45/31F	1995	
11	M211NDB	Scania N113DRB	East Lancashire	H45/31F	1995	
12	F112HNC	Scania N113DRB	Northern Counties	H47/32F	1989	
13	F113HNC	Scania N113DRB	Northern Counties	DPH47/30F	1989	
14	L114DNA	Scania N113DRB	East Lancashire	H47/31F	1993	
15	G115SBA	Scania N113DRB	Northern Counties	H47/32F	1989	
16	G116SBA	Scania N113DRB	Northern Counties	H47/32F	1989	
17	G117SBA	Scania N113DRB	Northern Counties	H47/32F	1989	
19	THX619S	Leyland Fleetline FE30ALR Sp	MCW	H44/31F	1978	Ex London Buses, 1991
21	A101DPB	Dennis Falcon HC SD407	Wadham Stringer(1987)	DP49F	1983	Ex Wycombe Bus, 1991
23w	LIW1323	Leyland Leopard PSU3B/4R	Willowbrook Warrior(1990)	B48F	1973	Ex Jowitt, Tankersley, 1990
24	KVO144W	Leyland Leopard PSU3E/4R	Willowbrook 003	C49F	1980	Ex Trent, 1994
25	NIB7625	Leyland Leopard PSU3C/2R	Willowbrook Warrior(1990)	B48F	1977	Ex Merthyr Tydfil, 1988
26	L26FNE	Dennis Dart 9.8SDL3035	Marshall C37	B40F	1994	
27	L27FNE	Dennis Dart 9.8SDL3035	Marshall C37	B40F	1994	
28	K28XBA	Dennis Dart 9.8SDL3012	Marshall Dartline	B40F	1992	
29	K29XBA	Dennis Dart 9.8SDL3012	Marshall Dartline	B40F	1993	
30	ULS663T	Leyland Fleetline FE30AGR	Eastern Coach Works	H43/32F	1979	Ex Clydeside 2000, 1992
31	THX601S	Leyland Fleetline FE30ALR Sp	Park Royal	H44/31F	1978	Ex London Buses, 1991
33	THX303S	Leyland Fleetline FE30ALR Sp	MCW	H44/31F	1978	Ex London Buses, 1991
34	THX594S	Leyland Fleetline FE30ALR Sp	Park Royal	H44/31F	1978	Ex London Buses, 1991
35	THX555S	Leyland Fleetline FE30ALR Sp	Park Royal	H44/31F	1978	Ex London Buses, 1991
40	KVO145W	Leyland Leopard PSU3E/4R	Willowbrook 003	C49F	1980	Ex Trent, 1994
41	GDZ3841	Leyland Leopard PSU3B/4R	Willowbrook Warrior(1990)	B51F	1974	Ex Perry, Bromyard, 1990
42	M42ONF	Scania L113CRL	Northern Counties Paladin	B51F	1994	
43	M113RNK	Scania L113CRL	Northern Counties Paladin	B51F	1994	Ex Scania demonstrator, 1995

Previously a demonstrator for Scania, M113RNK was supplied to Mayne along with a new example of the L113. Both carry Northern Counties Paladin bodywork and 43 is seen in Ashton-under-Lyne. *Roy Marshall*

Opposite, top: **Along with the pair of Scania L113s, Mayne operate eight Scania double-deck buses with a mixture of East Lancashire and Northern Counties bodies. Seen the service through Ashton to Carrbrook is 15, G115SBA, one of three Northern Counties examples from 1989.** *Paul Wigan*
Opposite, bottom: **Mayne operate two Bova coaches with a new Futura coach due in 1996. Pictured with property typical of the Manchester area is 58, IIL2258.** *Paul Wigan*

The Lancashire, Cumbria & Manchester Bus Handbook

44	A44YWJ	Dennis Falcon HC SD414	Marshall Camair	DP53F	1984	Ex Chesterfield, 1991
45	A45YWJ	Dennis Falcon HC SD414	Marshall Camair	B53F	1984	Ex Chesterfield, 1991
46	A46YWJ	Dennis Falcon HC SD414	Marshall Camair	B53F	1984	Ex Chesterfield, 1991
47	A47YWJ	Dennis Falcon HC SD414	Marshall Camair	B53F	1984	Ex Chesterfield, 1991
48	A48YWJ	Dennis Falcon HC SD414	Marshall Camair	B53F	1984	Ex Chesterfield, 1991
50	403BGO	Leyland Tiger TRCTLXCT/3RZ	Plaxton Paramount 3200	C57F	1985	
51	H51DVR	Dennis Javelin 8.5SDA1903	Duple 320	C37F	1991	
52	H52FDB	Dennis Javelin 11SDL1907	Duple 320	C55F	1991	
57	IIL2257	Bova FHD12/290	Bova Futura	C50FT	1990	
58	IIL2258	Bova FHD12/290	Bova Futura	C40FT	1990	
59	GIL3259	Leyland Leopard PSU5C/4R	Plaxton Supreme IV	C57F	1981	
60	GIL2160	Leyland Leopard PSU5C/4R	Plaxton Supreme IV	C57F	1981	
62	NIB4162	Leyland Leopard PSU5C/4R	Plaxton Supreme IV	C57F	1982	
63	MJI5763	Leyland Leopard PSU5C/4R	Plaxton Supreme IV	C57F	1982	
64	MJI5764	Leyland Leopard PSU5C/4R	Plaxton Supreme IV	C57F	1982	
65	MJI5765	Leyland Leopard PSU5C/4R	Plaxton Supreme IV	C57F	1982	
66	MJI5766	Leyland Leopard PSU3E/4R	Plaxton Supreme IV Express	C53F	1980	
67	N67YVR	Dennis Javelin 12SDA19..	UVG Unistar	C55F	1996	
68	N68YVR	Dennis Javelin 12SDA19..	UVG Unistar	C55F	1996	
69	SSV269	Leyland Tiger TRCTL11/3R	Plaxton Paramount 3500 E	C55F	1983	
70	TKU540	Leyland Tiger TRCTL11/3R	Plaxton Paramount 3500	C49FT	1984	
77	LIB6437	Leyland Tiger TRCTLXCT/3RZ	Plaxton Paramount 3500 II	C51FT	1986	
78	LIB6438	Leyland Tiger TRCTLXCT/3RZ	Plaxton Paramount 3500 II	C51FT	1986	
79	LIB6439	Leyland Tiger TRCTLXCT/3RZ	Plaxton Paramount 3200 II	C57F	1985	
	N	Scania N113DRB	East Lancashire Citizen	H45/31F	1996	
	N	Scania N113DRB	East Lancashire Citizen	H45/31F	1996	
	P	Scania N113DRB	East Lancashire Citizen	H45/31F	1996	
	P	Scania N113DRB	East Lancashire Citizen	H45/31F	1996	
	N	Bova FLC12.290	Bova Futura Cub	C55F	1996	

Barry Coopers Coaches:

1	OJD131R	Leyland Fleetline FE30AGR	Park Royal	H44/29F	1976	Ex Stevensons, 1984
4	GND505N	Daimler Fleetline CRG6LXB	Northern Counties	H43/32F	1974	Ex Greater Manchester, 1988
6	ULS666T	Leyland Fleetline FE30AGR	Eastern Coach Works	H43/32F	1979	Ex Clydeside 2000, 1992
8	YNA328M	Daimler Fleetline CRG6LXB	Northern Counties	H43/32F	1973	Ex Greater Manchester, 1987
10	KUC969P	Leyland Fleetline FE30ALR(6LXB)	MCW	H45/32F	1976	Ex Wilts & Dorset, 1990
17	VGU443	Leyland Leopard PSU5D/4R	Plaxton Supreme IV	C57F	1981	
18	YPL764	Leyland Tiger TRCTL11/3R	Plaxton Paramount 3500	C57F	1983	
19	YUC765	Leyland Tiger TRCTL11/3R	Duple Laser	C57F	1983	
21	EUK976	Leyland Tiger TRCTL11/3R	Plaxton Paramount 3500	C53FT	1984	
24	OED201	Leyland Tiger TRCTL11/3R	Plaxton Paramount 3200 II	C53F	1985	
25	UOL337	Leyland Tiger TRCTL11/3R	Plaxton Paramount 3200 II	C53F	1985	
26	LIB5440	Leyland Tiger TRCTLXCT/3RZ	Plaxton Paramount 3500 II	C51F	1986	
27	614BWU	DAF SB2305DHTD585	Duple 320	C57F	1989	
28	H28DVM	Dennis Javelin 11SDL1921	Duple 320	C55F	1991	
29	J29LBA	Dennis Javelin 11SDL1921	Duple 320	C55F	1991	
66	UCE665	Leyland Leopard PSU4A/4R	Plaxton Supreme IV (1982)	C53F	1968	Ex Midland Red, 1982
69	906GAU	Leyland Leopard PSU5C/4R	Plaxton Supreme IV	C57F	1980	
	EHB259G	Leyland Leopard PSU4A/2R	East Lancashire	B43F	1969	Ex Stonier, Goldenhill, 1988
	PCW680P	Leyland Leopard PSU3C/4R	Duple Dominant I	C49F	1976	Ex Whitecross, Warrington, 1994
	ARB134T	Leyland Leopard PSU3E/4R	Plaxton Supreme III Express	C49F	1978	Ex Trent, 1994
	KVO142W	Leyland Leopard PSU3E/4R	Willowbrook 003	C49F	1980	Ex Trent, 1994
	NMX643	Leyland Leopard PSU3F/5R	Plaxton Supreme IV	C53F	1980	
	289BUA	Leyland Leopard PSU5C/4R	Plaxton Supreme IV	C57F	1980	
	NIB3261	Leyland Leopard PSU5C/4R	Plaxton Supreme IV	C57F	1981	
	SCH149X	Leyland Leopard PSU3F/4R	Willowbrook 003	C49F	1982	Ex Trent, 1994

Previous Registrations:

289BUA	HDB356V	LIB5440	C426YBA	NIB4162	SNC362X
403BGO	B350RNA	LIB6437	C347YBA	NIB7625	NTX363R
614BWU	F27HNC	LIB6438	C348YBA	NMX643	HDB355V
906GAU	HDB357V	LIB6439	B349RNA	OED201	B424RNA
EUK978	A421KBA	LIW1322	NRE562L	SSV269	ANA368Y
GDZ3841	JVS928N	LIW1323	RBF987M	TKU540	A370HNC
GIL2160	MRJ360W	MJI5763	SNC363X	UCE665	WHA236H, SNC355X
GIL3259	MRJ359W	MJI5764	SNC364X	UOL337	B425RNA
IAZ4775	MNC487W	MJI5765	SNC365X	VGU443	ODJ417W
IAZ4776	MNC488W	MJI5766	MRJ358W	YPL764	A418HND
IIL2257	G57SBA	NIB3261	SNC361X	YUC785	A419HND
IIL2258	G58SBA				

MOUNTAIN GOAT

Mountain Goat Holidays, 10 Victoria Street, Windermere,
Cumbria, LA23 1AD

F946ORV	Ford Transit VE6	Coachcraft	M11	1989	Ex private owner, 1994
G218REC	Renault Master T35D	Dobson	M15	1990	
G963REC	Renault Master T35D	Dobson	M15	1990	
H487CEC	Renault Master T35D	Dobson	M15	1991	
M10MGH	Renault Master T35D	Cymric	M16	1994	
M6MGH	Renault Master T35D	Dobson	M16	1995	
M8MGH	Renault Master T35D	Dobson	M16	1995	

Livery: White and green

Mountain Goat has established itself as a provider of tours and minibus services over the various passes in English Lakeland, many of which would not support larger vehicles. A fleet based on the Renault Master has built up with conversion work being carried out over the winter. Seen outside the Studio in Grasmere is M10MGH, the only example to carry a Cymric conversion. *Brian Pritchard*

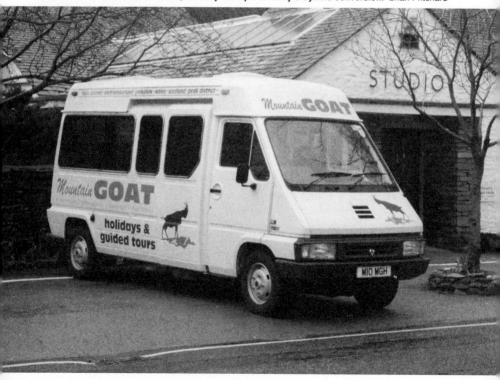

PHOENIX HANDYBUS

Phoenix North West Ltd, 38 The Corners, Cleveleys, Lancashire FY5 1LG

Depots:

801	H611CGG	Mercedes-Benz 709D	Dormobile Routemaker	B29F	1991	Ex Lofty's, Mickle Trafford, 1995
802	H612CGG	Mercedes-Benz 709D	Dormobile Routemaker	B29F	1991	Ex Lofty's, Mickle Trafford, 1995
803	H613CGG	Mercedes-Benz 709D	Dormobile Routemaker	B29F	1991	Ex Lofty's, Mickle Trafford, 1995
804	H804SFP	Mercedes-Benz 709D	Dormobile Routemaker	B29F	1992	Ex Kinch, Barrow-on-Soar, 1995
805	N	Mercedes-Benz 811D	Mellor	B31F	1996	
808	J608KGB	Mercedes-Benz 709D	Dormobile Routemaker	B27F	1992	Ex D&N Travel, Ystradgynlais, 1996

Livery: Black & yellow

Recently launched is the Phoenix Handybus service operated in association with Blackpool Transport. A fleet of five Mercedes-Benz 709s is to be joined by a new 811 with Mellor bodywork during 1996. Seen here is 802, H612CGG on the first day of operation, 13th January 1996. *Paul Wigan*

PIONEER

J M Whitehead, 10 Fairfax Drive, Smithybridge, Littleborough, OL15 8RA

Depot: Scot Industrial Park, Fishwick Street, Rochdale.

	RDV419H	Bristol RELH6G	Eastern Coach Works	DP45F	1970	Ex Southern National, 1994
w	289CLT	Leyland Leopard PSU3E/4R	Duple Dominant	C53F	1973	Ex Bradshaw, Middleton, 1992
	SSX601V	Seddon Pennine 7	Alexander AYS	B53F	1980	Ex Mayne, Manchester, 1993
	HSC161X	Leyland Cub CU435	Duple Dominant	B31F	1981	Ex Lothian, 1991
	HSC174X	Leyland Cub CU435	Duple Dominant	B31F	1981	Ex Lothian, 1991
	MSL155X	Leyland Leopard PSU3F/4RT	Willowbrook 003	C53F	1981	Ex Clydeside 2000, 1994
	RPB955X	Leyland Leopard PSU3G/4R	Eastern Coach Works B51	C49F	1982	Ex Stagecoach South, 1994
	VCW596Y	Dennis Lancet SD505	Marshall Camair	B51F	1982	Ex Tanat Valley, Pentrefelin, 1995
	PJI6069	Dennis Falcon V SDA404	Duple Goldliner	C47FT	1983	Ex Ashall, Levenshulme, 1995
	C41HDT	Dennis Domino SDA1201	Optare	B33F	1985	Ex Stevensons, 1994
	C46HDT	Dennis Domino SDA1201	Optare	B33F	1985	Ex Stevensons, 1994
	D972TKC	Renault-Dodge S56	Northern Counties	B22F	1987	Ex Merseybus, 1992
	D973TKC	Renault-Dodge S56	Northern Counties	B22F	1987	Ex Merseybus, 1992
	KUX774	Volkswagen LT55	Optare City Pacer	B25F	1987	Ex Kingston-upon-Hull, 1993
	E518PWR	Volkswagen LT55	Optare City Pacer	B25F	1987	Ex Elaine's, Gwersyllt, 1995
	E675KDG	MCW MetroRider MF150/61	MCW	DP25F	1987	Ex Cheltenham & Gloucester, 1995
	E236UWR	MCW MetroRider MF150/80	MCW	B23F	1988	Ex Yorkshire Rider, 1995

Previous Registrations:

289CLT	FAU48L	MSL155X	PRM629X, 588SC
KUX774	E941WWE	PJI6069	TWE81Y, 20VWC, ARR247Y

Note: MSL155X has all rear-facing seats (except the back row) as an experiment.

Livery: Purple and yellow.

Pioneer operate in the Littleborough area using a yellow and purple livery. Also unusual is VCW596Y, a Dennis Lancet once new to Blackpool which is seen at Rochdale bus station on the operator's service from its base. Another of the batch is seen in the colours of Bluebird on page 16. *Roy Marshall*

PRESTON

Preston Bus Ltd, 221 Deepdale Road, Preston, PR1 6NY

1-10		Optare MetroRider MR37		Optare		B25F		1994-95		
1	M401TCK	3	M403TCK	5	M405TCK	7	M407TCK	9	M409TCK
2	M402TCK	4	M404TCK	6	M406TCK	8	M408TCK	10	M410TCK

20-31		Optare MetroRider MR17		Optare		B29F		1995-96		
20	N420GBV	23	N423GBV	26	N426GBV	28	N428GBV	30	N430GBV
21	N421GBV	24	N424GBV	27	N427GBV	29	N429GBV	31	N431GBV
22	N422GBV	25	N425GBV						

41-74		Renault-Dodge S56		Northern Counties		B22F*		1987-88 *47-9 are B25F; 70/1 are DP22F		
41	D41AFV	47w	E47KBV	52	D752YCW	61	D761YCW	70	D870ABV
42	D42AFV	48w	E48MCK	54	D754YCW	62	D762YCW	71	D871ABV
43	D43AFV	49	E49MCK	58w	D758YCW	63	D763YCW	72	D72AFV
44	E44FFV	50w	D750YCW	59	D759YCW	64	D764YCW	73	D73AFV
45	E45GRN	51	D751YCW	60	D760YCW	66	D766YCW	74	D74AFV

75-92		Renault-Dodge S56		Northern Counties		B25F		1988-89		
75w	E75LFR	79	E79MHG	83	E83MHG	87	E87MHG	90	F90UHG
76	E76LFR	80	E80MHG	84	E84MHG	88	F88UHG	91	F91AHG
77	E77LFR	81	E81MHG	85w	E85MHG	89	F89UHG	92	F92AHG
78w	E78MHG	82	E82MHG	86	E86MHG				

Opposite: **Preston was renowned for its loyalty to Leyland products and here we see two examples of the last of the line. The Lynx followed the National in production at Lillyhall and is typified here by 217, G217KRN. The Lynx is the subject of a special book in this series. The Olympian chassis was also built in Cumbria though the body on 101, H101BFR is a Northern Counties example from Wigan.** *Paul Wigan*

Below: **Preston have started to replace their Renault-Dodge first generation minibuses with Optare MetroRiders with ten in service and more to follow. Photographed shortly after delivery is 7, M407TCK.** *Paul Wigan*

101	H101BFR	Leyland Olympian ON2R50C13Z4	Northern Counties	H47/30F	1991	
102	H102BFR	Leyland Olympian ON2R50C13Z4	Northern Counties	H47/30F	1991	
103	H103BFR	Leyland Olympian ON2R50C13Z4	Northern Counties	H47/30F	1991	
104	H104BFR	Leyland Olympian ON2R50C13Z4	Northern Counties	H47/30F	1991	
106	J976PRW	Leyland Olympian ON2R50C13Z4	Leyland	H47/31F	1991	Ex Volvo bus demonstrator, 1992

107-114

Leyland Olympian ON2R50C13Z4 Leyland H47/31F* 1991-92 *107/14 are DPH43/29F

107	J107KCW	**109**	J109KCW	**112**	J112KCW	**113**	J113KCW	**114**	J114KCW
108	J108KCW	**110**	J110KCW						

132	F32AHG	Leyland Olympian ONCL10/2RZ	Northern Counties	H51/34F	1989
133	A33MRN	Leyland Olympian ONTL11/2R	Eastern Coach Works	H47/25F	1984
134	G34OCK	Leyland Olympian ONCL10/1RZ	Eastern Coach Works	DPH43/29F	1990
135	G35OCK	Leyland Olympian ONCL10/1RZ	Eastern Coach Works	DPH43/29F	1990
136	G36OCK	Leyland Olympian ONCL10/1RZ	Eastern Coach Works	H47/31F	1990
137	G37OCK	Leyland Olympian ONCL10/1RZ	Eastern Coach Works	H47/31F	1990

141-150

Leyland Atlantean AN68A/2R Alexander AL H49/36F 1980

141	UHG141V	**143**	UHG143V	**145**	UHG145V	**148**	UHG148V	**150**	UHG150V
142	UHG142V	**144**	UHG144V	**147**	UHG147V	**149**	UHG149V		

151-157

Leyland Atlantean AN68B/2R East Lancashire H50/36F 1981

151	GFV151W	**153**	GFV153W	**155**	GFV155W	**156**	GFV156W	**157**	GFV157W
152	GFV152W	**154**	GFV154W						

158-165

Leyland Atlantean AN68C/2R East Lancashire H50/36F 1981

158	OBV158X	**160**	OBV160X	**162**	OBV162X	**164**	OBV164X	**165**	OBV165X
159	OBV159X	**161**	OBV161X	**163**	OBV163X				

166-177

Leyland Atlantean AN68D/2R East Lancashire H50/36F 1982-83

166	URN166Y	**169**	URN169Y	**172**	URN172Y	**174**	DRN174Y	**176**	DRN176Y
167	URN167Y	**170**	URN170Y	**173**	DRN173Y	**175**	DRN175Y	**177**	DRN177Y
168	URN168Y	**171**	URN171Y						

181	DRN1Y	Leyland Atlantean AN68D/2R	East Lancashire	H45/29F	1983
182	DRN2Y	Leyland Atlantean AN68D/2R	East Lancashire	H45/29F	1983
210	F210YHG	Leyland Lynx LX112L10ZR1R	Leyland Lynx	B47F	1989
211	F211YHG	Leyland Lynx LX112L10ZR1R	Leyland Lynx	B47F	1989
212	F212YHG	Leyland Lynx LX112L10ZR1R	Leyland Lynx	DP45F	1989
213	F213YHG	Leyland Lynx LX112L10ZR1R	Leyland Lynx	DP45F	1989

214-218

Leyland Lynx LX2R11C15Z4R Leyland Lynx DP45F 1989

214	G214KRN	**215**	G215KRN	**216**	G216KRN	**217**	G217KRN	**218**	G218KRN

223-229

Leyland Lynx LX2R11C15Z4R Leyland Lynx DP45F 1990

223	H23YBV	**226**	H26YBV	**227**	H27YBV	**228**	H28YBV	**229**	H29YBV
224	H24YBV								

309	PRN909	Leyland Tiger TRBTL11/2RP	Duple 320	C51F	1987

Livery: Blue and ivory

Previous Registrations:
PRN909   D40AFV

RIBBLE

Stagecoach Ribble, Frenchwood Avenue, Preston, PR1 4LU.

Depots : George Street, Blackburn; Goodwin Street, Bolton; Eaves Lane, Chorley; Pimlico Road, Clitheroe; Sidings Road, Fleetwood; Owen Road, Lancaster; Heysham Road, Morecambe and Selbourne Street, Preston. Outstations: Burnley; Garstang and Ingleton.

101-105

		Dennis Lance SLF 11SDA3201		Berkhof		B40F	1996		
101	N101...	102	N102...	103	N103...	104	N104...	105	N105...

135	F135SPX	Dennis Javelin 11SDL1914		Duple 300		B63F	1989	Ex Hampshire Bus, 1991	
136	F136SPX	Dennis Javelin 11SDL1914		Duple 300		B63F	1989	Ex Hampshire Bus, 1991	
137	F137SPX	Dennis Javelin 11SDL1914		Duple 300		B63F	1989	Ex Hampshire Bus, 1991	

138-144

		Dennis Javelin 11SDL2129		Plaxton Premiére Interurban DP47F			1993		
138	L138BFV	140	L140BFV	142	L142BFV	143	L143BFV	144	L144BFV
139	L139BFV	141	L141BFV						

145-161

		Dennis Javelin 11SDL2133		Plaxton Premiére Interurban DP47F			1993		
145	L145BFV	150	L150BFV	153	L153BFV	156	L156BFV	159	L159CCW
146	L146BFV	151	L151BFV	154	L154BFV	157	L157BFV	160	L160CCW
148	L148BFV	152	L152BFV	155	L155BFV	158	L158BFV	161	L161CCW
149	L149BFV								

162-168

		Dennis Javelin 11SDL2133		Plaxton Premiére Interurban DP47F			1994	Ex Stagecoach South, 1994	
162	L101SDY	164	L104SDY	166	L102SDY	167	L105SDY	168	L107SDY
163	L103SDY	165	L106SDY						

237-256

		Volvo B6-9.9M		Alexander Dash		DP40F	1993		
237	L237CCW	240	L240CCW	251	L251CCK	253	L253CCK	256	L256CCK
239	L239CCW	241	L242CCK	252	L252CCK	255	L255CCK		

257-265

		Volvo B6-9.9M		Alexander Dash		DP40F	1993	Ex Fife Scottish, 1994	
257	L667MSF	259	L669MSF	261	L661MSF	263	L663MSF	265	L665MSF
258	L668MSF	260	L660HKS	262	L662MSF	264	L664MSF		

277-283

		Volvo B6-9.9M		Alexander Dash		B40F	1993	Ex Cumberland 1994	
277	L277JAO	278	L278JAO	279	L279JAO	281	L281JAO	283	L283JAO

Stagecoach have extended their Express service network during 1995 with Ribble playing their part. With Blackpool Tower in the background Ribble 152, L152BFV shows the latest lettering as it prepares to commence the return X64 service to Bolton. During 1996 a bendibus version of this Plaxton style will enter service with the group, two Jonckheere-bodied examples are destined for Fife.
Paul Wigan

Bolton depot of Ribble operate over one in three of the remaining Leyland Nationals in the fleet. These have seen the gradual sale of older buses with National 2s coming in from other fleets within the group, the latest arriving from Fife. Shown in Blackhorse Street on the 471 to Bury is 394, SHH394X, a 1982 example from Cumberland. *Gerry Mead*

301	CHH214T	Leyland National 10351B/1R		B44F	1979	Ex Cumberland, 1993
311	AHH206T	Leyland National 10351B/1R		B44F	1979	Ex Cumberland, 1993
312	CHH210T	Leyland National 10351B/1R		B44F	1979	Ex Cumberland, 1993
346	NLS986W	Leyland National 2 NL116L11/1R		B52F	1980	Ex Fife Scottish, 1996
348	NLS988W	Leyland National 2 NL116L11/1R		B52F	1980	Ex Fife Scottish, 1996
357	KHH377W	Leyland National 2 NL116L11/1R		B52F	1980	Ex Cumberland, 1993
359	KHH375W	Leyland National 2 NL116L11/1R		B52F	1980	Ex Cumberland, 1993
370	HHH370V	Leyland National 2 NL116L11/1R		B52F	1980	Ex Cumberland, 1993
372	HHH372V	Leyland National 2 NL116L11/1R		B52F	1980	Ex Cumberland, 1993
373	HHH373V	Leyland National 2 NL116L11/1R		B52F	1980	Ex Cumberland, 1993
375	AHH209T	Leyland National 10351B/1R		B44F	1979	Ex Cumberland, 1993
378	KHH378W	Leyland National 2 NL116L11/1R		B52F	1980	Ex Cumberland, 1993
380	NHH380W	Leyland National 2 NL116AL11/1R		B52F	1981	Ex Cumberland, 1993
383	RRM383X	Leyland National 2 NL116AL11/1R		DP52F	1982	Ex Cumberland, 1993
384	CHH211T	Leyland National 10351B/1R		B44F	1979	Ex Cumberland, 1993
385	RRM384X	Leyland National 2 NL116AL11/1R		DP52F	1982	Ex Cumberland, 1993

386-394

		Leyland National 2 NL116AL11/1R		B52F	1981-82	Ex Cumberland, 1993

386	RRM386X	390	SHH390X	391	SHH391X	393	SHH393X	394	SHH394X
387	SHH387X								

396	WAO396Y	Leyland National 2 NL116HLXB/1R		B52F	1982	Ex Cumberland, 1993
398	WAO398Y	Leyland National 2 NL116HLXB/1R		B52F	1982	Ex Cumberland, 1993
399	SHH388X	Leyland National 2 NL116AL11/1R		B52F	1982	Ex Cumberland, 1993

Opposite: The colour selection this year for Ribble shows two examples allocated to Fleetwood. After a period of running only minibuses, full-size vehicles are again allocated to the depot. Shown here is 428, M782PRS which was registered by Stagecoach Scotland in readiness for the Glasgow operation. Around thirty Mercedes-Benz L608Ds now remain with Ribble, all destined to be replaced in the near future. Almost at its destination is 513, D513RCK. For many years the F-prefix routes operated local services in Fleetwood or Cleveleys. *Paul Wigan*

428-442 — Volvo B10M-55 — Alexander PS — DP48F — 1994-95

428	M782PRS	431	M231TBV	434	M234TBV	437	M794PRS	440	M797PRS
429	M783PRS	432	M232TBV	435	M235TBV	438	M795PRS	441	M798PRS
430	M230TBV	433	M233TBV	436	M236TBV	439	M796PRS	442	M799PRS

449	K449YCW	Optare MetroRider	Optare	B31F	1992	Ex Lancaster, 1993
450	K450YCW	Optare MetroRider	Optare	B31F	1992	Ex Lancaster, 1993

451-463 — Volvo B10M-55 — Alexander PS — B48F — 1995

451	M451VCW	454	M454VCW	457	M457VCW	460	M460VCW	462	M462VCW
452	M452VCW	455	M455VCW	458	M458VCW	461	M461VCW	463	M463VCW
453	M453VCW	456	M456VCW	459	M459VCW				

501-527 — Mercedes-Benz L608D — Reeve Burgess — DP19F* — 1986 — *527 is B20F — 527 ex Cumberland, 1991

501	D501RCK	507	D507RCK	510	D510RCK	513	D513RCK	521	D521RCK
502	D502RCK	508	D508RCK	512	D512RCK	515	D515RCK	527	D527RCK
505	D505RCK								

530	D672SHH	Mercedes-Benz 609D	Ribble/Cumbria Commercials	B20F	1986

536-564 — Mercedes-Benz L608D — Reeve Burgess — B20F — 1986 — 562 ex Cumberland, 1991

536	D536RCK	545	D545RCK	549	D549RCK	553	D553RCK	556	D556RCK
537	D537RCK	546	D546RCK	551	D551RCK	554	D554RCK	562	D562RCK
541	D541RCK	548	D548RCK	552	D552RCK	555	D555RCK	564	D564RCK
542	D542RCK								

565-592 — Mercedes-Benz 709D — Alexander Sprint — B23F* — 1990 — 579/80 ex Magicbus, 1990 — *567-572 are DP25F

565	G665PHH	571	G571PRM	577	G577PRM	583	G183PAO	588	G188PAO
566	G566PRM	572	G572PRM	578	G578PRM	584	G184PAO	589	G189PAO
567	G567PRM	573	G573PRM	579	G179PAO	585	G185PAO	590	G190PAO
568	G568PRM	574	G574PRM	580	G180PAO	586	G186PAO	591	G191PAO
569	G569PRM	575	G575PRM	581	G181PAO	587	G187PAO	592	G192PAO
570	G570PRM	576	G576PRM	582	G182PAO				

595-608 — Mercedes-Benz 709D — Alexander Sprint — B25F — 1993

595	K115XHG	598	K118XHG	600	K120XHG	604	K124XHG	607	L127DRN
596	K116XHG	599	L119DRN	602	L122DRN	605	L125DRN	608	L128DRN
597	K117XHG								

610-628 — Mercedes-Benz 709D — Alexander Sprint — B23F — 1992-93

610	K610UFR	614	K614UFR	617	K617UFR	620	K620UFR	625	K625UFR
611	K611UFR	615	K615UFR	618	K618UFR	621	K621UFR	627	K627UFR
612	K612UFR	616	K616UFR	619	K619UFR	624	K624UFR	628	K628UFR
613	K613UFR								

629-637 — Mercedes-Benz 709D — Alexander Sprint — B25F — 1993

629	L629BFV	631	L631BFV	633	L633BFV	635	L635BFV	637	K112XHG
630	L630BFV	632	L632BFV	634	L634BFV	636	L636BFV		

645	WAO645Y	Leyland Tiger TRCTL11/2R	Alexander TE	DP47F	1983	Ex Cumberland, 1991
646	WAO646Y	Leyland Tiger TRCTL11/2R	Alexander TE	DP47F	1983	Ex Cumberland, 1991
802	TRN802V	Leyland National 10351B/1R		B44F	1979	Ex Cumberland, 1993
806	TRN806V	Leyland National 10351B/1R		B44F	1979	Ex Cumberland, 1993
812	TRN812V	Leyland National 10351B/1R		B44F	1979	Ex Cumberland, 1993

All sixteen of the remaining Bristol VRs are based at Clitheroe and its Burnley outstation. Of these only two were new to Ribble, the majority of the others, like 2052, LFJ883W seen here heading for Burnley, were displaced by Devon General by the minibus revolution and came to Ribble from United Counties.

Buses operating on the Lancaster University services carry a Uni-Sprint livery of black and Gold. A variety of models have been painted in this scheme, the latest being the Leyland Olympian. Shown in Lancaster while heading south for the university is 2116, OFV16X. *Malc. McDonald*

813-843

			Leyland National 2 NL106L11/1R		B44F	1980	813/4/42 ex Cumberland, 1993		
813	YRN813V	819	YRN819V	828	DBV828W	833	DBV833W	839	DBV839W
814	YRN814V	820	YRN820V	829	DBV829W	834	DBV834W	841	DBV841W
815	YRN815V	822	YRN822V	830	DBV830W	835	DBV835W	842	DBV842W
817	YRN817V	825	BCW825V	831	DBV831W	837	DBV837W	843	DBV843W
818	YRN818V	826	BCW826V	832	DBV832W	838	DBV838W		

846-877

			Leyland National 2 NL106AL11/1R		B44F	1981	856/7 ex Cumberland, 1993		
846	JCK846W	856	LFR856X	859	LFR859X	868	LFR868X	871	LFR871X
847	JCK847W	857	LFR857X	866	LFR866X	870	LFR870X	877	LFR877X
848	JCK848W	858	LFR858X						

878-886

			Leyland National 2 NL116AL11/1R		B52F	1982	881 ex Cumberland, 1993		
878	RHG878X	879	RHG879X	881	RHG881X	884	RHG884X	886	RHG886X

888	ARN888Y	Leyland National 2 NL116HLXB/1R		B52F	1983
889	ARN889Y	Leyland National 2 NL116HLXB/1R		B52F	1983
890	ARN890Y	Leyland National 2 NL116HLXB/1R		B52F	1983
895	CEO720W	Leyland National 2 NL116L11/1R		B49F	1980	Ex Cumberland, 1993
896	CEO721W	Leyland National 2 NL116L11/1R		B49F	1980	Ex Cumberland, 1993
897	CEO722W	Leyland National 2 NL116L11/1R		B49F	1980	Ex Cumberland, 1993
900	B900WRN	Leyland Tiger TRCTL11/1R	Duple Dominant	B49F	1984
1122	J122AHH	Volvo B10M-60	Plaxton Expressliner	C46FT	1992	Ex Cumberland, 1995
1123	J123AHH	Volvo B10M-60	Plaxton Expressliner	C46FT	1992	Ex Cumberland, 1995
1124	J124AHH	Volvo B10M-60	Plaxton Expressliner	C46FT	1992	Ex Cumberland, 1995
1145	PSU775	Leyland Tiger TRCTL11/3RZ	Duple Caribbean 2	C48FT	1985	Ex Cumberland, 1995
1149	PSU788	Leyland Tiger TRCTL11/3RZ	Duple Caribbean 2	C48FT	1985	Ex Cumberland, 1995
1152	B152WRN	Leyland Tiger TRCTL11/3R	Duple Laser 2	C49F	1985
1157	927GTA	Leyland Tiger TRCTL11/3R	Duple Laser 2	C53F	1985
1158	B158WRN	Leyland Tiger TRCTL11/3R	Duple Laser 2	C53F	1985
1164	M164SCK	Volvo B10M-62	Plaxton Expressliner 2	C46FT	1994
1165	M165SCK	Volvo B10M-62	Plaxton Expressliner 2	C46FT	1994

1200	TCK200X	Leyland Atlantean AN68D/2R	East Lancashire	H50/36F	1982	Ex Lancaster, 1993
1205	LFV205X	Leyland Atlantean AN68C/2R	East Lancashire	H50/36F	1981	Ex Lancaster, 1993
1206	LFV206X	Leyland Atlantean AN68C/2R	East Lancashire	H50/36F	1981	Ex Lancaster, 1993
1212	TCK212X	Leyland Atlantean AN68D/2R	East Lancashire	H50/36F	1982	Ex Lancaster, 1993
1213	WCK213Y	Leyland Atlantean AN68D/2R	East Lancashire	H50/36F	1982	Ex Lancaster, 1993
1214	A214MCK	Leyland Atlantean AN68D/2R	East Lancashire	H50/36F	1984	Ex Lancaster, 1993
1215	WCK215Y	Leyland Atlantean AN68D/2R	East Lancashire	H50/36F	1982	Ex Lancaster, 1993
1221	BFV221Y	Leyland Atlantean AN68D/2R	East Lancashire	DPH45/32F	1983	Ex Lancaster, 1993
1222	BFV222Y	Leyland Atlantean AN68D/2R	East Lancashire	DPH45/32F	1983	Ex Lancaster, 1993

1476-1482

			Leyland Atlantean AN68A/1R		Eastern Coach Works	H43/31F	1980	Ex Cumberland, 1992-93	
1476	TRN476V	1478	TRN478V	1480	TRN480V	1481	TRN481V	1482	TRN482V

The express versions of the Leyland Olympian carried a variety of promotional liveries for Ribble since their inception. Recently seen in Bury, 2156, A156OFR is smartly turned out in standard Stagecoach livery.
Paul Wigan

2021	CBV21S	Bristol VRT/SL3/501(6LXB)	Eastern Coach Works	H43/31F	1977	
2030	DBV30W	Bristol VRT/SL3/6LXB	Eastern Coach Works	H43/31F	1980	
2034	URF662S	Bristol VRT/SL3/501(6LXB)	Eastern Coach Works	H43/31F	1977	Ex Potteries, 1982
2040	FDV813V	Bristol VRT/SL3/6LXB	Eastern Coach Works	H43/31F	1980	Ex Magicbus, 1990
2042	RRP858R	Bristol VRT/SL3/501	Eastern Coach Works	H43/31F	1977	Ex United Counties, 1990
2043	FDV817V	Bristol VRT/SL3/6LXB	Eastern Coach Works	H43/31F	1980	Ex Magicbus, 1990
2044	FDV833V	Bristol VRT/SL3/6LXB	Eastern Coach Works	H43/31F	1980	Ex Magicbus, 1990
2045	FDV784V	Bristol VRT/SL3/6LXB	Eastern Coach Works	H43/31F	1980	Ex Magicbus, 1990
2051	LFJ882W	Bristol VRT/SL3/6LXC	Eastern Coach Works	H43/31F	1980	Ex United Counties, 1993
2052	LFJ883W	Bristol VRT/SL3/6LXC	Eastern Coach Works	H43/31F	1980	Ex United Counties, 1993
2053	LFJ858W	Bristol VRT/SL3/6LXB	Eastern Coach Works	H43/31F	1980	Ex United Counties, 1993
2054	LFJ859W	Bristol VRT/SL3/6LXB	Eastern Coach Works	H43/31F	1980	Ex United Counties, 1993
2055	LFJ885W	Bristol VRT/SL3/6LXC	Eastern Coach Works	H43/31F	1980	Ex United Counties, 1993
2056	LFJ866W	Bristol VRT/SL3/6LXB	Eastern Coach Works	H43/31F	1980	Ex United Counties, 1993
2057	LFJ861W	Bristol VRT/SL3/6LXB	Eastern Coach Works	H43/31F	1980	Ex United Counties, 1993
2058	LFJ884W	Bristol VRT/SL3/6LXC	Eastern Coach Works	H43/31F	1980	Ex United Counties, 1993
2100	DBV100W	Leyland Olympian B45.02	Eastern Coach Works	H45/33F	1980	

2101-2137

Leyland Olympian ONLXB/1R*   Eastern Coach Works   H45/32F   1981-83 *2124-30 are ONLXBT/1R

2101	GFR101W	2108	JFR8W	2115	OFV15X	2122	OFV22X	2128	VRN828Y
2102	JFR2W	2109	JFR9W	2116	OFV16X	2123	OFV23X	2129	VRN829Y
2103	JFR3W	2110	JFR10W	2117	OFV17X	2124	SCK224X	2130	VRN830Y
2104	JFR4W	2111	JFR11W	2118	OFV18X	2125	SCK225X	2131	DBV131Y
2105	JFR5W	2112	JFR12W	2119	OFV19X	2126	SCK226X	2132	DBV132Y
2106	JFR6W	2113	JFR13W	2120	OFV20X	2127	VRN827Y	2137	DBV137Y
2107	JFR7W	2114	OFV14X	2121	OFV21X				

2138-2152

Leyland Olympian ONLXB/1R   Eastern Coach Works   H45/32F   1984

2138	A138MRN	2142	A142MRN	2143	A143MRN	2145	A145MRN	2152	B152TRN

2156-2179

Leyland Olympian ONLXB/1R   Eastern Coach Works   DPH41/26F 1984-85

2156	A156OFR	2159	A159OFR	2171	C171ECK	2173	C173ECK	2178	C178ECK
2157	A157OFR	2170	C170ECK	2172	C172ECK	2174	C174ECK	2179	C179ECK
2158	A158OFR							

2180-2189

Leyland Olympian ON2R50G16Z4 Alexander RL   DPH51/31F 1989

2180	G180JHG	2182	G182JHG	2184	G184JHG	2186	G186JHG	2188	G188JHG
2181	G181JHG	2183	G183JHG	2185	G185JHG	2187	G187JHG	2189	G189JHG

2191-2197

Leyland Olympian ON2R50G16Z4 Alexander RL   H51/34F   1990

2191	H191WFR	2193	H193WFR	2195	H195WFR	2196	H196WFR	2197	H197WFR
2192	H192WFR	2194	H194WFR						

2198-2210

Leyland Olympian ON2R56G13Z4 Alexander RL   DPH43/27F* 1991   *2204/8-10 are DPH47/27F

2198	J198HFR	2202	J202HFR	2205	J205HFR	2207	J207HFR	2209	J209HFR
2199	J199HFR	2203	J203HFR	2206	J206HFR	2208	J208HFR	2210	J210HFR
2201	J201HFR	2204	J204HFR						

2211-2223

Leyland Olympian ONLXB/1R   Alexander RL   H45/32F   1984-85 Ex Highland Scottish, 1991

2211	A975OST	2214	A979OST	2217	B893UAS	2220	B896UAS	2222	B898UAS
2212	A977OST	2215	B891UAS	2218	B894UAS	2221	B897UAS	2223	B899UAS
2213	A978OST	2216	B892UAS	2219	B895UAS				

Previous Registrations:

927GTA	B157WRN	K450YCW	K200LCT	PSU788	B146ACK
K449YCW	K300LCT	PSU775	B148ACK		

Livery: National Express 1122-4/64/5; red (Coachline) 1145/9

ROBINSONS

Ribblesdale Coachways Ltd, Park Garage, Great Harwood,
Lancashire, BB6 7SP

222-226		DAF MB230LT615		Van Hool Alizée		C51FT	1989		
222	F222YHG	223	F223YHG	224	F224YHG	225	F225YHG	226	F226YHG

227-231		DAF MB230LT615		Van Hool Alizée		C49FT	1990		
227	G227NCW	228	G228NCW	229	G229NCW	230	G230NCW	231	G231NCW

236-247		DAF MB230LT615		Van Hool Alizée		C49FT	1991-92		
236	H236AFV	239	H239AFV	242	H242AFV	244	J244LFR	246	J246LFR
237	H237AFV	240	H140AFV	243	J243LFR	245	J245LFR	247	J247LFR
238	H238AFV	241	H241AFV						

248	L248JBV	Volvo B10M-62	Jonckheere Deauville	C48FT	1994
249	L249JBV	Volvo B10M-62	Jonckheere Deauville	C48FT	1994
250	L250JBV	Volvo B10M-62	Jonckheere Deauville	C48FT	1994
251	N251	Volvo B10M-62	Plaxton Premiére 350	C49FT	1996
252	N252	Volvo B10M-62	Plaxton Premiére 350	C49FT	1996
253	N253	Volvo B10M-62	Plaxton Premiére 350	C49FT	1996
254	N254	Volvo B10M-62	Plaxton Premiére 350	C49FT	1996

Livery: Green and black.

ROBINSON'S

P R Elliott, Station Road Garage, Appleby-in-Westmorland, Cumbria, CA16 6TX

CHA460K	Leyland Leopard PSU3B/4R	Plaxton Panorama	C47F	1971	Ex Midland Red, 1981
KBD21V	Bristol LHS6L	Eastern Coach Works	DP35F	1979	Ex Bedlington, Ashington, 1994
SIB2632	DAF MB200DKTL600	Plaxton Supreme IV	C53F	1980	Ex Harris Bus, West Thurrock, 1991
SIB2633	Volvo B58-56	Plaxton Supreme IV	C53F	1980	Ex Hilton, Newton-le-Willows, 1995
NUS333Y	Bedford YNT	Wright TT	B53F	1983	Ex Goodwin, Stockport, 1991
A745DRM	Volkswagen Transporter	Devon Conversions	M10	1984	Ex private owner, 1990
9884TR	DAF MB200DKFL600	LAG Galaxy	C51F	1985	
3937TR	Mercedes-Benz 0303	Mercedes-Benz	C49FT	1986	
SWS768S	Bristol LH6L	Eastern Coach Works	B45F	1987	Ex Bristol, 1984
4761TR	DAF SB3000DKS585	Van Hool Alizée	C53F	1988	
F842EHH	Ford Transit VE6	Mellor	B16F	1988	Ex Swallow, Sheffield, 1989
990ENR	Volvo B10M-61	Van Hool Alizée	C53F	1988	Ex Excelsior, 1991
3927TR	Volvo B10M-61	Van Hool Alizée	C53F	1989	Ex Excelsior, 1994
3179TR	Volvo B10M-61	Van Hool Alizée	C53F	1989	Ex Excelsior, 1994
M785PAO	LDV 400	LDV	M16	1995	

Livery: Silver and green

Previous Registrations:

3179TR	G500CJT, XEL254, G307GJT	9884TR	From new
3927TR	G501CJT, XEL606, G303GJT	990ENR	E303OPR, XEL55S, E406SEL
3937TR	From new	SIB2632	NEV773V
4761TR	From new	SIB2633	LUA255V, AFJ405A

Robinsons livery of black and green is familiar to many in the north west. After years of dedication to Leyland, the DAF product was used until 1994 when three Jonckheere-bodied Volvo B10Ms were supplied. Pictured on tour in Llanberis is 227, G227NCW a DAF MB230 also with Belgian bodywork this time by Van Hool. *Ralph Stephens*

Robinson's of Applleby in Westmorland is represented by 4761TR, a rear-engined DAF SB3000 chassis with a Van Hool Alizée body. *Andrew Jarosz*

ROSSENDALE

Rossendale Transport Ltd; Ellen Smith (Tours) Ltd
35 Bacup Road, Rawtenstall, Lancashire, BB4 7NG

Depots: Bacup Road, Rawtenstall and Mandale Park, Rochdale.

1	F91CWG	MCW MetroRider MF150/105	MCW	B23F	1988	Ex Bee Line Bus, 1991
2	F92CWG	MCW MetroRider MF150/105	MCW	B23F	1988	Ex Bee Line Bus, 1991
3	F93CWG	MCW MetroRider MF150/105	MCW	B23F	1988	Ex Bee Line Bus, 1991
4	F94CWG	MCW MetroRider MF150/105`	MCW	B23F	1988	Ex Bee Line Bus, 1991
5	D21CFL	MCW MetroRider MF150/23	MCW	DP25F	1987	Ex Robinson, Kimbolton, 1992
6	E519YWF	MCW MetroRider MF150/35	MCW	B23F	1987	Ex Smith, Prenton, 1989
7	E674DCU	MCW MetroRider MF150/62	MCW	B23F	1987	Ex Moor-Dale, Newcastle, 1990
8	E248UWR	MCW MetroRider MF150/80	MCW	B23F	1988	Ex Yorkshire Rider, 1993
9	D859LND	Renault-Dodge S56	Northern Counties	B20F	1986	Ex Evans, Tregaron, 1992
10	D901MDB	Renault-Dodge S56	Northern Counties	B20F	1987	Ex GM Buses, 1992
11	L911ECW	Optare MetroRider MR09	Optare	B23F	1993	
12	L912ECW	Optare MetroRider MR09	Optare	B23F	1993	
13	L813KCW	Optare MetroRider MR31	Optare	B25F	1994	
14	L814KCW	Optare MetroRider MR31	Optare	B25F	1994	

17-23		Leyland Atlantean AN68A/1R	East Lancashire	H43/32F	1977-79

17	PTD417S	**18**	STE18S	**19**	STE19S	**22**	ABN722V	**23**	ABN723V

24	DDK24W	Leyland Atlantean AN68B/1R	East Lancashire	H43/32F	1980	
25	DDK25W	Leyland Atlantean AN68B/1R	East Lancashire	H43/32F	1980	
26	DDK26W	Leyland Atlantean AN68B/1R	East Lancashire	H43/32F	1980	
27	SND27X	Leyland Atlantean AN68D/1R	East Lancashire	DPH43/27F	1982	
28	SND28X	Leyland Atlantean AN68D/1R	East Lancashire	H43/32F	1982	
29	M529RHG	Volvo Olympian YN2RV18Z4	Alexander Royale RH	H43/29F	1994	
30	M530RHG	Volvo Olympian YN2RV18Z4	Alexander Royale RH	H43/29F	1994	
31	B101PHC	Leyland Olympian ONLXCT/2R	East Lancashire	H47/35F	1985	Ex Stevensons, 1993
32	B102PHC	Leyland Olympian ONLXCT/2R	East Lancashire	H47/35F	1985	Ex Stevensons, 1993
39	F103YWO	MCW MetroRider MF151/104	MCW	DP25F	1988	Ex Rhondda, 1996
40	F113YWO	MCW MetroRider MF151/103	MCW	DP23F	1988	Ex Rhondda, 1996
41	F111YWO	MCW MetroRider MF151/103	MCW	DP23F	1988	Ex Rhondda, 1995
42	F115YWO	MCW MetroRider MF151/103	MCW	DP23F	1988	Ex Rhondda, 1995
43	E143KYW	MCW MetroRider MF151/38	MCW	B25F	1987	Ex Rhondda, 1995
44	E144KYW	MCW MetroRider MF151/38	MCW	B25F	1987	Ex Rhondda, 1995
45	D601AFR	MCW MetroRider MF151/4	MCW	B23F	1987	Ex Blackburn, 1995
46	RJA705R	Leyland Atlantean AN68A/1R	Northern Counties	H43/32F	1977	Ex GM Buses, 1990
47	SRJ740R	Leyland Atlantean AN68A/1R	Northern Counties	H43/32F	1977	Ex GM Buses, 1990
48	ONF684R	Leyland Atlantean AN68A/1R	Northern Counties	H43/32F	1976	Ex GM Buses, 1990
49	ONF692R	Leyland Atlantean AN68A/1R	Northern Counties	H43/32F	1977	Ex GM Buses, 1990
50	SND550X	Bristol LHS6L	East Lancashire	B28F	1982	
51w	SND551X	Bristol LHS6L	East Lancashire	B28F	1982	
52	E481CNM	MCW MetroRider MF150/72	MCW	B23F	1988	Ex Sovereign, 1995
53	E483CNM	MCW MetroRider MF150/72	MCW	B23F	1988	Ex Sovereign, 1995
54	E979DGS	MCW MetroRider MF150/72	MCW	B23F	1988	Ex Sovereign, 1995
55	E980DGS	MCW MetroRider MF150/72	MCW	B23F	1988	Ex Sovereign, 1995
56	E56KHG	MCW MetroRider MF151/8	MCW	B23F	1988	
58	E58KHG	MCW MetroRider MF151/8	MCW	B23F	1988	
59	E59KHG	MCW MetroRider MF151/8	MCW	B23F	1988	
60	F60ARN	MCW MetroRider MF150/106	MCW	B23F	1989	
61	F61ARN	MCW MetroRider MF150/106	MCW	B23F	1989	
62	F62ARN	MCW MetroRider MF150/106	MCW	B23F	1989	
63	F63ARN	MCW MetroRider MF150/120	MCW	B25F	1989	

Opposite, top: **Rossendale have built up a fleet of new and pre-owned MetroRiders, the latest arrivals coming from Rhondda early in 1996. Seen on the Bury ring road is 8, E248UWR, an example from Yorkshire Rider in 1993.** *Richard Godfrey*
Opposite, bottom: **Coaching and tour work for Rossendale continues the Ellen Smith name and traditional tiger motif. Waiting time at Fleetwood is Tiger 84, LIB1184 lettered for the Lancashire town service X69 and X79. This vehicle carries a Plaxton Supreme IV body with shallow side windows.** *Mark Bailey*

The withdrawal from Rochdale and Tameside by Greater Manchester Buses left the areas open to others. Rossendale now have a considerable presence in Rochdale where 118, BAJ118Y is seen on service 435. Previously with Trimdon Motor Services, it is one of five Duple bus-bodied Leyland Tigers now operated. *Richard Godfrey*

Two Volvo Olympians with Alexander Royale bodies joined the Rossendale fleet in 1994. Photographed on the main 464 service between Bacup and Accrington is 29, M529RHG. *Roy Marshall*

The Dennis Dart has become a favourite for mid-size buses, this example being built by Duple and completed by Carlyle in 1990. Pictured in Rochdale is 103, H103VFV. *Richard Godfrey*

64	F164DET	MCW MetroRider MF150/120	MCW	B25F	1989	Ex Liverbus, 1993
65	F165DET	MCW MetroRider MF150/120	MCW	B25F	1989	Ex Liverbus, 1993
66	E977DGS	MCW MetroRider MF150/72	MCW	B23F	1988	Ex Sovereign, 1995
67	F171DET	MCW MetroRider MF150/106	MCW	B25F	1989	Ex Liverbus, 1993
68	F168DET	MCW MetroRider MF150/120	MCW	B25F	1989	Ex Liverbus, 1993
69	F169DET	MCW MetroRider MF150/120	MCW	B25F	1989	Ex Liverbus, 1993
70	PJI9170	Leyland Leopard PSU4D/2R	East Lancs EL2000(1993)	B47F	1977	Ex National Welsh, 1989
71	PJI9171	Leyland Leopard PSU4D/2R	East Lancs EL2000(1993)	B47F	1977	Ex National Welsh, 1989
75	PJI9175	Leyland Leopard PSU3E/4R	East Lancs EL2000 (1993)	DP49F	1980	Ex Blue Bus, Horwich, 1993
76	PJI9176	Leyland Leopard PSU3E/4R	East Lancs EL2000 (1992)	B51F	1977	Ex South Lancs, St Helens, 1993
77	PJI9177	Leyland Leopard PSU3C/4R	East Lancs EL2000 (1992)	B51F	1977	Ex Ellen Smith, Rochdale, 1991
78	PJI9178	Leyland Leopard PSU3E/4R	East Lancs EL2000 (1992)	B51F	1979	Ex Ribble, 1987
79	PJI9179	Leyland Leopard PSU3E/4R	East Lancs EL2000 (1992)	B51F	1980	Ex Cooper, Stockton Heath, 1980
92	F92XBV	Leyland Tiger TRBTL11/2RP	East Lancashire	DP49F	1989	
93	F93XBV	Leyland Tiger TRBTL11/2RP	East Lancashire	B51F	1989	
94	F94XBV	Leyland Tiger TRBTL11/2RP	East Lancashire	B51F	1989	
95	F95XBV	Leyland Tiger TRBTL11/2RP	East Lancashire	B51F	1989	
96	A196WGE	Leyland Tiger TRCTL11/2R	Duple Dominant	B51F	1984	Ex Hutchison, Overtown, 1988
99	OGE9Y	Leyland Tiger TRCTL11/2R	Duple Dominant	B55F	1983	Ex Hutchison, Overtown, 1988
101	H101VFV	Dennis Dart 9SDL3002	Duple/Carlyle Dartline	B36F	1990	
102	H102VFV	Dennis Dart 9SDL3002	Duple/Carlyle Dartline	B36F	1990	
103	H103VFV	Dennis Dart 9SDL3002	Duple/Carlyle Dartline	B36F	1990	
104	H104CHG	Dennis Dart 9SDL3002	Reeve Burgess Pointer	B35F	1991	
105	H105CHG	Dennis Dart 9SDL3002	Reeve Burgess Pointer	B35F	1991	
106	N106	Dennis Dart 9SDL3	East Lancashire	B F	1996	
107	N107	Dennis Dart 9SDL3	East Lancashire	B F	1996	
108	N108	Dennis Dart 9SDL3	East Lancashire	B F	1996	
109	N109	Dennis Dart 9SDL3	East Lancashire	B F	1996	
118	BAJ118Y	Leyland Tiger TRCTL11/2R	Duple Dominant	B53F	1983	Ex Trimdon MS, 1988
119	BAJ119Y	Leyland Tiger TRCTL11/2R	Duple Dominant	B53F	1983	Ex Trimdon MS, 1988
120	BAJ120Y	Leyland Tiger TRCTL11/2R	Duple Dominant	B53F	1983	Ex Trimdon MS, 1988
128	VDY528T	Leyland Atlantean AN68A/2R	East Lancashire	H47/35F	1978	Ex Hastings Top Line, 1989
129	VDY529T	Leyland Atlantean AN68A/2R	East Lancashire	H47/35F	1978	Ex Hastings Top Line, 1989
130	VDY530T	Leyland Atlantean AN68A/2R	East Lancashire	H47/35F	1978	Ex Hastings Top Line, 1989
131	VDY531T	Leyland Atlantean AN68A/2R	East Lancashire	H47/35F	1978	Ex Hastings Top Line, 1989
136	CJK36V	Leyland Atlantean AN68B/1R	East Lancashire	H43/31F	1980	Ex Hastings Top Line, 1989
137	CJK37V	Leyland Atlantean AN68B/1R	East Lancashire	H43/31F	1980	Ex Hastings Top Line, 1989

		Leyland Atlantean AN68B/1R	Alexander AL	H45/33F	1981	Ex South Yorkshire's Transport, 1991

188	JKW288W	191	JKW291W	194	JKW294W	196	JKW296W	197	JKW297W
190	JKW290W	193	JKW293W						

Num	Reg	Chassis	Body	Seating	Year	History
199	E764KJX	Peugeot-Talbot Freeway	Talbot	B15FL	1988	Ex Employment Service, Sheffield, 1995
300	N300EST	Dennis Javelin 12SDA2159	Plaxton Premiére 350	C48FT	1996	
301	OIW5801	Leyland Tiger TRCTL11/3RZ	Van Hool Alizée	C49FT	1985	Ex Lodge, High Easter, 1994
303	OIB5403	Leyland Tiger TRCTL11/3RZ	Plaxton Paramount 3200 II	C53F	1985	Ex Ellen Smith, Rochdale, 1991
304	OIB3604	Leyland Tiger TRCTL11/3R	Plaxton Paramount 3200	C53F	1984	Ex Ellen Smith, Rochdale, 1991
305	OIB6205	Leyland Tiger TRCTL11/3R	Plaxton Paramount 3200	C53F	1983	Ex Ellen Smith, Rochdale, 1991
307	OIB6207	Leyland Leopard PSU5C/5R	Plaxton Supreme IV	C53F	1980	Ex Ellen Smith, Rochdale, 1991
308	OIB3608	Leyland Leopard PSU3E/4R	Plaxton Supreme IV	C49F	1979	Ex Ellen Smith, Rochdale, 1991
317	NIW6517	Volvo B10M-61	Van Hool Alizée	C49FT	1987	Ex Shearings, 1991
318	NIW6518	Volvo B10M-61	Van Hool Alizée	C53F	1986	Ex Shearings, 1991
319	NIW6519	Volvo B10M-61	Van Hool Alizée	C51FT	1988	Ex Rothwell, Heywood, 1993
320	RJI8720	Volvo B10M-61	Van Hool Alizée	C49FT	1989	Ex Shearings, 1993
321	RJI8721	Volvo B10M-60	Van Hool Alizée	C51FT	1989	Ex Bruce, Overtown, 1993
322	RJI8722	Volvo B10M-61	Van Hool Alizée	C53F	1987	Ex Clarkson, South Elmsall, 1993
323	RJI8723	Volvo B10M-61	Van Hool Alizée	C49FT	1989	Ex Limebourne, London, 1994
324	G94VFP	Volvo B10M-60	Van Hool Alizée	C51FT	1989	Ex Starline, Wootton, 1995
380	LIB1180	Leyland Tiger TRCTL11/3RZ	Plaxton Paramount 3500 II	C49FT	1985	Ex Ribble, 1988
381	LIB1181	Leyland Leopard PSU3F/5R	Plaxton Supreme IV Express	C53F	1981	Ex Hill's, Tredegar, 1985
382	AAL468A	Leyland Leopard PSU5D/4R	Plaxton P3200 III (1988)	C53F	1980	Ex Border, Burnley, 1993
383	LIB1183	Leyland Tiger TRCTL11/2R	Plaxton Supreme VI Express	C49F	1982	Ex Hill's, Tredegar, 1986
384	LIB1184	Leyland Tiger TRCTL11/2R	Plaxton Supreme VI Express	C53F	1982	Ex Hill's, Tredegar, 1986
387	OIB1287	Leyland Tiger TRCTL11/2RH	Plaxton Paramount 3200 E	C53F	1984	Ex Kentish Bus, 1990
389	LIW4289	Leyland Tiger TRCTL11/3R	Plaxton Paramount 3200 E	C51F	1984	Ex Kentish Bus, 1990
390	170BHR	MCW MetroRider MF150/6	MCW	C16F	1987	Ex Capital, West Drayton, 1990
392	NSU181	MCW MetroRider MF150/9	MCW	DP25F	1986	Ex Patrick Collection, Birmingham, 1992
393	B183FDM	Volvo B10M-50	East Lancashire	CH45/33F	1985	Ex The Wright Company, Wrexham, 1993

Previous Registrations:

170BHR	D741ALR	NSU181	D87EDH		PJI9175	WCK139V	
AAL468A	BUH225V	OIB1287	A133EPA		PJI9176	VAJ784S	
LIB1180	B66YFV	OIB3604	A886OND		PJI9177	UGG369R	
LIB1181	GBO243W	OIB3608	LFS487T		PJI9178	WCK123V	
LIB1183	NDW149X	OIB5403	B887WRJ		PJI9179	GRF268V	
LIB1184	NDW148X	OIB6205	FJA400Y		RJI8720	F763ENE	
LIW4289	A148EPA	OIB6207	UFS690V		RJI8721	F348JSU	
NIW6517	D537MVR	OIW5801	C396DML		RJI8722	D561MVR, MIW2422, D709NYG	
NIW6518	C532DND	PJI9170	PHB362R		RJI8723	F887SMU	
NIW6519	E329OMG	PJI9171	PHB363R				

Livery: Cream, red and green (buses); red and white (coaches); white, red and gold (Ellen Smith)

ROYAL MAIL POST BUS

Royal Mail, North West & North Wales, 2 Weston Road, Crewe, CW1 1AN

Vehicles are based at Ulverston, Broughton-in-Furness, and Penrith.

1750049	J153LRN	Leyland DAF 400	Post Office	M11	1991	Ulverston-Grizedale
1750050	J154LRN	Leyland DAF 400	Post Office	M11	1991	Broughton-in-Furness
1750051	J155LRN	Leyland DAF 400	Post Office	M11	1991	Barrow reserve
3760001	L720JFA	Peugeot 405	Peugeot	M4	1994	Brampton
3780019	K865CEH	Leyland DAF 400	Post Office	M11	1994	Carlisle
	L750PFA	Leyland DAF 400	Post Office	M11	1994	Penrith-Martindale/Patterdale

Livery: Post Office red and yellow

SHAW HADWIN

J Shaw & Son (Silverdale) Ltd, Stoneleigh, Silverdale, Lancashire, LA5 0RA
Hadwin's Tours Ltd, Billings Road, Dalton-in-Furness, Cumbria, CA16 6TX

Depots and outstations are located at Bowness, Carnforth and Billcape Road, Dalton

FAP9	Bedford OB	Duple Vista	C29F	1949	Ex Hardy, Heathfield, 1995
LTF346	Bedford OB	Duple Vista	C29F	1950	Ex Topp-Line, Liverpool, 1995
SND83X	Leyland Leopard PSU3B/4R	Duple Dominant II(1981)	C51F	1974	Ex Chester, 1994
6682WY	Volvo B58-56	Plaxton P3200 (1984)	C53F	1977	Ex Goodwin, Stockport, 1988
XDO32	Volvo B58-56	Plaxton P3200 (1984)	C53F	1977	Ex Goodwin, Stockport, 1988
UIA7087	Volvo B58-61	Plaxton Supreme III	C57F	1978	
GIL3016	Volvo B58-61	Plaxton Supreme IV	C57F	1980	
OVR409W	Ford Transit 190	Ford	M5L	1980	Ex Manchester MB, 1988
HSC164X	Leyland Cub CU435	Duple Dominant	B33F	1981	Ex Munro, Uddingston, 1995
GTU606X	Ford Transit 190	Steedrive	M8L	1982	Ex Salford MB, 1989
LSU939	Volvo B58-61	Plaxton Supreme VI	C57F	1982	Ex Mountain Goat, Windermere, 1994
THH288X	Mercedes-Benz L508D	Reeve Burgess	C16F	1982	Ex Seaview, Askham, 1986
HIL8916	Leyland Leopard PSU3G/4R	Eastern Coach Works B51	C38FL	1982	Ex Lancaster, 1993
BYP985	DAF MB200DKFL600	Jonckheere Jubilee	C51FT	1983	Ex Hutchison, Overtown, 1985
5129UA	Volvo B10M-61	Jonckheere Jubilee P599	C49FT	1983	Ex Rotherham Travel, 1991
6267UA	Volvo B10M-61	Jonckheere Jubilee P599	C51FT	1983	
824HAO	Volvo B10M-61	Jonckheere Jubilee P599	C51FT	1983	Ex Rotherham Travel, 1991
899CAN	Volvo B10M-61	Jonckheere Jubilee	C51FT	1983	
A383HFK	Ford Transit 190	Deansgate	M8L	1983	Ex Dudley MB, 1994
KBZ5749	Volvo B10M-61	Duple Dominant IV	C57F	1984	Ex Browns, Ambleside, 1994
UWR294	DAF MB200DKFL600	Plaxton Paramount 3200	C49FT	1984	Ex Mountain Goat, Windermere, 1987
HIL8917	Leyland Tiger TRCTL11/3RH	Plaxton Paramount 3500	C53F	1984	Ex Lancaster, 1993
UIB4751	Leyland Tiger TRCTL11/3RH	Duple Laser 2	C57F	1985	Ex Lancaster, 1993
B59AOP	Ford Transit 190	Carlyle	B16F	1985	Ex Lancaster, 1993
JIL2045	Mercedes-Benz L608D	PMT Hanbridge	C21F	1985	Ex Lancaster, 1993
JIL2047	Mercedes-Benz L608D	PMT Hanbridge	C21F	1985	Ex Lancaster, 1993
C963END	Ford Transit VE6	Steedrive	M16L	1986	Ex Gwynedd CC, 1993
C489PHG	Ford Transit VE6	Ford	M8L	1986	Ex McBurney, Larne, 1993
D69ONS	Bedford YMP	Plaxton Paramount 3200 II	C35F	1986	Ex Blue Line, Hereford, 1993
HIL9311	MAN MT8.136	G C Smith	C28F	1986	Ex Lancaster, 1993
IIL3198	Leyland Tiger TRCTL11/3RH	320	C57F	1986	Ex Lancaster, 1993
UIB4752	Leyland Tiger TRCTL11/3RH	Duple Laser 2	C57F	1986	Ex Lancaster, 1993
HIL8915	Leyland Tiger TRCTL11/3RZ	Plaxton Paramount 3500 III	C53F	1987	Ex Lancaster, 1993
E403WRH	Ford Transit VE6	Ford	M8	1987	Ex private owner, 1994
JIB3515	Volvo B10M-61	Plaxton Paramount 3200 III	C57F	1987	Ex Express Travel, 1995
509EBL	Volvo B10M-61	Plaxton Paramount 3200 III	C49FT	1987	Ex Express Travel, 1995
XJF386	Volvo B10M-61	Plaxton Paramount 3500 III	C50FT	1988	Ex Wallace Arnold, 1992
RIB5093	Volvo B10M-61	Plaxton Paramount 3500 III	C49FT	1988	Ex Wallace Arnold, 1992
E119UEC	Renault Master T35D	Dobson	M15	1988	Ex Browns, Ambleside, 1994
RIB4323	DAF SB2305DHTD585	Plaxton Paramount 3200 III	C57F	1988	
YFG333	DAF SB2305DHTD585	Duple 320	C57F	1988	
525XPD	DAF SB3000DKV601	Van Hool Alizée	C49FT	1988	Ex Wharfedale Cs, Yeadon, 1993
E775WEC	Mercedes-Benz L307D	Mercedes-Benz	M8	1988	Ex Barrow Travel, 1991
F371JTN	Mercedes-Benz 407D	Reeve Burgess	M15	1988	Ex Target, Cramlington, 1993
F485CKU	Mercedes-Benz 609D	Whittaker-Europa	C24F	1988	
F664DRN	Aüwaerter Neoplan N122/3	Aüwaerter Skyliner	CH57/20CT	1989	Ex Mandale, Greystoke, 1993
4150RU	Volvo B10M-60	Duple 340	C57F	1989	Ex Baker, Bidduplh, 1995
G581PVU	Ford Transit VE6	Ford	M8	1990	Ex Tarmac Construction, 1993
H176ANE	Ford Transit VE6	Deansgate	M14	1990	
H251ANE	Ford Transit VE6	Deansgate	M14	1990	
H493BND	Mercedes-Benz 811D	Made-to-Measure	C28F	1990	
H882JFA	Mercedes-Benz 811D	PMT Ami	C33F	1991	Ex PMT demonstrator, 1992

The picturesque setting of HIL8915 is no less than the Liverpool Gyratory. On the windscreen is the Lonsdale name of the former Lancaster coaching unit, and one of several fleet names used by the company including Shaw's, Browns, Hadwins and Shaw Hadwin International. *Paul Wigan*

H538SEO	Volvo B10M-60	Plaxton Expressliner	C46FT	1991	
H539SEO	Volvo B10M-60	Plaxton Expressliner	C46FT	1991	
6137RU	Volvo B10M-60	Plaxton Paramount 3200 III	C57F	1992	
K615EEO	Volvo B10M-60	Van Hool Alizée	C46FT	1993	
K36OUY	Volvo B10M-60	Plaxton Premiére 350	C49FT	1993	Ex Go-Whittle, Kidderminster, 1995
M208SCK	Volvo B10M-62	Plaxton Premiére 320	C53FT	1994	
M209SCK	Volvo B10M-62	Plaxton Premiére 320	C53FT	1994	
M338EEC	Volvo B10M-62	Plaxton Premiére 350	C49FT	1995	
M339EEC	Volvo B10M-62	Plaxton Premiére 350	C51FT	1995	
N160GRN	Volvo B10M-62	Plaxton Premiére 350	C48FT	1995	
N781PEC	Volvo B10M-62	Plaxton Premiére 350	C53F	1996	

Previous Registrations:

509EBL	D443CNR	FAP9	From new	LTF346	From new
525XPD	F217RJX	GIL3016	YEC21W, 6SVK	RIB4323	E651EEO
824HAO	A309XHE	HIL8915	D120GWS	RIB5093	E902UNW
899CAN	A539BEC	HIL8916	UKE829X	SND83X	HNE643N
4150RU	F477WFX, 9530RU, F515WFA	HIL8917	A203OCW	UIA7087	FEC952T
5129UA	A305XHE	HIL9311	C854VRY	UIB4751	B99YRN
6137RU	J728KBC	IIL3198	D98SCW	UIB4752	C913XEO
6267UA	A538BEC, XDO32	JIB3515	D446CNR, NXI900n, D997UKA	UWR294	A739JAY
6682WY	PYT153R, A184UJD	JIL2045	B926DTU	XDO32	PYT152R, A183UJD, 6267UA
BYP985	NNV611Y	JIL2047	B902DTU	XJF386	E901UNW, RIB5092
C489PHG	JIB3515	KBZ5749	A287FEC	YFG333	E467FEO, PIB9452
F664DRN	F619CWJ, 4150RU	LSU939	TRB25X		

Livery: White, cream and gold; National Express: H538/9SEO, RIB5093, 6137RU, K615EEO

Opposite: Shaw Hadwin operate several National Express contracts. Seen in Blackpool in Rapide livery is H538SEO one of the earlier Plaxton Expressliners based on a Volvo B10M chassis. Also working National Express service when photographed was 5129UA, another Volvo B10M, this time with Jonckheere Jubilee bodywork. *Paul Wigan*

The Lancashire, Cumbria & Manchester Bus Handbook

SHEARINGS

Shearings Ltd, Miry Lane, Wigan, WN3 4AG

Depots : Lockett Road, Bryn; Bayton Road, Exhall; Mill Road, Whitwood, Normanton; Alexandra Road, Gorseinon and Lamberts Road, Tunbridge Wells.

156-169 — Volvo B10M-60 — Van Hool Alizée — C49FT — 1992

156	H156DVM	159	H159DVM	162	H162DVM	165	H165DVM	168	H168DVM
157	H157DVM	160	H160DVM	163	H163DVM	166	H166DVM	169	H169DVM
158	H158DVM	161	H161DVM	164	H564DVM	167	H167DVM		

181-200 — Volvo B10M-60 — Van Hool Alizée — C53F — 1992

181	H181DVM	185	H185DVM	189	CAZ2819	193	H193DVM	197	H197DVM
182	H182DVM	186	H186DVM	190	CAZ3190	194	H194DVM	198	H198DVM
183	H183DVM	187	H187DVM	191	H191DVM	195	H195DVM	199	H199DVM
184	H184DVM	188	CAZ2818	192	H192DVM	196	H196DVM	200	H501DVM

206-257 — Volvo B10M-60 — Van Hool Alizée — C49FT* — 1992 — *246-257 are C53F

206	J206NNC	218	J218NNC	228	J228NNC	238	J238NNC	248	J248NNC
207	J207NNC	219	J219NNC	229	J229NNC	239	J239NNC	249	J249NNC
208	J208NNC	220	J220NNC	231	J231NNC	241	J241NNC	251	J251NNC
209	J209NNC	221	J221NNC	232	J232NNC	242	J242NNC	252	J252NNC
210	J210NNC	223	J223NNC	233	J233NNC	243	J243NNC	253	J253NNC
211	J211NNC	224	J224NNC	234	J234NNC	244	J244NNC	254	J254NNC
212	J212NNC	225	J225NNC	235	J235NNC	245	J245NNC	255	J255NNC
215	J215NNC	226	J226NNC	236	J236NNC	246	J246NNC	256	J256NNC
217	J217NNC	227	J227NNC	237	J237NNC	247	J247NNC	257	J257NNC

258-268 — Volvo B10M-60 — Plaxton Première 350 — C47FT — 1992

258	J258NNC	261	J261NNC	263	J263NNC	265	J265NNC	267	J267NNC
259	J259NNC	262	J262NNC	264	J264NNC	266	J266NNC	268	J268NNC

269-299 — Scania K93CRB — Plaxton Première 320 — C53F — 1992

269	J269NNC	275	J275NNC	282	J282NNC	288	J288NNC	294	J294NNC
270	J270NNC	276	J276NNC	283	J283NNC	289	J289NNC	295	J295NNC
271	J271NNC	277	J277NNC	284	J284NNC	290	J290NNC	296	J296NNC
272	J272NNC	278	J278NNC	285	J285NNC	291	J291NNC	297	J297NNC
273	J273NNC	279	J279NNC	286	J286NNC	292	J292NNC	298	J298NNC
274	J274NNC	281	J281NNC	287	J287NNC	293	J293NNC	299	J299NNC

301	SPR124	Volvo B10M-60	Van Hool Alizée	C46FT	1992
302	YTP749	Volvo B10M-60	Van Hool Alizée	C46FT	1992

451-485 — Volvo B10M-60 — Van Hool Alizée — C46FT — 1993

451	K451VVR	458	K458VVR	465	K465VVR	473	K473VVR	480	K80VVR
452	K452VVR	459	K459VVR	466	K466VVR	474	K474VVR	481	K481VVR
453	K453VVR	460	K460VVR	467	K467VVR	475	K475VVR	482	K482VVR
454	K454VVR	461	K461VVR	468	K468VVR	476	K476VVR	483	K483VVR
455	K455VVR	462	K462VVR	469	K469VVR	477	K477VVR	484	K484VVR
456	K456VVR	463	K463VVR	471	K471VVR	478	K478VVR	485	K485VVR
457	K457VVR	464	K464VVR	472	K472VVR	479	K479VVR		

Opposite: **1995 saw the introduction to Shearings of Jonckheere bodied Volvo B10Ms in addition to the other Belgian supplier, Van Hool. Photographed in the Belgian town of Brugge - just north of the Jonckheere factory - is 568, L568FND, a Scania K113 with Van Hool Alizée bodywork. A similar body on the Volvo B10M chassis shows the repositioning of the offside door to the rear.**
Bill Potter/Lee Whitehead

The Plaxton Première 320 and 350 are represented in the Shearings fleet, the taller vehicle also featuring air conditioning for continental touring work. The 320 examples are normally found on the British tours. Shown here is one of these, 272, J272NNC. *Colin Lloyd*

486-495 — Volvo B10M-60 — Van Hool Alizée — C53F — 1993

486	K486VVR	488	K488VVR	490	K490VVR	492	K492VVR	494	K494VVR
487	K487VVR	489	K489VVR	491	K491VVR	493	K493VVR	495	K495VVR

496	K496VVR	Volvo B10M-62		Van Hool Alizée	C53F	1993

561-569 — Scania K113CRB — Van Hool Alizée — C46FT — 1994

561	L561FND	563	L563FND	565	L565FND	567	L567FND	569	L569FND
562	L562FND	564	L564FND	566	L566FND	568	L568FND		

570	L570FND	Volvo B10M-62		Plaxton Excalibur	C46FT	1994

601-630 — Volvo B10M-62 — Jonckheere Deauville 45 — C53F* — 1995 — *621-30 are C46FT

601	M601ORJ	607	M607ORJ	613	M613ORJ	619	M619ORJ	625	M625ORJ
602	M602ORJ	608	M608ORJ	614	M614ORJ	620	M620ORJ	626	M626ORJ
603	M603ORJ	609	M609ORJ	615	M615ORJ	621	M621ORJ	627	M627ORJ
604	M604ORJ	610	M610ORJ	616	M616ORJ	622	M622ORJ	628	M628ORJ
605	M605ORJ	611	M611ORJ	617	M617ORJ	623	M623ORJ	629	M629ORJ
606	M606ORJ	612	M612ORJ	618	M618ORJ	624	M624ORJ	630	M630ORJ

631-688 — Volvo B10M-62 — Van Hool Alizée — C46FT — 1995

631	M631MVU	643	M643MVU	655	M655MVU	667	M667MVU	678	M678MVU
632	M632MVU	644	M644MVU	656	M656MVU	668	M668MVU	679	M679MVU
633	M633MVU	645	M645MVU	657	M657MVU	669	M669MVU	680	M680MVU
634	M634MVU	646	M646MVU	658	M658MVU	670	M670MVU	681	M681MVU
635	M635MVU	647	M647MVU	659	M659MVU	671	M671MVU	682	M682MVU
636	M636MVU	648	M648MVU	660	M660MVU	672	M672MVU	683	M683MVU
637	M637MVU	649	M649MVU	661	M661MVU	673	M673MVU	684	M684MVU
638	M638MVU	650	M650MVU	662	M662MVU	674	M674MVU	685	M685MVU
639	M639MVU	651	M651MVU	663	M663MVU	675	M675MVU	686	M686MVU
640	M640MVU	652	M652MVU	664	M664MVU	676	M676MVU	687	M687MVU
641	M641MVU	653	M653MVU	665	M665MVU	677	M677MVU	688	M688MVU
642	M642MVU	654	M654MVU	666	SPR35				

A line up of Shearings coaches at Llandudno shows Plaxton and Van Hool products. The Plaxton Paramount 3200 914, H914DRJ, is based on a Leyland Tiger chassis while the two Alizée coaches 730 and 736 are based on Volvo chassis. *Ralph Stephens*

701-720

				Volvo B10M-62		Van Hool Alizée	C46FT	1996		
701	N701UVR	705	N705UVR	709	N709UVR	713	N713UVR	717	N717UVR
702	N702UVR	706	N706UVR	710	N710UVR	714	N714UVR	718	N718UVR
703	N703UVR	707	N707UVR	711	N711UVR	715	N715UVR	719	N719UVR
704	N704UVR	708	N708UVR	712	N712UVR	716	N716UVR	720	N720UVR

721-735

				Volvo B10M-62		Jonckheere Deauville 45	C46FT	1996		
721	N721UVR	724	N724UVR	727	N727UVR	730	N730UVR	733	N733UVR
722	N722UVR	725	N725UVR	728	N728UVR	731	N731UVR	734	N734UVR
723	N723UVR	726	N726UVR	729	N729UVR	732	N732UVR	735	N735UVR

774	M774VCW	Volkswagon Caravelle	Volkswagon	M8	1995
775	M774VCW	Volkswagon Caravelle	Volkswagon	M8	1995

846-865

				Volvo B10M-60		Van Hool Alizée	C53F	1990		
846	BAZ6516	850	BAZ6170	854	BAZ7054	858	BAZ7058	862	BAZ7912
847	BAZ6527	851	BAZ6851	855	BAZ7055	859	BAZ7059	863	BAZ7918
848	BAZ6528	852	BAZ7052	856	BAZ7056	860	BAZ7360	864	BAZ7914
849	BAZ7049	853	BAZ7053	857	BAZ7057	861	BAZ7901	865	BAZ7917

Livery: Miami blue, orange and white; 451 is metallic blue

Previous Registrations:

BAZ6170	G850RNC	BAZ7055	G855RNC	BAZ7917	G865RNC
BAZ6516	G846RNC	BAZ7056	G856RNC	BAZ7918	G863RNC
BAZ6527	G847RNC	BAZ7057	G857RNC	CAZ2818	H188DVM
BAZ6528	G848RNC	BAZ7058	G858RNC	CAZ2819	H189DVM
BAZ6851	G851RNC	BAZ7059	G859RNC	CAZ3190	H590DVM
BAZ7049	G849RNC	BAZ7360	G860RNC	ESU121	-
BAZ7052	G852RNC	BAZ7901	G861RNC	SPR35	From new
BAZ7053	G853RNC	BAZ7912	G862RNC	SPR124	J301PND
BAZ7054	G854RNC	BAZ7914	G864RNC	YTP749	J302RNE

SIM

J & B Sim, Hunholme Garage, Boot, Eskdale, Cumbria, CA19 1TF

C590NRM	Mercedes-Benz L608D	PMT Hanbridge	C21F	1985	
ENF555Y	Volvo B10M-61	Duple Dominant IV	C53F	1983	Ex Shearings, 1988
F355JAO	Scania K92CRB	Duple 320	C55F	1989	
F130AEL	Volvo B10M-60	Plaxton Paramount 3200 III	C49F	1989	Ex Excelsior, 1995
219DLV	DAF MB230LB615	Caetano Algarve	C53F	1989	Ex Abbeyways, Halifax, 1991
WXI5865	Van Hool T815H	Van Hool Alizée	C51F	1990	Ex Peter & Carol, Bristol, 1994
H538EVM	Mercedes-Benz 709D	Made-to-Measure	C24F	1991	
J767BHH	Mercedes-Benz 811D	Plaxton Beaver	C33F	1992	
N298VRM	Mercedes-Benz 814D	K&L	C..F	1995	

Livery: White, red and plum

Previous Registrations:

219DLV	F234RJX	F130AEL	F458WFX, A18EXC	WXI5865	G731XHY

SOUTH MANCHESTER

South Manchester Transport, Adamson Ind Est, Raglan Street, Hyde, Tameside, SK14 2DX

7u	KDW707P	Bristol RESL6L	East Lancashire	B47F	1975	Ex Cambrian Coast, Abergynolwyn, 1994
12w	JDK912P	Bristol RESL6L	East Lancashire	DP42F	1975	Ex Rossendale, 1994
14	JDK914P	Bristol RESL6L	East Lancashire	B45F	1975	Ex Rossendale, 1994
24	PKA724S	Leyland Atlantean AN68A/1R	MCW	H43/32F	1978	Ex Merseybus, 1994
28	WWM928W	Leyland Atlantean AN68B/1R	Willowbrook	H45/33F	1981	Ex PMT, 1994
32	WWM932W	Leyland Atlantean AN68B/1R	Willowbrook	H45/33F	1981	Ex PMT, 1994
59	PHF559T	Leyland Atlantean AN68A/1R	MCW	H43/32F	1978	Ex Merseybus, 1994
64	ONF664R	Leyland Atlantean AN68A/1R	Northern Counties	H43/32F	1976	Ex Blue Buses (Fylde), 1995
67	ONF667R	Leyland Atlantean AN68A/1R	Northern Counties	H43/32F	1976	Ex Blue Buses (Fylde), 1995
69	ONF659R	Leyland Atlantean AN68A/1R	Northern Counties	H43/32F	1976	Ex Blue Buses (Fylde), 1995
80	AFY180X	Leyland Atlantean AN68B/1R	Willowbrook	H45/33F	1981	Ex Tame Valley, Hyde, 1994
82	YNA282M	Daimler Fleetline CRG6LXB	Northern Counties	H43/32F	1973	Ex Stotts, Oldham, 1995
122	DAR122T	Leyland National 11351A/1R		B49F	1978	Ex MTL, 1995
143	THX143S	Leyland National 10351/2R		B36D	1977	Ex Smith, Sittingbourne, 1995
346	AYR346T	Leyland National 10351/2R		B36D	1979	Ex Barnard Kirtonian, Lindsey, 1995

Livery: Green and yellow

SPRINGFIELD COACHWAYS

W & E Trezise, 24 Douglas Bank Drive, Wigan, WN6 7NH

XBF58S	Leyland Leopard PSU3E/4R	Duple Dominant I	C49F	1978	Ex PMT, 1990
MFR420T	Ford R1114	Plaxton Supreme III	C53F	1978	Ex Ericsway, Eccles, 1988
JMB331T	Leyland Leopard PSU3E/4R	Duple Dominant II Express	C49F	1979	Ex PMT, 1990
LAO627W	Leyland Leopard PSU3F/4R	Duple Dominant II Express	C53F	1980	Ex Cumberland, 1993
GHR301W	Leyland Leopard PSU3F/4R	Duple Dominant II Express	C53F	1981	Ex Thamesdown, 1993
A717GJA	Leyland Royal Tiger B50	Roe Doyen	C44FT	1983	Ex East End Travel, Burstwick, 1995
C150LWA	Leyland Royal Tiger RT	Plaxton Paramount 3500 II	C49FT	1986	Ex Roe, Stainforth, 1993
D349JUM	Volkswagen LT55	Optare City Pacer	B23F	1986	Ex London Buses, 1992
D359JUM	Volkswagen LT55	Optare City Pacer	B23F	1986	Ex London Buses, 1992
RJX318	DAF SB2300DHS585	Duple 340	C53F	1987	Ex Hughes DAF, 1990
H129YGG	Mercedes-Benz 709D	Dormobile Routemaker	B29F	1991	Ex Timeline, 1995

Previous Registrations:

RJX318	D624YCX

Livery: Blue and white.

SIM operate F355JAO, a Scania with Duple 320 bodywork. This was one of only 25 Scania chassis to be bodied by Duple, all of which have the 320 product. This body was introduced by Scania to provide a less-expensive product than the imported bodies and in line with this theme only offered the smaller engined K92 and K93 chassis. *David Donati collection*

Some distance away from South Manchester's operating centre at Hyde is Wilmslow Road, Fallowfield once described as the bus photographers paradise with around twelve operators providing services. Seen here is South Manchester YNA282M, a Northern Counties-bodied Daimler Fleetline. *Richard Godfrey*

STOTTS

Stotts Tours (Oldham) Ltd, 144 Lees Road, Oldham, OL4 1HT

XJA549L	Daimler Fleetline CRG6LXB	Park Royal	H43/32F	1973	Ex GM Buses, 1988
YNA281M	Daimler Fleetline CRG6LXB	Northern Counties	H43/32F	1973	Ex GM Buses, 1988
YNA284Mw	Daimler Fleetline CRG6LXB	Northern Counties	H43/32F	1973	Ex GM Buses, 1988
YNA287M	Daimler Fleetline CRG6LXB	Northern Counties	H43/32F	1973	Ex GM Buses, 1988
YNA300M	Daimler Fleetline CRG6LXB	Northern Counties	H43/32F	1973	Ex GM Buses, 1988
YNA303M	Daimler Fleetline CRG6LXB	Northern Counties	H43/32F	1974	Ex GM Buses, 1987
YNA345Mw	Daimler Fleetline CRG6LXB	Northern Counties	H43/32F	1974	Ex R & R, Luton, 1990
BNE741N	Daimler Fleetline CRG6LXB	Northern Counties	H43/32F	1974	Ex GM Buses, 1988
RWU52R	Leyland Fleetline FE30AGR	Roe	H43/33F	1976	Ex Yorkshire Rider, 1990
NOC603R	Leyland Fleetline FE30AGR	Park Royal	H43/33F	1976	Ex West Midlands Travel, 1989
TET747S	Leyland Fleetline FE30AGR	Roe	H43/33F	1977	Ex South Yorkshire's Transport, 1987
TET746S	Leyland Fleetline FE30AGR	Roe	H43/33F	1977	Ex South Yorkshire's Transport, 1987
SDA512S	Leyland Fleetline FE30AGR	MCW	H43/33F	1977	Ex West Midlands Travel, 1989
WDA975T	Leyland Fleetline FE30AGR	MCW	H43/33F	1978	Ex West Midlands Travel, 1989
XSJ652T	Leyland Fleetline FE30AGR	Northern Counties	H43/32F	1979	Ex Western Scottish, 1992
ANA47T	Leyland Fleetline FE30AGR	Northern Counties	H43/32F	1979	Ex Topp-Line, Wavertree, 1995
ANC932T	Leyland Atlantean AN68A/1R	Park Royal	H44/31F	1979	Ex A1 Service, (Brown), 1995
CWG766V	Leyland Atlantean AN68A/1R	Roe	H45/29D	1979	Ex Mainline, 1994
CWG705V	Leyland Atlantean AN68A/1R	Alexander AL	H45/33F	1979	Ex South Yorkshire's Transport, 1991
CWG726V	Leyland Atlantean AN68A/1R	Alexander AL	H45/33F	1980	Ex South Yorkshire's Transport, 1991
CWG727V	Leyland Atlantean AN68A/1R	Alexander AL	H45/33F	1980	Ex South Yorkshire's Transport, 1991
ECS875V	Leyland Fleetline FE30AGR	Northern Counties	H44/31F	1979	Ex Clydeside 2000, 1993
JKW281W	Leyland Atlantean AN68B/1R	Alexander AL	H45/33F	1981	Ex Mainline, 1994
JKW292W	Leyland Atlantean AN68B/1R	Alexander AL	H45/33F	1981	Ex South Yorkshire's Transport, 1991
JKW298W	Leyland Atlantean AN68B/1R	Alexander AL	H45/33F	1981	Ex South Yorkshire's Transport, 1991
JKW304W	Leyland Atlantean AN68B/1R	Alexander AL	H45/33F	1981	Ex South Yorkshire's Transport, 1991
JKW315W	Leyland Atlantean AN68B/1R	Marshall	H45/29D	1981	Ex Mainline, 1995
JKW321W	Leyland Atlantean AN68B/1R	Marshall	H45/29D	1981	Ex Mainline, 1995
JKW332W	Leyland Atlantean AN68B/1R	Marshall	H45/29D	1981	Ex Mainline, 1995
DWH700W	Leyland Fleetline FE30AGR	Northern Counties	H43/32F	1979	Ex Village, Garston, 1995
TYS256W	Dennis Dominator DD135B	Alexander RL	H45/34F	1981	Ex Clydeside 2000, 1993
TYS257W	Dennis Dominator DD135B	Alexander RL	H45/34F	1981	Ex Clydeside 2000, 1993
TYS258W	Dennis Dominator DD135B	Alexander RL	H45/34F	1981	Ex Clydeside 2000, 1993
TYS259W	Dennis Dominator DD135B	Alexander RL	H45/34F	1981	Ex Clydeside 2000, 1993
AFY182X	Leyland Atlantean AN68B/1R	Willowbrook	H45/34F	1981	Ex Somerbus, Paulton, 1994
AFY183X	Leyland Atlantean AN68B/1R	Willowbrook	H45/33F	1981	Ex Merseybus, 1994
AFY184X	Leyland Atlantean AN68B/1R	Willowbrook	H45/33F	1981	Ex Merseybus, 1994
AFY189X	Leyland Atlantean AN68B/1R	Willowbrook	H45/33F	1982	Ex Somerbus, Paulton, 1994
AFY190X	Leyland Atlantean AN68B/1R	Willowbrook	H45/33F	1982	Ex Merseybus, 1994
GSB146Y	Dennis Dominator DD163	Alexander RL	H45/34F	1983	Ex Clydeside 2000, 1993
GSB147Y	Dennis Dominator DD163	Alexander RL	H45/34F	1983	Ex Clydeside 2000, 1993
GIB1437	Leyland Tiger TRCTL11/3RZ	Plaxton Paramount 3200 II	C53F	1985	Ex Hill's, Tredegar, 1991
D143RAK	Renault-Dodge S56	Reeve Burgess	B25F	1987	Ex Mainline, 1994
D144RAK	Renault-Dodge S56	Reeve Burgess	B25F	1987	Ex Mainline, 1994
D160RAK	Renault-Dodge S56	Reeve Burgess	B25F	1987	Ex Mainline, 1994
D171PYB	Leyland Tiger TRCTL11/3RZ	Plaxton Paramount 3200 II	C53F	1987	Ex Denslow, Chard, 1990
E172UWF	Renault-Dodge S56	Reeve Burgess	B25F	1987	Ex Mainline, 1994
E175UWF	Renault-Dodge S56	Reeve Burgess	B25F	1987	Ex Mainline, 1995
E189UWF	Renault-Dodge S56	Reeve Burgess	B25F	1987	Ex Mainline, 1995
F995HGE	Volvo B10M-60	Plaxton Paramount 3500 III	C53F	1985	Ex Park's, Hamilton, 1990

Previous Registration: GIB1437   B614CKG

Livery: Cream, red and black

Still resplendent as shown in this photograph with full autumn glow is Stotts oldest vehicle, Daimler Fleetline XJA549L. New to Selnec South it carries a Park Royal body and is heading out of Oldham for Grotton. *Richard Godfrey*

In contrast to the Daimler is Leyland Atlantean AFY182X also seen on Lord Street, Oldham. This vehicle carries a Willowbrook body from a batch new to Merseyside PTE. Examples of the type are now with other operators in the area covered by this book, including Hyndburn and South Manchester. *Richard Godfrey*

STUARTS

Stuarts Bus & Coach Co Ltd, Rothsesey Garage, Broadway,
Dukinfield, Tameside, SK16 4UU

33	SXI9033	Leyland Tiger TRCTL11/3R	Duple Dominant IV	C48FT	1982	Ex Gath, Dewsbury, 1989
34	SXI9034	Leyland Leopard PSU5D/4R	Plaxton Supreme V	C48FT	1982	Ex Midland Red North, 1989
35	YEL95Y	Leyland Leopard PSU5E/4R	Eastern Coach Works B51	DP57F	1982	Ex Midland Red North, 1989
36	SXI3627	DAF MB200DKFL600	Caetano Algarve	C48FT	1984	Ex Brewers, 1991
37	SXI9037	Leyland Leopard PSU3E/4R	Duple Dominant II	C53F	1979	Ex Reliance, Gt Gonerby, 1990
39	SXI9039	DAF MB200DKFL600	LAG Galaxy	C49FT	1984	Ex Elsey, Gosberton, 1991
40	MIW4840	DAF MB200DKFL600	LAG Galaxy	C49FT	1986	Ex Brewers, 1990
41	MIW4841	Bova EL26-581	Bova Europa	C53F	1981	Ex Enterprise, Darlington, 1991
42	628ELX	Leyland Tiger TRCTL11/3R	Duple Dominant IV	C46F	1983	Ex Walls, Wigan, 1993
103	ABM801A	Leyland Atlantean AN68/1R	Alexander AL	H45/29D	1974	Ex Grampian, 1987
106	SGA710N	Leyland Atlantean AN68/1R	Alexander AL	H45/31F	1974	Ex London Country NE, 1988
116	WDA680T	Leyland Fleetline FE30AGR	Park Royal	H43/33F	1979	Ex West Midlands Travel, 1990
117	WDA980T	Leyland Fleetline FE30AGR	MCW	H43/33F	1979	Ex West Midlands Travel, 1990
118	WDA981T	Leyland Fleetline FE30AGR	MCW	H43/33F	1979	Ex West Midlands Travel, 1991
119	SDA613S	Leyland Fleetline FE30AGR	Park Royal	H43/33F	1977	Ex West Midlands Travel, 1990
120	D109OWG	Renault-Dodge S56	Reeve Burgess Beaver	B25F	1987	Ex South Yorkshire's Transport, 1991
123	K123TCP	DAF SB220LC550	Ikarus Citi Bus	B48F	1992	
124	K124TCP	DAF SB220LC550	Ikarus Citi Bus	B48F	1992	
125	EWF469V	MCW Metrobus DR102/13	MCW	H46/27D	1980	Ex Stevensons, 1993
126	JKW310W	Leyland Atlantean AN68B/1R	Marshall	H45/29D	1981	Ex A1 Service, (Steele), 1994
127	JKW322W	Leyland Atlantean AN68B/1R	Marshall	H45/29D	1981	Ex A1 Service, (Steele), 1994
128	JKW335W	Leyland Atlantean AN68B/1R	Marshall	H45/29D	1981	Ex A1 Service, (Steele), 1994
129	ULS614X	MCW Metrobus DR102/28	MCW	H45/33F	1982	Ex Bullock, Cheadle, 1994
130	D912VCN	Freight Rover Sherpa	Dormobile	B18F	1987	Ex Northumbria, 1994
131	JKW316W	Leyland Atlantean AN68B/1R	Marshall	H45/29D	1981	Ex A1 Service, (Steele), 1994
132	N132XND	Dennis Dart 9.8SDL3054	Plaxton Pointer	B40F	1995	
133	N133XND	Dennis Dart 9.8SDL3054	Plaxton Pointer	B40F	1995	
134	N134XND	Dennis Dart 9.8SDL3054	Plaxton Pointer	B40F	1995	

Previous Registrations:

628ELX	FWH22Y	SXI3627	A504WTH, 948RJO, A659XWN		
ABM801A	NRG173M	SXI9033	NVH961X	SXI9037	CTM408T
MIW4840	C950GTH	SXI9034	SND298X	SXI9039	B596LJU
MIW4841	RSF10Y				

Livery: White, green, red and yellow.

LAG Galaxy is the body type seen on Stuarts DAF MB200 pictured here at Liverpool operating with a Merseyrail rail replacement service board The Galaxy was replaced by the Panoramic integral coach in 1987 having appeared on Leyland Tiger, Volvo B10M and DAF chassis in the UK.
Ralph Stevens

The main bus services operated by Stuarts serve Tameside and in particular the Hyde area on routes once provided by the PTE's Tameside depot. On the 208 from Manchester to Newton we see 124, K124TCP, a DAF SB220 with Ikarus CitiBus bodywork.

TAYLORS COACHES

Taymor Contracts Ltd, Yew Tree Garage, Great Strickland,
Penrith, Cumbria, CA10 3DF

CEC14W	Volvo B58-56	Duple Dominant III	C53F	1981	
PHH24W	Bedford YMQ	Plaxton Supreme IV	C45F	1981	Ex Borderbus, Carlisle, 1993
A196MNE	Volvo B10M-61	Van Hool Alizée	C49F	1984	Ex Shearings, 1989
B358UCW	Volvo B10M-61	Duple Caribbean	C49F	1984	Ex Hestair Duple, 1984
F899SMU	Mercedes-Benz 811D	Reeve Burgess Beaver	C33F	1989	Ex G P Travel, London, 1991
G337PAO	Hestair Duple 425	Duple 425	C53F	1990	

Livery: Yellow, gold and brown.

Previous Registrations:
PHH24W   SUM131W, USU642

Taylors Coaches operate a small coach fleet based in the market town of Penrith. Seen here is
CEC14W, a Volvo B58 with Duple Dominant III bodywork, a design which copied the American
Greyhound style though not very popular in this country. *John Curwen*

The Lancashire, Cumbria & Manchester Bus Handbook

TOWN BUS

C D Mather, Wyre Bank Garage, Cocker Avenue,
Poulton-le-Fylde, FY6 8JU

JWU248N	Leyland Leopard PSU4C/4R	Plaxton Derwent	DP43F	1975	Ex Henshall, Ashton, 1994
KON336P	Leyland Fleetline FE30ALR	MCW	H43/33F	1976	Ex Western Scottish, 1995
NOC450R	Leyland Fleetline FE30AGR	MCW	H43/33F	1977	Ex Western Scottish, 1995
OCS114R	Daimler Fleetline CRG6LXB	Alexander AD	H44/31F	1976	Ex Western Scottish, 1995
THX566S	Leyland Fleetline FE30ALR	Park Royal	H44/27D	1978	Ex Midland Fox, 1995
THX569S	Leyland Fleetline FE30ALR	Park Royal	H44/27D	1978	Ex Midland Fox, 1994
VKW999S	Bedford YLQ	Duple Dominant II	C45F	1978	Ex OR Jones, Llanfaethlu, 1994
C829CBU	Renault-Dodge S56	Northern Counties	B20F	1986	Ex Scott, Stanley, 1993
D122NON	Freight Rover Sherpa	Carlyle	B20F	1987	Ex Midland Fox, 1995

Livery: White and maroon

Town Bus operates tendered services and school contracts from the Fylde market town of Poulton-le-Fylde using a mixture of double-deck buses, saloons and minibuses. Seen heading for Staining is OCS114R, an Alexander-bodied Fleetline and one recently acquired from Western Scottish along with two others which had been taken into that fleet with the acquisition of A1 Services by Stagecoach in January 1995. *Paul Wigan*

TIMELINE

Timeline Travel Ltd, 12 Bold Street, Leigh, WN7 1AL

Depots Gas Street, Bolton; Moss Ind Est Lowton, Leigh; Railway Yard, Shifnal and GEC Complex, Trafford Park, Manchester.

1	TNA161J	Leyland Leopard PSU3/3R	Alexander AYS	B53F	1971	Ex Shearings, 1992	
3	PFS561M	Leyland Leopard PSU3/3R	Alexander AYS	B53F	1974	Ex Progress, Chorley, 1992	
6	DRJ897L	Leyland Leopard PSU3/3R	Alexander AYS	B53F	1973	Ex Shearings, 1992	
16w	JND256V	Leyland Leopard PSU5C/4R	Duple Dominant II	C53F	1980	Ex Ribble, 1992	
20w	NNH187Y	Leyland Leopard PSU5C/4R	Duple Dominant IV	C57F	1983	Ex United Counties, 1993	
24	OIB8606	Leyland Tiger TRCTL11/3R	Duple Dominant IV	C57F	1981	Ex Rossendale, 1994	
37	F37FNF	Leyland Tiger TRBL10/3ARZA	Alexander N	B55F	1988	Ex Shearings, 1992	
38	F38FNF	Leyland Tiger TRBL10/3ARZA	Alexander N	B55F	1988	Ex Shearings, 1992	

49-72

Leyland Tiger TRBL10/3ARZA Alexander N B55F 1989 Ex Shearings, 1992

49w	F49FNF	56	G56RND	61	G61RND	65	G65RND	69	G69RND
50	F50FNF	57	G57RND	62	G62RND	66	G66RND	70	G70RND
53	G53RND	58	G58RND	63	G63RND	67	G67RND	71	G71RND
54	G54RND	59	G59RND	64	G64RND	68	G68RND	72	G72RND
55	G55RND	60	G60RND					

73-88

Volvo Citybus B10M-50 Alexander Q B55F 1990 Ex Shearings, 1992

73	H73DVM	77	H577DVM	80	H580DVM	83	H83DVM	86	H86DVM
74	H74DVM	78	H78DVM	81	H81DVM	84	H84DVM	87	H87DVM
75	H575DVM	79	H79DVM	82	H82DVM	85	H85DVM	88	H588DVM
76	H76DVM							

92	H522FSB	Mercedes-Benz 709D	Reeve Burgess Beaver	B25F	1990	Ex West Coast, Campbeltown, 1994
94	H564OOK	Mercedes-Benz 709D	Carlyle	B27F	1991	Ex The Wright Company, Wrexham, 1993
95	H415BVR	Mercedes-Benz 709D	Carlyle	B27F	1991	Ex Davidson, Whitburn, 1995
104	F135KAO	Mercedes-Benz 609D	Reeve Burgess Beaver	B19F	1989	Ex North Western, 1994
105	F545EJA	Mercedes-Benz 709D	PMT	DP23F	1988	Ex Wall, Sharston, 1993
106	H406BVR	Mercedes-Benz 709D	Carlyle	B27F	1990	Ex Starline, Knutsford, 1992

107-112

Mercedes-Benz 609D Reeve Burgess B19F 1989-90 Ex Shearings, 1992

107	G107RND	108	G108RND	109	H109DVM	110	H110DVM	112	H112DVM

140	F394DOA	Peugeot-Talbot Pullman	Talbot	B18F	1989	Ex Pathfinder, Newark, 1993
141	L141JVR	Peugeot-Talbot Pullman	TBP	B18F	1994	
142	L142JVR	Peugeot-Talbot Pullman	TBP	B18F	1994	
151	L151DRJ	Mercedes-Benz 709D	Alexander Sprint	B23F	1993	
152	L152DRJ	Mercedes-Benz 709D	Alexander Sprint	B23F	1993	
153	L153DRJ	Mercedes-Benz 709D	Alexander Sprint	B23F	1993	
154	L154DRJ	Mercedes-Benz 709D	Alexander Sprint	B23F	1993	

156-161

Mercedes-Benz 811D Alexander Sprint B33F 1994

156	M156LNC	158	M158LNC	159	M159LNC	160	M160LNC	161	M161LNC
157	M157LNC							

162-177

Mercedes-Benz 709D Alexander Sprint B23F 1994-95

162	M162LNC	166	M166LNC	169	N169WNF	172	N172WNF	175	N175WNF
163	M163LNC	167	M167LNC	170	N170WNF	173	N173WNF	176	N176WNF
164	M164LNC	168	N168WNF	171	N171WNF	174	N174WNF	177	N177WNF
165	M165LNC							

Opposite: **Timeline have taken many new buses into the fleet since the last edition including 210, N210WBA, a Volvo B6 with Alexander Dash bodywork. Also working service 137 to Bury, this time at the Bury end of the service, is 70, G70RND. This Leyland Tiger has Alexander N-type bodywork which was produced at the Belfast plant of the company.** *Paul Wigan/Richard Godfrey*

The latest arrivals with Timeline are six Volvo B10Ls with Alexander Ultra bodywork. This low floor model uses the Säffle designed body, Säffle being a bodybuilder in Sweden that is a subsidiary of Volvo. The six vehicles are to be used on the Bolton - Harwood - Bury services 508 and 565.

201-212

Volvo B6.9M   Alexander Dash   B38F   1994-95

201	M201LNC	204	M204LNC	207	N207WBA	209	N209WBA	211	N211WBA
202	M202LNC	205	M205LNC	208	N208WBA	210	N210WBA	212	N212WBA
203	M203LNC	206	M206LNC						

301-306

Volvo B10L   Alexander Ultra   B43F   1995-96

| 301 | N301WNF | 303 | N303WNF | 304 | N304WNF | 305 | N305WNF | 306 | N306WNF |
| 302 | N302WNF | | | | | | | | |

901-917

Dennis Javelin 12SDA2158   Aüwaerter Transliner   C53F   1995

901	M901OVR	905	M905OVR	909	M909OVR	912	M912OVR	915	M915OVR
902	M902OVR	906	M906OVR	910	M910OVR	913	M913OVR	916	M916OVR
903	M903OVR	907	M907OVR	911	M911OVR	914	M914OVR	917	M917OVR
904	M904OVR	908	M908OVR						

Previous Registrations:

| DRJ897L | BSG526L, 205CCH, DRJ851L, 5140RU | OIB8606 | FTD758W |
| TNA161J | RSD732J, SPR35 | | |

Livery: Yellow, cream and white; cream, yellow and red 901-17

TITTERINGTONS

G, S, I, P & C Titterington, The Garage, Blencow, Penrith, Cumbria, CA11 0DG

XAP956	Leyland Leopard PSU3C/4R	Plaxton Supreme III	C53F	1976	Ex Holmeswoord, Rufford, 1987
AXI8323	Leyland Leopard PSU3F/5R	Duple Dominant II	C53F	1981	Ex Holmeswood, Rufford, 1993
890TTE	Leyland Leopard PSU3F/4R	Plaxton Supreme IV	C53F	1981	Ex Johnson, Hodthorpe, 1987
212VPF	Leyland Tiger TRCTL11/3R	Duple	C51F	1984	
C196OHH	Volkswagen Caravelle	Volkswagen	M8	1986	
OZ4688	Volvo B10M-61	Plaxton Paramount 3500 III	C53F	1986	Ex Clarkes of London, 1992
CUI925	Volvo B10M-61	Plaxton Paramount 3500 III	C49FT	1986	Ex National Travel East, 1987
XOU692	LAG G355Z	LAG Panoramic	C49FT	1988	
368SHX	Dennis Javelin 12SDA1907	Duple 320	C57F	1988	
TYT653	LAG G355Z	LAG Panoramic	C49FT	1989	
G39ORM	LAG G355Z	LAG Panoramic	C49FT	1990	
G57OHH	LAG G355Z	LAG Panoramic	C49FT	1990	
G647ONH	Volvo B10M-60	Jonckheere Deauville P599	C51FT	1990	Ex Tellings-Golden Miller, 1993
M949RHH	Volvo B10M-62	Van Hool Alizée	C49FT	1995	
M950RHH	Volvo B10M-62	Van Hool Alizée	C49FT	1994	

Previous Registrations:

212VPF	B342GRM	AXI8323	PWK8W	TYT653	F432GHH
368SHX	E592CAO	CUI925	C450CWR	XAP956	LOT779R
890TTE	PNW342W	OZ4688	C178LWB	XOU692	E804ARM

Titteringtons have built up a coach fleet with many vehicles being supplied new. Of the older coaches, two Plaxton Supreme-bodied Leyland Leopards are kept. Shown in its home town of Penrith XAP956 is displaying the Supreme III version of this Plaxton style. *John Curwen*

VALE OF MANCHESTER

Vales Coaches (Manchester) Ltd, 49 Broughton Street, Manchester, M8 8AN

BAZ7284	Leyland Leopard PSU3B/4R	Plaxton Elite III Express	C53F	1974	Ex Yorkshire Rider, 1994
URN12V	Leyland Leopard PSU3E/4R	Duple Dominant II Express	C53F	1979	Ex Lancaster, 1991
SSX599V	Seddon Pennine 7	Alexander AYS	B53F	1980	Ex Stevensons, 1992
YSG651W	Seddon Pennine 7	Alexander AYS	B53F	1982	Ex Stevensons, 1992
JFS978X	Seddon Pennine 7	Alexander AYS	B53F	1982	Ex Stonier, Turnstall, 1992
TPL762X	Leyland Tiger TRCTL11/2R	Plaxton Supreme V Express	C53F	1982	Ex Yorkshire Rider, 1994
CAH880Y	Leyland Leopard PSU3G/4R	Eastern Coach Works B51	DP51F	1982	Ex Yorkshire Rider, 1994
NNH191Y	Leyland Leopard PSU5C/4R	Duple Dominant IV	C57F	1983	Ex Timeline, 1995
B739YUD	Ford Transit 190	Carlyle	B20F	1985	Ex Yorkshire Rider, 1994
D142NUS	Mercedes-Benz L608D	Alexander AM	B21F	1986	Ex Timeline, 1995
D143NUS	Mercedes-Benz L608D	Alexander AM	B21F	1986	Ex Timeline, 1994
E183CNE	Iveco Daily 49.10	Northern Counties	B22F	1988	Ex GM Buses, 1989
E185CNE	Iveco Daily 49.10	Northern Counties	B22F	1988	Ex GM Buses, 1989
E878LHV	Iveco Daily 49.10	Robin Hood City Nippy	B21F	1987	Ex Nat-West Bank, 1990
E458TYG	Iveco Daily 49.10	Robin Hood City Nippy	B19F	1988	Ex Yorkshire Rider, 1994
F358FNB	Iveco Daily 49.10	Northern Counties	B22F	1988	
F359FNB	Iveco Daily 49.10	Northern Counties	B22F	1988	
F360FNB	Iveco Daily 49.10	Northern Counties	B22F	1988	
F623YCW	Iveco Daily 49.10	Northern Counties	DP22F	1989	
F624YCW	Iveco Daily 49.10	Northern Counties	B22F	1989	
G874DSC	Mercedes-Benz 609D	Alexander AM	DP25F	1989	Ex Transfleet Services, Coventry, 1993
G150MMA	Iveco Daily 49.10	Robin Hood City Nippy	B21F	1989	Ex Iveco-Ford demonstrator, 1991

Previous Registrations:
BAZ7284   VLB662M, 26BMR, ANW266M

Livery: Blue and cream

Another operator to ply Wilmslow Road is Vale of Manchester. Previously with Yorkshire Rider was CAH880Y, seen turning out of Oldham Street into Piccadilly, Manchester. This vehicle carries the B51 design of Eastern Coach Works body, one showing much influence from National Bus, the dominant operator of the time. *Richard Godfrey*

WALL'S BUSES

M J Wall, Paston Road, Sharston Ind Est, Northenden, Manchester, M22 4TF

	LNA367	Bedford OB	Duple Vista	C29F	1950	Ex Maypole, Lathom, 1991
w	YSV205	Daimler Fleetline CRG6LXB	Northern Counties	H43/32F	1973	Ex Greater Manchester, 1986
	BNE740N	Daimler Fleetline CRG6LXB	Northern Counties	H43/32F	1975	Ex Mayne, Manchester, 1992
	JBN540N	Daimler Fleetline CRG6LXB	Northern Counties	H43/32F	1974	Ex Hulme Hall, Cheadle Hulme, 1993
	YNA307M	Daimler Fleetline CRG6LXB	Northern Counties	H43/32F	1974	Ex Warrington, 1994
w	GNC294N	Daimler Fleetline CRG6LXB	Northern Counties	H43/32F	1975	Ex Mayne, Manchester, 1992
w	YSV605	Daimler Fleetline CRG6LXB	Northern Counties	H43/32F	1975	Ex Greater Manchester, 1986
	YSV589	Daimler Fleetline CRG6LXB	Northern Counties	H43/32F	1975	Ex Greater Manchester, 1986
	YSV426	Daimler Fleetline CRG6LXB	Northern Counties	H43/32F	1975	Ex Greater Manchester, 1986
	955WAL	Daimler Fleetline CRG6LXB	Northern Counties	H43/32F	1975	Ex Greater Manchester, 1986
	168WAL	Daimler Fleetline CRG6LXB	Northern Counties	H43/32F	1975	Ex Greater Manchester, 1986
	452WAL	Daimler Fleetline CRG6LXB	Northern Counties	H43/32F	1975	Ex Greater Manchester, 1986
	LJA473P	Daimler Fleetline CRG6LXB	Northern Counties	H43/32F	1975	Ex Warrington, 1994
	LJA480P	Daimler Fleetline CRG6LXB	Northern Counties	H43/32F	1976	Ex Warrington, 1994
	LJA484P	Daimler Fleetline CRG6LXB	Northern Counties	H43/32F	1976	Ex Warrington, 1994
	YSV662	Leyland Fleetline FE30AGR	MCW	H43/33F	1975	Ex West Midlands Travel, 1990
w	KON332P	Leyland Fleetline FE30AGR	MCW	H43/33F	1975	Ex West Midlands Travel, 1990
	RVB977S	Bristol VRT/SL3/6LXB	Willowbrook	O43/31F	1978	Ex East Kent, 1992
	GGM76W	Bristol VRT/SL3/6LXB	Eastern Coach Works	H43/31F	1981	Ex Partridge, Hadleigh, 1992
	GGM109W	Bristol VRT/SL3/6LXB	Eastern Coach Works	H43/31F	1981	Ex Partridge, Hadleigh, 1992
	F823KRJ	Mercedes-Benz 811D	Robin Hood	DP29F	1989	
	G251EHD	DAF SB220LC550	Optare Delta	B49F	1989	
	G252EHD	DAF SB220LC550	Optare Delta	B49F	1989	
	G253EHD	DAF SB220LC550	Optare Delta	B49F	1989	
	G315YHJ	DAF SB220LC550	Optare Delta	B47F	1989	Ex Harris Bus, West Thurrock, 1990
	G316YHJ	DAF SB220LC550	Optare Delta	B47F	1989	Ex Harris Bus, West Thurrock, 1990
	H534YCX	DAF SB220LC550	Optare Delta	B49F	1990	Ex OK, Bishop Auckland, 1992
	H536YCX	DAF SB220LC550	Optare Delta	B49F	1990	Ex OK, Bishop Auckland, 1992
	H537YCX	DAF SB220LC550	Optare Delta	B49F	1990	Ex OK, Bishop Auckland, 1992
	H538YCX	DAF SB220LC550	Optare Delta	B49F	1990	Ex OK, Bishop Auckland, 1992
	H611CVM	Ford Transit VE6	Asquith	M12	1991	
	H220TCP	DAF SB220LC550	Ikarus CitiBus	B50F	1991	Ex Pride of the Road, 1992
	M15WAL	DAF SB220LC550	Ikarus CitiBus	B48F	1994	
	M16WAL	DAF SB220LC550	Ikarus CitiBus	B48F	1994	
	M17WAL	DAF DB250RS505	Northern Counties Palatine	H47/30F	1995	
	M18WAL	DAF DB250RS505	Northern Counties Palatine	H47/30F	1995	
	M19WAL	DAF DB250RS505	Northern Counties Palatine	H47/30F	1995	
	M20WAL	DAF DB250RS505	Northern Counties Palatine	H47/30F	1995	
	N10WAL	DAF DE02LTSB220	Ikarus CitiBus	B49F	1995	
	N12WAL	DAF DE02LTSB220	Ikarus CitiBus	B49F	1995	
	N13WAL	DAF DB250RS505	Northern Counties Palatine	H47/30F	1995	
	N14WAL	DAF DB250RS505	Northern Counties Palatine	H47/30F	1995	
	N15WAL	DAF DE02LTSB220	Ikarus CitiBus	B49F	1995	
	N16WAL	DAF DE02LTSB220	Ikarus CitiBus	B49F	1995	

Previous Registrations:

168WAL	KBU907P	LNA367	From new	YSV589	LJA471P
452WAL	KBU910P	YSV205	KBU909P	YSV605	YNA357M
955WAL	KBU906P	YSV426	KBU908P	YSV662	KON363P
JBN540N	GDB165N, CSU917				

Livery: Green and white.

Wall's Buses have received many DAF buses, both single-and double-decks. Representing the additions are, above, M15WAL, a DAF SB220 with Ikarus CitiBus bodywork while below is M18WAL, a DB250 with a Northern Counties Palatine II body. Both vehicles are seen on the Wilmslow Road service W2. *Paul Wigan/Tony Wilson*

WRIGHT BROS

Wright Brothers (Coaches) Ltd, Central Garage, Nenthead,
Alston, Cumbria, CA9 3NP

Depots: Central Garage, Nenthead and West Road, Blucher, Tyne & Wear

FUN319	Crossley SD42/7	Burlingham	C33F	1949	Ex Patterson, Beadnell, 1959
RRM915M	Bedford YRQ	Plaxton Elite III Express	C45F	1974	
VRM73S	Bedford YLQ	Plaxton Supreme III Express	C45F	1978	
JAO400V	Bedford YMT	Plaxton Supreme IV Express	C53F	1980	
OEH930W	Leyland Leopard PSU5C/4R	Duple Dominant IV	C57F	1980	Ex Proctor, Fenton, 1992
UGE807W	Volvo B10M-61	Plaxton Supreme IV	C57F	1981	Ex McPhail, Newart Hill, 1992
LTG271X	Volvo B58-56	Plaxton Supreme IV	C53F	1981	Ex Capitol, Cwmbran, 1994
SAO466X	Bedford YNT	Plaxton Supreme V Express	C53F	1982	
SAO467X	Bedford YMP	Plaxton Supreme V Express	C45F	1982	
CIW290	Volvo B10M-56	Van Hool Alizée	C49DT	1984	Ex Park's, 1988
TSV807	Volvo B10M-61	Plaxton Paramount 3500	C14FT	1983	Ex Cantabrica, Watford, 1990
C166VRE	Ford Transit 190	PMT	B16F	1986	Ex Scandle, Prudhoe, 1991
C61WBF	Ford Transit 190	Dormobile	B16F	1986	Ex Midland Red North, 1991
UDX921	Volvo B10M-53	Jonckheere Jubilee P95	CH52/6FT	1986	Ex Team Travel, Horseforth, 1992
G852NUP	Scania K113TRB	Van Hool Astrabel	CH53/14CT	1990	Ex Busways, 1994
H917PTG	Volvo B10M-50	Ikarus Blue Danube	C49FT	1991	Ex Thames Transit, 1995

Livery: Cream, gold and black

Previous Registrations:

CIW290	A604UGD	TSV807	BJU857Y
G852NUP	G31WTY, 813VPU	UDX921	C363SVV

Representing the Wright Bros. fleet is EHH915V, a recently withdrawn Bedford with Plaxton Supreme bodywork. *Brian Pritchard*

Vehicle Index

Reg	Operator	Reg	Operator	Reg	Operator	Reg	Operator
5AAX	Holmeswood	A44YWJ	Mayne	A676HNB	G M N	A742NNA	G M N
10RU	Finglands	A45YWJ	Mayne	A677HNB	G M N	A743NNA	GMS Buses
109DRM	Cumberland	A46YWJ	Mayne	A678HNB	GMS Buses	A744NNA	GMS Buses
168WAL	Wall's	A47YWJ	Mayne	A679HNB	GMS Buses	A745DRM	Robinson's
170BHR	Rossendale	A48YWJ	Mayne	A680HNB	GMS Buses	A745NNA	GMS Buses
201SC	Holmeswood	A50LHG	Hyndburn	A681HNB	G M N	A746NNA	G M N
212VPF	Titteringtons	A72VTX	Blue Bus	A682HNB	G M N	A747NNA	GMS Buses
219DLV	Sim	A73VTX	Blue Bus	A683HNB	GMS Buses	A748NNA	GMS Buses
289BUA	Mayne	A101DPB	Mayne	A684HNB	GMS Buses	A749NNA	GMS Buses
289CLT	Pioneer	A102DAO	Cumberland	A685HNB	G M N	A750NNA	GMS Buses
318EVO	Brownrigg's	A138MRN	Ribble	A686HNB	G M N	A751NNA	GMS Buses
357CLT	Blackpool	A142MRN	Ribble	A687HNB	GMS Buses	A752NNA	GMS Buses
368SHX	Titteringtons	A143MRN	Ribble	A688HNB	GMS Buses	A753NNA	G M N
403BGO	Mayne	A145MRN	Ribble	A689HNB	G M N	A754NNA	GMS Buses
452WAL	Wall's	A156OFR	Ribble	A690HNB	GMS Buses	A755NNA	G M N
466YMG	Holmeswood	A157OFR	Ribble	A691HNB	G M N	A756NNA	G M N
476CEL	GMS Buses	A158OFR	Ribble	A692HNB	G M N	A757NNA	GMS Buses
509EBL	Shaw Hadwin	A159OFR	Ribble	A693HNB	GMS Buses	A758NNA	G M N
513ERH	Borderbus	A196MNE	Taylors Cs	A694HNB	GMS Buses	A759NNA	GMS Buses
515VTB	GMS Buses	A196WGE	Rossendale	A695HNB	GMS Buses	A760NNA	G M N
525XPD	Shaw Hadwin	A214MCK	Ribble	A696HNB	GMS Buses	A761NNA	GMS Buses
563UM	Brownrigg's	A301JFA	R Bullock	A697HNB	G M N	A762NNA	GMS Buses
583CLT	Blackpool	A303JFA	R Bullock	A698HNB	GMS Buses	A763NNA	G M N
583TD	GMS Buses	A355HHG	Blackpool	A699HNB	GMS Buses	A764NNA	GMS Buses
614BWU	Mayne	A356HHG	Blackpool	A700HNB	GMS Buses	A765NNA	G M N
627DYE	Blackpool	A357HHG	Blackpool	A701LNC	G M N	A777RBV	Abbott's
628ELX	Stuart's	A358HHG	Blackpool	A702LNC	GMS Buses	A914RRN	Holmeswood
640DYE	Blackpool	A359HHG	Blackpool	A703LNC	G M N	A975OST	Ribble
647JOE	Finglands	A360HHG	Blackpool	A704LNC	GMS Buses	A977OST	Ribble
650DYE	Blackpool	A361HHG	Blackpool	A705LNC	GMS Buses	A978OST	Ribble
735DYE	Blackpool	A362HHG	Blackpool	A706LNC	GMS Buses	A979OST	Ribble
824HAO	Shaw Hadwin	A383HFK	Shaw Hadwin	A707LNC	G M N	AAL468A	Rossendale
890TTE	Titteringtons	A462LFV	Fishwick	A708LNC	GMS Buses	AAX300A	Holmeswood
899CAN	Shaw Hadwin	A471HNC	GMS Buses	A709LNC	G M N	ABA15T	GMS Buses
906GAU	Mayne	A472HNC	GMS Buses	A710LNC	GMS Buses	ABA17T	GMS Buses
927GTA	Ribble	A473HNC	GMS Buses	A711LNC	GMS Buses	ABA19T	GMS Buses
955WAL	Wall's	A547HBV	Abbott's	A712LNC	G M N	ABA22T	G M N
990ENR	Robinson's	A576HDB	G M N	A713LNC	G M N	ABA24T	GMS Buses
3179TR	Robinson's	A577HDB	G M N	A714LNC	GMS Buses	ABA26T	G M N
3927TR	Robinson's	A578HDB	G M N	A715LNC	GMS Buses	ABA27T	G M N
3937TR	Robinson's	A579HDB	G M N	A716LNC	G M N	ABA28T	G M N
4150RU	Shaw Hadwin	A580HDB	G M N	A717GJA	Springfield Cs	ABA30T	GMS Buses
4761TR	Robinson's	A581HDB	GMS Buses	A717LNC	G M N	ABM801A	Stuart's
5129UA	Shaw Hadwin	A582HDB	GMS Buses	A718LNC	G M N	ABN721V	Border
6137RU	Shaw Hadwin	A583HDB	GMS Buses	A719LNC	GMS Buses	ABN722V	Rossendale
6267UA	Shaw Hadwin	A584HDB	GMS Buses	A720LNC	G M N	ABN723V	Rossendale
6682WY	Shaw Hadwin	A585HDB	GMS Buses	A721LNC	G M N	ABV43B	Blackburn
9884TR	Robinson's	A656HNB	G M N	A722LNC	GMS Buses	ABV939Y	Fishwick
A4HWD	Holmeswood	A657HNB	GMS Buses	A723LNC	G M N	AFM1W	Hyndburn
A21HNC	GMS Buses	A658HNB	G M N	A724LNC	G M N	AFM5W	Blackburn
A22HNC	GMS Buses	A659HNB	G M N	A725LNC	GMS Buses	AFY180X	South Manchester
A23HNC	GMS Buses	A660HNB	GMS Buses	A726LNC	GMS Buses	AFY181X	Hyndburn
A23JBV	Blackburn	A661HNB	GMS Buses	A727LNC	G M N	AFY182X	Stotts
A24HNC	GMS Buses	A662HNB	G M N	A728LNC	G M N	AFY183X	Stotts
A25HNC	GMS Buses	A663HNB	G M N	A729LNC	G M N	AFY184X	Stotts
A26JBV	Blackburn	A664HNB	GMS Buses	A730LNC	GMS Buses	AFY189X	Stotts
A26ORJ	GMS Buses	A665HNB	GMS Buses	A731NNA	G M N	AFY190X	Stotts
A27ORJ	GMS Buses	A666HNB	G M N	A732NNA	G M N	AFY191X	Hyndburn
A28JBV	Blackburn	A667HNB	G M N	A733NNA	G M N	AHG331V	Blackpool
A28ORJ	GMS Buses	A668HNB	GMS Buses	A734NNA	GMS Buses	AHG332V	Blackpool
A29JBV	Blackburn	A669HNB	GMS Buses	A735NNA	GMS Buses	AHG333V	Blackpool
A29ORJ	GMS Buses	A670HNB	G M N	A736NNA	G M N	AHG334V	Blackpool
A30ORJ	GMS Buses	A671HNB	GMS Buses	A737NNA	G M N	AHG336V	Blackpool
A31ORJ	GMS Buses	A672HNB	G M N	A738NNA	G M N	AHG337V	Blackpool
A32ORJ	GMS Buses	A673HNB	G M N	A739NNA	G M N	AHG338V	Blackpool
A33MRN	Preston	A674HNB	GMS Buses	A740NNA	G M N	AHG339V	Blackpool
A33ORJ	GMS Buses	A675HNB	GMS Buses	A741NNA	GMS Buses	AHG340V	Blackpool

When index numbers reverted to the A-prefix the first of the main-block commenced with Hxx letters. Blackburn's first 'reversed' letters were on a batch of Leyland Atlanteans with East Lancashire bodywork. Photographed arriving in Accrington is 23, A23JBV. *Gerry Mead*

AHH206T	Ribble	ANA165Y	GMS Buses	ANA218T	GMS Buses	ANA544Y	GMS Buses
AHH209T	Ribble	ANA166Y	G M N	ANA220T	GMS Buses	ANA546Y	GMS Buses
AHN394T	Brownrigg's	ANA167Y	G M N	ANA221T	G M N	ANA547Y	G M N
AJF405A	Robinson's	ANA168Y	G M N	ANA222T	GMS Buses	ANA548Y	G M N
ALD966B	Blackpool	ANA169Y	G M N	ANA223T	G M N	ANA549Y	G M N
ALD989B	Blackpool	ANA170Y	GMS Buses	ANA224B	G M N	ANA550Y	GMS Buses
ALM71B	Blackpool	ANA171Y	G M N	ANA225T	GMS Buses	ANA551Y	G M N
ALM89B	Blackpool	ANA172Y	G M N	ANA226T	G M N	ANA552Y	GMS Buses
ANA1Y	GMS Buses	ANA173Y	GMS Buses	ANA227T	GMS Buses	ANA553Y	GMS Buses
ANA2Y	GMS Buses	ANA174Y	G M N	ANA228T	G M N	ANA554Y	G M N
ANA3Y	GMS Buses	ANA175Y	G M N	ANA229T	G M N	ANA555Y	G M N
ANA4Y	GMS Buses	ANA176Y	G M N	ANA230T	GMS Buses	ANA556Y	G M N
ANA5Y	GMS Buses	ANA177Y	G M N	ANA231T	GMS Buses	ANA557Y	G M N
ANA6Y	GMS Buses	ANA178Y	G M N	ANA232T	G M N	ANA558Y	G M N
ANA7Y	GMS Buses	ANA179Y	GMS Buses	ANA233T	G M N	ANA559Y	GMS Buses
ANA8Y	GMS Buses	ANA180Y	GMS Buses	ANA234T	GMS Buses	ANA560Y	G M N
ANA9Y	GMS Buses	ANA181Y	G M N	ANA235T	GMS Buses	ANA561Y	G M N
ANA10Y	GMS Buses	ANA182Y	G M N	ANA236T	GMS Buses	ANA562Y	G M N
ANA26T	G M N	ANA183Y	G M N	ANA237T	GMS Buses	ANA563Y	G M N
ANA39T	G M N	ANA184Y	G M N	ANA238T	G M N	ANA564Y	GMS Buses
ANA47T	Stotts	ANA185Y	G M N	ANA239T	G M N	ANA566Y	G M N
ANA50T	G M N	ANA186Y	G M N	ANA241T	GMS Buses	ANA567Y	G M N
ANA151Y	G M N	ANA187Y	G M N	ANA531Y	G M N	ANA568Y	GMS Buses
ANA152Y	G M N	ANA188Y	G M N	ANA532Y	G M N	ANA569Y	GMS Buses
ANA153Y	GMS Buses	ANA189Y	G M N	ANA533Y	GMS Buses	ANA570Y	G M N
ANA154Y	GMS Buses	ANA190Y	GMS Buses	ANA534Y	G M N	ANA571Y	G M N
ANA155Y	GMS Buses	ANA207T	G M N	ANA535Y	G M N	ANA572Y	GMS Buses
ANA156Y	G M N	ANA208T	G M N	ANA536Y	G M N	ANA573Y	G M N
ANA157Y	GMS Buses	ANA209T	G M N	ANA537Y	GMS Buses	ANA574Y	G M N
ANA158Y	GMS Buses	ANA210T	GMS Buses	ANA538Y	GMS Buses	ANA575Y	G M N
ANA159Y	GMS Buses	ANA212T	GMS Buses	ANA539Y	G M N	ANA576Y	G M N
ANA160Y	GMS Buses	ANA213T	G M N	ANA540Y	G M N	ANA577Y	GMS Buses
ANA161Y	GMS Buses	ANA214T	GMS Buses	ANA541Y	G M N	ANA578Y	G M N
ANA162Y	GMS Buses	ANA215T	GMS Buses	ANA542Y	G M N	ANA579Y	GMS Buses
ANA163Y	GMS Buses	ANA216T	G M N	ANA543Y	GMS Buses	ANA580Y	G M N
ANA164Y	GMS Buses	ANA217T	GMS Buses	ANA544Y	G M N	ANA581Y	G M N

Reg	Operator	Reg	Operator	Reg	Operator	Reg	Operator
ANA582Y	GMS Buses	ANA655Y	G M N	B74PJA	GMS Buses	B142WNB	G M N
ANA583Y	G M N	ANC904T	G M N	B75PJA	G M N	B143WNB	GMS Buses
ANA584Y	G M N	ANC911T	G M N	B76PJA	G M N	B144WNB	G M N
ANA585Y	GMS Buses	ANC912T	GMS Buses	B77PJA	GMS Buses	B145WNB	GMS Buses
ANA586Y	GMS Buses	ANC913T	GMS Buses	B78PJA	G M N	B146XNA	GMS Buses
ANA587Y	G M N	ANC928T	G M N	B79PJA	G M N	B147XNA	GMS Buses
ANA588Y	G M N	ANC932T	Stotts	B80PJA	GMS Buses	B148XNA	G M N
ANA589Y	GMS Buses	ARB134T	Mayne	B81PJA	G M N	B149XNA	GMS Buses
ANA590Y	G M N	ARH301K	Blackpool	B82PJA	GMS Buses	B150XNA	GMS Buses
ANA591Y	G M N	ARH304K	Blackpool	B83PJA	G M N	B151WRN	Cumberland
ANA592Y	GMS Buses	ARH306K	Blackpool	B84PJA	GMS Buses	B151XNA	G M N
ANA593Y	GMS Buses	ARH308K	Blackpool	B85PJA	G M N	B152TRN	Ribble
ANA594Y	G M N	ARH309K	Blackpool	B86SJA	GMS Buses	B152WRN	Ribble
ANA595Y	G M N	ARH314K	Blackpool	B87SJA	GMS Buses	B152XNA	G M N
ANA596Y	GMS Buses	ARN888Y	Ribble	B88SJA	GMS Buses	B153WRN	Cumberland
ANA597Y	GMS Buses	ARN889Y	Ribble	B89SJA	GMS Buses	B153XNA	GMS Buses
ANA598Y	G M N	ARN890Y	Ribble	B90SJA	G M N	B154WRN	Cumberland
ANA599Y	G M N	ASD31T	Blue Note	B91SJA	GMS Buses	B154XNA	GMS Buses
ANA600Y	GMS Buses	ATD281J	Blackpool	B92SJA	G M N	B155XNA	GMS Buses
ANA601Y	GMS Buses	AXI8323	Titteringtons	B93SJA	G M N	B158WRN	Ribble
ANA602Y	G M N	AYR354T	Blackburn	B94SJA	GMS Buses	B162WRN	Cumberland
ANA603Y	G M N	B21TVU	GMS Buses	B95SJA	GMS Buses	B183FDM	Rossendale
ANA604Y	GMS Buses	B22TVU	GMS Buses	B96SJA	G M N	B350PJA	G M N
ANA605Y	GMS Buses	B23TVU	GMS Buses	B97SJA	G M N	B351PJA	G M N
ANA606Y	G M N	B24TVU	GMS Buses	B98SJA	G M N	B357UCW	Abbott's
ANA607Y	G M N	B25ADW	Blue Bus	B99SJA	G M N	B358UCW	Taylors Cs
ANA608Y	GMS Buses	B25TVU	GMS Buses	B100SJA	G M N	B363UBV	Blackpool
ANA609Y	GMS Buses	B26TVU	GMS Buses	B101PHC	Rossendale	B364UBV	Blackpool
ANA610Y	G M N	B27TVU	GMS Buses	B101SJA	G M N	B417CMC	Blackburn
ANA611Y	G M N	B28TVU	GMS Buses	B102PHC	Rossendale	B512PRF	Kirkby Lonsdale
ANA612Y	GMS Buses	B29TVU	GMS Buses	B102SJA	G M N	B739YUD	Vale of Manchester
ANA613Y	GMS Buses	B30TVU	GMS Buses	B103HAO	Cumberland	B845SEC	Holmeswood
ANA614Y	G M N	B34PJA	GMS Buses	B103SJA	G M N	B891UAS	Ribble
ANA615Y	G M N	B35PJA	GMS Buses	B104SJA	G M N	B892UAS	Ribble
ANA616Y	G M N	B36PJA	GMS Buses	B105HAO	Cumberland	B893UAS	Ribble
ANA617Y	G M N	B37PJA	G M N	B105SJA	G M N	B894UAS	Ribble
ANA618Y	G M N	B38PJA	G M N	B106HAO	Cumberland	B895UAS	Ribble
ANA619Y	G M N	B39PJA	GMS Buses	B106SJA	G M N	B896UAS	Ribble
ANA620Y	GMS Buses	B40PJA	G M N	B107SJA	G M N	B897UAS	Ribble
ANA621Y	G M N	B41PJA	G M N	B108SJA	G M N	B898UAS	Ribble
ANA622Y	G M N	B42PJA	G M N	B109SJA	G M N	B899UAS	Ribble
ANA623Y	G M N	B43MAO	Cumberland	B110SJA	GMS Buses	B900WRN	Ribble
ANA624Y	GMS Buses	B43PJA	G M N	B111SJA	G M N	B901TVR	GMS Buses
ANA625Y	GMS Buses	B44PJA	G M N	B112SJA	G M N	B902TVR	GMS Buses
ANA626Y	G M N	B45PJA	G M N	B113SJA	G M N	B903TVR	GMS Buses
ANA627Y	GMS Buses	B46PJA	G M N	B114SJA	GMS Buses	B904TVR	GMS Buses
ANA628Y	G M N	B47PJA	G M N	B115SJA	G M N	B905TVR	GMS Buses
ANA629Y	G M N	B48PJA	G M N	B116TVU	G M N	B906TVR	GMS Buses
ANA630Y	GMS Buses	B49PJA	GMS Buses	B117TVU	GMS Buses	B907TVR	GMS Buses
ANA631Y	GMS Buses	B51XFV	Hyndburn	B118TVU	GMS Buses	B908TVR	GMS Buses
ANA633Y	G M N	B52PJA	G M N	B119TVU	GMS Buses	B909BGA	Kirkby Lonsdale
ANA633Y	GMS Buses	B53PJA	GMS Buses	B120TVU	G M N	B909TVR	GMS Buses
ANA634Y	G M N	B54PJA	G M N	B121TVU	GMS Buses	B910TVR	GMS Buses
ANA635Y	G M N	B55PJA	GMS Buses	B122TVU	GMS Buses	B911TVR	GMS Buses
ANA636Y	G M N	B56PJA	GMS Buses	B123TVU	G M N	B912TVR	GMS Buses
ANA637Y	GMS Buses	B57PJA	GMS Buses	B124TVU	GMS Buses	B913TVR	GMS Buses
ANA638Y	G M N	B58PJA	GMS Buses	B125TVU	GMS Buses	B914TVR	GMS Buses
ANA639Y	GMS Buses	B59AOP	Shaw Hadwin	B126WNB	GMS Buses	B915TVR	GMS Buses
ANA640Y	G M N	B59PJA	G M N	B127WNB	G M N	B916TVR	GMS Buses
ANA641Y	G M N	B60PJA	GMS Buses	B128WNB	G M N	B917TVR	GMS Buses
ANA642Y	G M N	B61PJA	G M N	B129WNB	G M N	B918TVR	GMS Buses
ANA643Y	G M N	B62PJA	G M N	B130WNB	G M N	B919TVR	GMS Buses
ANA644Y	GMS Buses	B63PJA	G M N	B131WNB	G M N	B920TVR	GMS Buses
ANA645Y	G M N	B64PJA	G M N	B132WNB	GMS Buses	B931YCW	Darwen Coach
ANA646Y	GMS Buses	B65PJA	GMS Buses	B133WNB	GMS Buses	BAJ118Y	Rossendale
ANA647Y	GMS Buses	B66PJA	G M N	B134WNB	G M N	BAJ119Y	Rossendale
ANA648Y	G M N	B67PJA	GMS Buses	B135WNB	GMS Buses	BAJ120Y	Rossendale
ANA649Y	G M N	B68PJA	G M N	B136WNB	G M N	BAZ6170	Shearings
ANA650Y	G M N	B69PJA	GMS Buses	B137WNB	GMS Buses	BAZ6516	Shearings
ANA651Y	GMS Buses	B70PJA	GMS Buses	B138WNB	GMS Buses	BAZ6527	Shearings
ANA652Y	G M N	B71PJA	G M N	B139WNB	GMS Buses	BAZ6528	Shearings
ANA653Y	GMS Buses	B72PJA	GMS Buses	B140WNB	G M N	BAZ6851	Shearings
ANA654Y	G M N	B73PJA	G M N	B141WNB	G M N	BAZ7049	Shearings

Reg	Operator	Reg	Operator	Reg	Operator	Reg	Operator
BAZ7052	Shearings	BYP985	Shaw Hadwin	C205FVU	G M N	C751YBA	GMS Buses
BAZ7053	Shearings	BYW361V	Blackburn	C206CBU	G M N	C752YBA	GMS Buses
BAZ7054	Shearings	BYW362V	R Bullock	C206FVU	G M N	C753YBA	GMS Buses
BAZ7055	Shearings	C41HDT	Pioneer	C207CBU	GMS Buses	C754YBA	GMS Buses
BAZ7056	Shearings	C46HDT	Pioneer	C207FVU	G M N	C755YBA	GMS Buses
BAZ7057	Shearings	C61WBF	Wright Bros	C208CBU	GMS Buses	C756YBA	GMS Buses
BAZ7058	Shearings	C80OCW	Burnley & Pendle	C208FVU	G M N	C757YBA	GMS Buses
BAZ7059	Shearings	C150LWA	Springfield Cs	C209CBU	G M N	C758YBA	GMS Buses
BAZ7284	Vale of Manchester	C156YBA	GMS Buses	C209FVU	G M N	C760YBA	GMS Buses
BAZ7360	Shearings	C157YBA	G M N	C210CBU	GMS Buses	C761YBA	GMS Buses
BAZ7901	Shearings	C158YBA	GMS Buses	C210FVU	G M N	C762YBA	GMS Buses
BAZ7912	Shearings	C159YBA	G M N	C211CBU	G M N	C763YBA	GMS Buses
BAZ7914	Shearings	C160YBA	G M N	C212CBU	GMS Buses	C764YBA	GMS Buses
BAZ7917	Shearings	C161YBA	G M N	C213CBU	GMS Buses	C765YBA	GMS Buses
BAZ7918	Shearings	C162YBA	G M N	C214CBU	GMS Buses	C766YBA	GMS Buses
BCB614V	G M N	C163YBA	G M N	C215CBU	GMS Buses	C768YBA	GMS Buses
BCB615V	G M N	C164YBA	GMS Buses	C216CBU	GMS Buses	C769YBA	GMS Buses
BCB616V	G M N	C165YBA	GMS Buses	C217CBU	G M N	C801CBU	Knight B & C
BCW825V	Ribble	C166VRE	Wright Bros	C218CBU	G M N	C810CBU	Knight B & C
BCW826V	Ribble	C166YBA	GMS Buses	C219CBU	G M N	C813CBU	Knight B & C
BFV221Y	Ribble	C167YBA	GMS Buses	C220CBU	G M N	C828CBU	Knight B & C
BFV222Y	Ribble	C168YBA	G M N	C221CBU	GMS Buses	C829CBU	Town Bus
BFV861R	Blackburn	C169YBA	GMS Buses	C222CBU	G M N	C875JMB	City Nippy
BHF291A	Holmeswood	C170ECK	Ribble	C223CBU	G M N	C963END	Shaw Hadwin
BKJ150T	Hyndburn	C170YBA	GMS Buses	C224CBU	GMS Buses	CAH880Y	Vale of Manchester
BNC929T	GMS Buses	C171ECK	Ribble	C225CBU	G M N	CAU113T	Border
BNC937T	G M N	C171YBA	G M N	C226ENE	GMS Buses	CAZ2818	Shearings
BNC941T	GMS Buses	C172ECK	Ribble	C227ENE	G M N	CAZ2819	Shearings
BNC944T	GMS Buses	C172YBA	GMS Buses	C228ENE	G M N	CAZ3190	Shearings
BNC947T	Finglands	C173ECK	Ribble	C229ENE	G M N	CBV2S	Cumberland
BNC951T	G M N	C173YBA	GMS Buses	C230ENE	GMS Buses	CBV21S	Ribble
BNC954T	GMS Buses	C174ECK	Ribble	C231ENE	G M N	CEC14W	Taylors Cs
BNC956T	GMS Buses	C174YBA	GMS Buses	C232ENE	G M N	CEO720W	Ribble
BNC959T	GMS Buses	C175ECK	Cumberland	C233ENE	G M N	CEO721W	Ribble
BNE736N	R Bullock	C175YBA	GMS Buses	C234ENE	GMS Buses	CEO722W	Ribble
BNE740N	Wall's	C176ECK	Cumberland	C235ENE	G M N	CFR384V	Apex Travel
BNE741N	Stotts	C176YBA	GMS Buses	C236EVU	GMS Buses	CFR489V	Blackburn
BTB928	Blackpool	C177ECK	Cumberland	C237EVU	G M N	CFS264S	Border
BUH239V	Burnley & Pendle	C177YBA	G M N	C238EVU	G M N	CGV159	Borderbus
BUH240V	Burnley & Pendle	C178ECK	Ribble	C239EVU	G M N	CHA480K	Robinson's
BUH241V	Burnley & Pendle	C178YBA	GMS Buses	C240EVU	G M N	CHH210T	Ribble
BUI1133	R Bullock	C179ECK	Ribble	C241EVU	G M N	CHH211T	Ribble
BUI1300	R Bullock	C179YBA	GMS Buses	C242EVU	G M N	CHH214T	Ribble
BUI1424	R Bullock	C180YBA	G M N	C243EVU	G M N	CIB3202	Finglands
BUI1484	R Bullock	C181YBA	GMS Buses	C244EVU	G M N	CIW290	Wright Bros
BUI1610	R Bullock	C182YBA	G M N	C245EVU	G M N	CJK36V	Rossendale
BUI1675	R Bullock	C183YBA	G M N	C246FRJ	G M N	CJK37V	Rossendale
BVP807V	Blackburn	C184YBA	GMS Buses	C247FRJ	G M N	CKB161X	G M N
BVR51T	G M N	C185YBA	GMS Buses	C248FRJ	G M N	CKB162X	G M N
BVR54T	G M N	C186YBA	G M N	C249FRJ	G M N	CKB163X	G M N
BVR56T	G M N	C187YBA	G M N	C250FRJ	G M N	CKB164X	G M N
BVR57T	G M N	C188YBA	G M N	C251FRJ	G M N	CNH171X	Atherton Bus
BVR58T	G M N	C189YBA	G M N	C252FRJ	G M N	CSU917	Hulme Hall
BVR60T	G M N	C190YBA	G M N	C253FRJ	G M N	CUI925	Titteringtons
BVR62T	G M N	C191YBA	GMS Buses	C254FRJ	G M N	CWG683V	Blue Bus
BVR63T	G M N	C192YBA	G M N	C255FRJ	G M N	CWG691V	Blue Bus
BVR64T	G M N	C193YBA	GMS Buses	C281BBP	GMS Buses	CWG705V	Stotts
BVR72T	G M N	C194YBA	G M N	C282BBP	R Bullock	CWG726V	Stotts
BVR73T	G M N	C195YBA	GMS Buses	C283BBP	R Bullock	CWG727V	Stotts
BVR74T	G M N	C196OHH	Titteringtons	C284BBP	R Bullock	CWG766V	Stotts
BVR75T	G M N	C196YBA	GMS Buses	C285BBP	R Bullock	CWR525Y	Hyndburn
BVR77T	G M N	C197YBA	GMS Buses	C310ENA	GMS Buses	CWR526Y	Hyndburn
BVR78T	G M N	C198YBA	GMS Buses	C360BRJ	Hulme Hall	D21CFL	Rossendale
BVR79T	G M N	C200YBA	G M N	C382SAO	Cumberland	D25VCW	Fishwick
BVR81T	G M N	C201CBU	G M N	C383SAO	Cumberland	D30VCW	Fishwick
BVR84T	G M N	C201FVU	G M N	C481CBU	G M N	D32YCW	Fishwick
BVR86T	G M N	C202CBU	G M N	C482CBU	G M N	D33YCW	Fishwick
BVR88T	G M N	C202FVU	G M N	C483CBU	G M N	D35UAO	Cumberland
BVR90T	G M N	C203CBU	G M N	C489PHG	Shaw Hadwin	D36UAO	Cumberland
BVR91T	G M N	C203FVU	G M N	C515DYM	Darwen Minibus	D37TKA	Knight B & C
BVR93T	G M N	C204CBU	G M N	C544RAO	Cumberland	D37UAO	Cumberland
BVR95T	G M N	C204FVU	G M N	C590NRM	Sim	D38UAO	Cumberland
BVR96T	G M N	C205CBU	GMS Buses	C664BEX	Darwen Minibus	D39UAO	Cumberland

Reg	Operator	Reg	Operator	Reg	Operator	Reg	Operator
D41AFV	Preston	D308SDS	Knight B & C	D602AFR	Blackburn	D672NNE	GMS Buses
D42AFV	Preston	D309JVR	G M N	D602MDB	GMS Buses	D672SHH	Ribble
D42UAO	Cumberland	D310JVR	G M N	D603AFR	Blackburn	D673NNE	GMS Buses
D43AFV	Preston	D311LNB	G M N	D603MDB	GMS Buses	D674NNE	GMS Buses
D43UAO	Cumberland	D312LNB	G M N	D604MDB	GMS Buses	D675NNE	GMS Buses
D44UAO	Cumberland	D313LNB	G M N	D605MDB	GMS Buses	D676NNE	GMS Buses
D45UAO	Cumberland	D314LNB	G M N	D606MDB	GMS Buses	D677NNE	GMS Buses
D46UAO	Cumberland	D315LNB	G M N	D607AFR	Blackburn	D678NNE	GMS Buses
D52RJA	R Bullock	D316LNB	G M N	D607MDB	GMS Buses	D679NNE	GMS Buses
D53RJA	R Bullock	D317LNB	G M N	D608AFR	Blackburn	D680NNE	GMS Buses
D54RJA	R Bullock	D318LNB	G M N	D608MDB	GMS Buses	D693SEM	G M N
D69ONS	Shaw Hadwin	D319LNB	G M N	D609AFR	Blackburn	D699THF	Bu-Val
D72AFV	Preston	D319NEC	Blackburn	D609MDB	GMS Buses	D711HUA	Darwen Coach
D73AFV	Preston	D320LNB	G M N	D611AFR	Blackburn	D750YCW	Preston
D74AFV	Preston	D320NEC	Blackburn	D611MDB	GMS Buses	D751YCW	Preston
D81UFV	Burnley & Pendle	D327VVV	Abbott's	D612MDB	GMS Buses	D752YCW	Preston
D82UFV	Burnley & Pendle	D337VBB	City Nippy	D613MDB	GMS Buses	D754YCW	Preston
D83UFV	Burnley & Pendle	D349JUM	Springfield Cs	D614MDB	GMS Buses	D758YCW	Preston
D84BLF	Fishwick	D359JUM	Springfield Cs	D615BCK	B & D Coaches	D759YCW	Preston
D93VCC	Dennis's	D380XRS	Cumberland	D616MDB	G M N	D760YCW	Preston
D95VCC	Dennis's	D381XRS	Cumberland	D617MDB	GMS Buses	D761YCW	Preston
D97VCC	Dennis's	D384XAO	Cumberland	D618MDB	GMS Buses	D762YCW	Preston
D104AFV	Blackpool	D405FRV	Brownrigg's	D619MDB	GMS Buses	D763YCW	Preston
D105AFV	Blackpool	D447NNA	Darwen Coach	D620MDB	GMS Buses	D764YCW	Preston
D109OWG	Stuart's	D501LNA	G M N	D621MDB	GMS Buses	D766YCW	Preston
D117NON	Darwen Coach	D501RCK	Ribble	D622MDB	G M N	D772RBU	GMS Buses
D122NON	Town Bus	D502LNA	G M N	D623MDB	GMS Buses	D773RBU	GMS Buses
D137OWG	G M N	D502MJA	B & D Coaches	D624MDB	GMS Buses	D774RBU	GMS Buses
D140NUS	Kirkby Lonsdale	D502RCK	Ribble	D625MDB	G M N	D776RBU	GMS Buses
D142NUS	Vale of Manchester	D503LNA	G M N	D626MDB	GMS Buses	D781RBU	GMS Buses
D143NUS	Vale of Manchester	D504LNA	G M N	D627MDB	GMS Buses	D783RBU	GMS Buses
D143RAK	Stotts	D505RCK	Ribble	D628MDB	GMS Buses	D831RYS	Darwen Minibus
D144RAK	Stotts	D507RCK	Ribble	D629MDB	GMS Buses	D843LND	GMS Buses
D159RAK	Darwen Coach	D508RCK	Ribble	D630MDB	GMS Buses	D845LND	G M N
D160RAK	Stotts	D510RCK	Ribble	D631MDB	G M N	D846LND	G M N
D171PYB	Stotts	D511MJA	B & D Coaches	D632MDB	GMS Buses	D852LND	G M N
D178LTA	B & D Coaches	D512RCK	Ribble	D633MDB	GMS Buses	D854MUA	Blackpool
D181LTA	B & D Coaches	D513RCK	Ribble	D634MDB	GMS Buses	D857LND	G M N
D181NON	Darwen Coach	D515RCK	Ribble	D635MDB	GMS Buses	D857XBV	Abbott's
D210OKY	Fishwick	D520RCK	Cumberland	D636MDB	GMS Buses	D859LND	Rossendale
D256JVR	G M N	D521RCK	Ribble	D638MDB	GMS Buses	D860FOT	Hyndburn
D256PEP	G M N	D525RCK	Cumberland	D639MDB	GMS Buses	D864LND	G M N
D257JVR	G M N	D527RCK	Ribble	D640MDB	GMS Buses	D870ABV	Preston
D258JVR	G M N	D528RCK	Cumberland	D641MDB	GMS Buses	D871ABV	Preston
D259JVR	G M N	D529RCK	Cumberland	D642MDB	GMS Buses	D874MDB	G M N
D260JVR	GMS Buses	D530RCK	Cumberland	D643MDB	GMS Buses	D875MDB	G M N
D260PEP	G M N	D531RCK	Cumberland	D644MDB	GMS Buses	D876MDB	G M N
D261JVR	G M N	D533RCK	Cumberland	D645MDB	GMS Buses	D879MDB	G M N
D262JVR	G M N	D534RCK	Cumberland	D646MDB	GMS Buses	D885MDB	G M N
D263JVR	G M N	D535XBC	Dennis's	D647MDB	GMS Buses	D889MDB	G M N
D264JVR	G M N	D536RCK	Ribble	D648MDB	GMS Buses	D891MDB	GMS Buses
D265JVR	G M N	D537RCK	Ribble	D649MDB	GMS Buses	D892MDB	GMS Buses
D266JVR	G M N	D541RCK	Ribble	D650MDB	GMS Buses	D894MDB	G M N
D266OOJ	G M N	D542RCK	Ribble	D651NNE	GMS Buses	D897MDB	G M N
D267JVR	G M N	D545RCK	Ribble	D652NNE	GMS Buses	D898NUA	Blackpool
D268JVR	GMS Buses	D546RCK	Ribble	D653NNE	GMS Buses	D899MDB	G M N
D269JVR	GMS Buses	D548RCK	Ribble	D654NNE	GMS Buses	D901MDB	Rossendale
D270JVR	G M N	D549RCK	Ribble	D655NNE	GMS Buses	D904MDB	G M N
D271JVR	G M N	D551RCK	Ribble	D656NNE	GMS Buses	D906NDB	G M N
D272JVR	GMS Buses	D552MOK	Apex Travel	D657NNE	GMS Buses	D908NDB	G M N
D273JVR	G M N	D552RCK	Ribble	D658NNE	GMS Buses	D909NDB	G M N
D274JVR	G M N	D553RCK	Ribble	D659NNE	GMS Buses	D912VCN	Stuart's
D275JVR	G M N	D554RCK	Ribble	D661NNE	GMS Buses	D916NDB	G M N
D276JVR	G M N	D555RCK	Ribble	D662NNE	GMS Buses	D917NDB	GMS Buses
D277JVR	GMS Buses	D556RCK	Ribble	D663NNE	GMS Buses	D920NDB	G M N
D301JVR	G M N	D558RCK	Cumberland	D664NNE	GMS Buses	D921NDB	GMS Buses
D302JVR	G M N	D559RCK	Cumberland	D665NNE	GMS Buses	D922NDB	GMS Buses
D303JVR	G M N	D560RCK	Cumberland	D666NNE	GMS Buses	D930NDB	G M N
D304JVR	G M N	D562RCK	Ribble	D667NNE	GMS Buses	D932NDB	G M N
D305JVR	G M N	D564RCK	Ribble	D668NNE	GMS Buses	D933NDB	G M N
D306JVR	G M N	D601AFR	Rossendale	D670NNE	GMS Buses	D941NDB	G M N
D307JVR	G M N	D601MDB	GMS Buses	D671NNE	GMS Buses	D944NDB	GMS Buses
D308JVR	G M N					D945NDB	G M N

Reg	Operator	Reg	Operator	Reg	Operator	Reg	Operator
D947NDB	G M N	DWH692W	G M N	E112LCW	Blackpool	E393SWX	R Bullock
D948NDB	G M N	DWH693W	G M N	E113LCW	Blackpool	E403WRH	Shaw Hadwin
D949NDB	G M N	DWH695W	G M N	E114LCW	Blackpool	E419YLG	R Bullock
D952NDB	G M N	DWH697W	G M N	E119UEC	Shaw Hadwin	E430YLG	Kirkby Lonsdale
D954NDB	G M N	DWH698W	G M N	E120RDW	G M N	E458TYG	Vale of Manchester
D956PJA	G M N	DWH700W	Stotts	E121RDW	G M N	E473SON	Finglands
D958PJA	G M N	DWH701W	G M N	E122RDW	G M N	E474SON	Finglands
D963PJA	GMS Buses	DWH702W	G M N	E123RDW	G M N	E476SON	Finglands
D970PJA	GMS Buses	DWH703W	G M N	E124RDW	G M N	E477SON	Finglands
D971PJA	GMS Buses	DWH704W	G M N	E125RDW	G M N	E480UOF	Finglands
D972TKC	Pioneer	DWH705W	G M N	E126RDW	G M N	E481CNM	Rossendale
D973PJA	G M N	DWH706W	G M N	E127RDW	G M N	E483CNM	Rossendale
D973TKC	Pioneer	DWU295T	Fishwick	E128RDW	G M N	E510PVV	Cumberland
D977PJA	G M N	E24GCK	Hyndburn	E143KYW	Rossendale	E511PVV	Cumberland
D979PJA	G M N	E25GCK	Hyndburn	E144KYW	Rossendale	E512PVV	Cumberland
D979TKC	Bu-Val	E26GCK	Hyndburn	E144RAX	Darwen Coach	E518PWR	Pioneer
DBA227C	Blackpool	E27GCK	Hyndburn	E148KYW	G M N	E519YWF	Rossendale
DBV24W	Cumberland	E28GCK	Hyndburn	E150KYW	G M N	E553GFR	Blackpool
DBV30W	Ribble	E29GCK	Hyndburn	E157RNY	Glossopdale	E554GFR	Blackpool
DBV32W	Cumberland	E44FFV	Preston	E164CNC	Blackpool	E555GFR	Blackpool
DBV38W	Burnley & Pendle	E45GRN	Preston	E165CNC	Blackpool	E556GFR	Blackpool
DBV39W	Burnley & Pendle	E45HBV	Fishwick	E172UWF	Stotts	E557GFR	Blackpool
DBV40W	Burnley & Pendle	E46HBV	Fishwick	E175UWF	Stotts	E558GFR	Blackpool
DBV41W	Burnley & Pendle	E47CHH	Cumberland	E176TWO	Glossopdale	E559GFR	Blackpool
DBV42W	Burnley & Pendle	E47HBV	Fishwick	E177UWF	Darwen Coach	E567GFR	Blackpool
DBV43W	Burnley & Pendle	E47KBV	Preston	E178UWF	G M N	E568GFR	Blackpool
DBV100W	Ribble	E48CHH	Cumberland	E181CNE	Bu-Val	E569OCW	Blackpool
DBV131Y	Ribble	E48MCK	Preston	E183CNE	Vale of Manchester	E570OCW	Blackpool
DBV132Y	Ribble	E49CHH	Cumberland	E185CNE	Vale of Manchester	E632VBA	Brownrigg's
DBV134Y	Cumberland	E49MCK	Preston	E186CNE	Bu-Val	E636KYW	G M N
DBV137Y	Ribble	E50CHH	Cumberland	E187CNE	Bu-Val	E637KYW	G M N
DBV143W	Blackburn	E56KHG	Rossendale	E189CNE	Bluebird	E638KYW	G M N
DBV144W	Blackburn	E58KHG	Rossendale	E189UWF	Stotts	E674DCU	Rossendale
DBV145W	Blackburn	E59KHG	Rossendale	E200SVR	GMS Buses	E675KDG	Pioneer
DBV146W	Blackburn	E61JFV	Burnley & Pendle	E216WVM	City Nippy	E709MFV	Cumberland
DBV147W	Blackburn	E62JFV	Burnley & Pendle	E236UWR	Pioneer	E717BSU	Kirkby Lonsdale
DBV199W	Hyndburn	E63JFV	Burnley & Pendle	E237UWR	G M N	E754CHH	Brownrigg's
DBV828W	Ribble	E64JFV	Burnley & Pendle	E238UWR	Bu-Val	E758OWY	R Bullock
DBV829W	Ribble	E65JFV	Burnley & Pendle	E239UWR	G M N	E764KJX	Rossendale
DBV830W	Ribble	E66JFV	Burnley & Pendle	E240UWR	G M N	E775WEC	Shaw Hadwin
DBV831W	Ribble	E71XKW	Brownrigg's	E241UWR	G M N	E791SJA	GMS Buses
DBV832W	Ribble	E75LFR	Preston	E242UWR	G M N	E792SJA	GMS Buses
DBV833W	Ribble	E76LFR	Preston	E243UWR	G M N	E793SJA	GMS Buses
DBV834W	Ribble	E77LFR	Preston	E244UWR	G M N	E797SJA	GMS Buses
DBV835W	Ribble	E78MHG	Preston	E245UWR	Bu-Val	E815JSX	Darwen Minibus
DBV837W	Ribble	E79MHG	Preston	E246UWR	G M N	E878LHV	Vale of Manchester
DBV838W	Ribble	E80MHG	Preston	E247UWR	G M N	E919HHG	Darwen Minibus
DBV839W	Ribble	E81MHG	Preston	E248UWR	Rossendale	E929KYR	G M N
DBV841W	Ribble	E82MHG	Preston	E250UWR	G M N	E949GFV	G M N
DBV842W	Ribble	E83MHG	Preston	E251UWR	G M N	E977DGS	Rossendale
DBV843W	Ribble	E84HRN	Burnley & Pendle	E253UWR	Bu-Val	E979DGS	Rossendale
DDK24W	Rossendale	E84MHG	Preston	E254REP	G M N	E980DGS	Rossendale
DDK25W	Rossendale	E84OUH	Glossopdale	E254UWR	Bu-Val	E981SJA	GMS Buses
DDK26W	Rossendale	E85HRN	Burnley & Pendle	E255REP	G M N	E983SJA	G M N
DDM30X	Blue Bus	E85MHG	Preston	E255UWR	Bu-Val	E984SJA	G M N
DHC784E	Blackpool	E86HRN	Burnley & Pendle	E256UWR	Bu-Val	E985SJA	G M N
DRJ897L	Timeline	E86MHG	Preston	E257UWR	Bu-Val	E987SJA	G M N
DRN1Y	Preston	E87HRN	Burnley & Pendle	E258REP	G M N	E990SJA	GMS Buses
DRN2Y	Preston	E87MHG	Preston	E259REP	G M N	E994SJA	G M N
DRN173Y	Preston	E88HRN	Burnley & Pendle	E263REP	G M N	E996SJA	G M N
DRN174Y	Preston	E89HRN	Burnley & Pendle	E264REP	G M N	E996VYS	Dennis's
DRN175Y	Preston	E90JHG	Burnley & Pendle	E265REP	G M N	E997SJA	G M N
DRN176Y	Preston	E91LBV	Burnley & Pendle	E266REP	G M N	E999SJA	GMS Buses
DRN177Y	Preston	E92LHG	Burnley & Pendle	E267REP	G M N	ECK865E	Holmeswood
DSV943	Cumberland	E93LHG	Burnley & Pendle	E268REP	G M N	ECS875V	Stotts
DUI4760	Kirkby Lonsdale	E94LHG	Burnley & Pendle	E271REP	G M N	EFR97W	Abbott's
DWH683W	G M N	E100MFV	Fishwick	E272REP	G M N	EFR107W	Abbott's
DWH686W	G M N	E101JFV	Burnley & Pendle	E273REP	G M N	EGB51T	Blue Bus
DWH687W	G M N	E102JFV	Burnley & Pendle	E274REP	G M N	EGB60T	Blue Bus
DWH688W	G M N	E107OUH	Glossopdale	E275REP	G M N	EHB259G	Mayne
DWH689W	G M N	E108LCW	Blackpool	E276REP	G M N	EHG43S	Hyndburn
DWH690W	G M N	E110LCW	Blackpool	E277REP	G M N	EHG44S	Hyndburn
DWH691W	G M N	E111LCW	Blackpool	E357KPO	City Nippy	EHG45S	Hyndburn

Reg	Operator	Reg	Operator	Reg	Operator	Reg	Operator
EHG46S	Hyndburn	F225YHG	Robinsons	F597FAM	G M N	FFR167S	Burnley & Pendle
ENF555Y	Sim	F226FNE	Bu-Val	F598FAM	G M N	FFR168S	Burnley & Pendle
ERV251D	Cumberland	F226YHG	Robinsons	F616UBV	Blackburn	FFR172S	Burnley & Pendle
ESK978	Borderbus	F229BAX	Glossopdale	F617UBV	Blackburn	FFR173S	Burnley & Pendle
EUK976	Mayne	F241FNE	Bu-Val	F617UBV	Blackburn	FFR174S	Burnley & Pendle
EWF469V	Stuart's	F242FNE	Bluebird	F619UBV	Blackburn	FIL7287	Hyndburn
EYN165	Hyndburn	F242MBA	Finglands	F620UBV	Blackburn	FTV10L	Borderbus
F32AHG	Preston	F243FNE	Bu-Val	F621UBV	Blackburn	FUH32V	Burnley & Pendle
F37FNF	Timeline	F248KVU	B & D Coaches	F622UBV	Blackburn	FUH33V	Burnley & Pendle
F38FNF	Timeline	F249KVU	B & D Coaches	F623UBV	Blackburn	FUH34V	Burnley & Pendle
F49FNF	Timeline	F251JRM	Cumberland	F623YCW	Vale of Manchester	FUN319	Wright Bros
F50FNF	Timeline	F252JRM	Cumberland	F624UBV	Blackburn	FUT6V	Blackburn
F60ARN	Rossendale	F253KAO	Cumberland	F624YCW	Vale of Manchester	FVR240V	G M N
F61ARN	Rossendale	F278DRJ	G M N	F625UBV	Blackburn	FVR242V	GMS Buses
F62ARN	Rossendale	F279DRJ	G M N	F626OHD	Holmeswood	FVR243V	G M N
F63ARN	Rossendale	F280DRJ	G M N	F626UBV	Blackburn	FVR244V	G M N
F88UHG	Preston	F281DRJ	G M N	F638HVU	City Nippy	FVR245V	GMS Buses
F89UHG	Preston	F282DRJ	GMS Buses	F639HVU	City Nippy	FVR246V	GMS Buses
F90UHG	Preston	F283DRJ	GMS Buses	F642NVU	Bluebird	FVR247V	GMS Buses
F91AHG	Preston	F284DRJ	G M N	F664DRN	Shaw Hadwin	FVR249V	GMS Buses
F91CWG	Rossendale	F285DRJ	GMS Buses	F699ENE	Blackpool	FVR250V	GMS Buses
F92AHG	Preston	F286DRJ	G M N	F700ENE	Blackpool	FVR251V	G M N
F92CWG	Rossendale	F287DRJ	G M N	F701ENE	Blue Bus	FVR252V	GMS Buses
F92XBV	Rossendale	F288DRJ	G M N	F702ENE	Blue Bus	FVR254V	G M N
F93CWG	Rossendale	F288FLG	Bluebird	F703ENE	Blackpool	FVR255V	G M N
F93XBV	Rossendale	F289DRJ	GMS Buses	F705WFV	Fishwick	FVR256V	G M N
F94AEL	Burnley & Pendle	F290DRJ	G M N	F706WFV	Fishwick	FVR257V	G M N
F94CWG	Rossendale	F291DRJ	GMS Buses	F726DNB	City Nippy	FVR258V	G M N
F94XBV	Rossendale	F292DRJ	G M N	F727VAC	Abbott's	FVR259V	GMS Buses
F95XBV	Rossendale	F293DRJ	G M N	F803FAO	Cumberland	FVR260V	G M N
F103XCW	Burnley & Pendle	F294DRJ	GMS Buses	F804FAO	Cumberland	FVR261V	G M N
F103YWO	Rossendale	F295DRJ	GMS Buses	F805FAO	Cumberland	FVR263V	G M N
F104XCW	Burnley & Pendle	F296DRJ	GMS Buses	F806FAO	Cumberland	FVR264V	GMS Buses
F105XCW	Burnley & Pendle	F297DRJ	GMS Buses	F807FAO	Cumberland	FVR265V	G M N
F106XCW	Burnley & Pendle	F298DRJ	G M N	F808FAO	Cumberland	FVR266V	G M N
F107XCW	Burnley & Pendle	F299DRJ	G M N	F809FAO	Cumberland	FVR268V	G M N
F108XCW	Burnley & Pendle	F300DRJ	GMS Buses	F810FAO	Cumberland	FVR269V	G M N
F109XCW	Burnley & Pendle	F301DRJ	GMS Buses	F811FAO	Cumberland	FVR271V	G M N
F110XCW	Burnley & Pendle	F301JNC	Finglands	F823KRJ	Wall's	FVR272V	G M N
F111XCW	Burnley & Pendle	F302DRJ	G M N	F842EHH	Robinson's	FVR273V	G M N
F111YWO	Rossendale	F302JNC	Finglands	F882CJC	Hyndburn	FVR274V	G M N
F112HNC	Mayne	F303DRJ	G M N	F883CJC	Hyndburn	FVR275V	G M N
F112XCW	Burnley & Pendle	F303JNC	Finglands	F899SMU	Taylors Cs	FVR276V	G M N
F113HNC	Mayne	F304DRJ	GMS Buses	F913HTU	Hyndburn	FVR277V	G M N
F113YWO	Rossendale	F305DRJ	G M N	F914HTU	Hyndburn	FVR278V	G M N
F115YWO	Rossendale	F355JAO	Sim	F926HAL	R Bullock	FVR279V	G M N
F120UFR	Blackpool	F358FNB	Vale of Manchester	F934AWW	Blackpool	FVR280V	GMS Buses
F130AEL	Sim	F359FNB	Vale of Manchester	F946ORV	Mountain Goat	FVR281V	GMS Buses
F135KAO	Timeline	F360FNB	Vale of Manchester	F948CUA	Darwen Coach	FVR282V	G M N
F135SPX	Ribble	F368AFR	Blackpool	F956WCK	Darwen Minibus	FVR283V	GMS Buses
F136SPX	Ribble	F369AFR	Blackpool	F984HGE	Blackburn	FVR284V	G M N
F137SPX	Ribble	F370AFR	Blackpool	F995HGE	Stotts	FVR285V	G M N
F141UFR	Blackpool	F371AFR	Blackpool	FAO420V	Cumberland	FVR286V	G M N
F142UFR	Blackpool	F371JTN	Shaw Hadwin	FAO421V	Cumberland	FVR287V	G M N
F143UFR	Blackpool	F372AFR	Blackpool	FAO422V	Cumberland	FVR288V	G M N
F144UFR	Blackpool	F373AFR	Blackpool	FAO423V	Cumberland	FVR289V	G M N
F145UFR	Blackpool	F378UCP	Darwen Minibus	FAO424V	Cumberland	FVR290V	GMS Buses
F164DET	Rossendale	F394DOA	Timeline	FAO425V	Cumberland	FVR291V	GMS Buses
F165DET	Rossendale	F452FDB	R Bullock	FAO426V	Cumberland	FVR292V	G M N
F168DET	Rossendale	F485CKU	Shaw Hadwin	FAO427V	Cumberland	FVR293V	G M N
F169DET	Rossendale	F545EJA	Timeline	FAO428V	Cumberland	FVR294V	GMS Buses
F171DET	Rossendale	F571RCW	Blackpool	FAP9	Shaw Hadwin	FVR295V	GMS Buses
F201FHH	Cumberland	F572RCW	Blackpool	FBV524S	Fishwick	FVR296V	G M N
F202FHH	Cumberland	F573RCW	Blackpool	FBV525S	Fishwick	FVR297V	G M N
F210YHG	Preston	F574RCW	Glossopdale	FCK24Y	Blackburn	FVR298V	G M N
F211YHG	Preston	F575RCW	Blackpool	FCK25Y	Blackburn	FVR299V	G M N
F212YHG	Preston	F576RCW	Blackpool	FCK27Y	Blackburn	FVR300V	G M N
F213YHG	Preston	F577RCW	Blackpool	FDV784V	Ribble	FWA474V	G M N
F217AKG	Darwen Coach	F578RCW	Blackpool	FDV799V	Cumberland	FWH461Y	GMS Buses
F220JBB	Dennis's	F579WCW	Blackpool	FDV813V	Ribble	FWH462Y	GMS Buses
F222YHG	Robinsons	F580WCW	Blackpool	FDV817V	Ribble	G34OCK	Preston
F223YHG	Robinsons	F581WCW	Blackpool	FDV833V	Ribble	G35OCK	Preston
F224YHG	Robinsons	F582WCW	Blackpool	FFR166S	Burnley & Pendle	G36OCK	Preston

Reg	Operator	Reg	Operator	Reg	Operator	Reg	Operator
G37OCK	Preston	G192PAO	Ribble	G996RKN	Blackburn	GXI613	Burnley & Pendle
G39ORM	Titteringtons	G214KRN	Preston	G999RKN	Blackburn	H1FBT	Blackpool
G41XBK	Hyndburn	G215KRN	Preston	GAS656N	Borderbus	H2FBT	Blackpool
G53RND	Timeline	G216KRN	Preston	GBU11V	G M N	H3FBT	Blackpool
G54RND	Timeline	G217KRN	Preston	GBU12V	G M N	H10BUL	R Bullock
G55RND	Timeline	G218KRN	Preston	GBU13V	G M N	H23YBV	Preston
G56RND	Timeline	G218REC	Mountain Goat	GBU14V	G M N	H24YBV	Preston
G57OHH	Titteringtons	G227NCW	Robinsons	GBU15V	G M N	H26YBV	Preston
G57RND	Timeline	G228NCW	Robinsons	GBU17V	GMS Buses	H27YBV	Preston
G58RND	Timeline	G229NCW	Robinsons	GBU20V	GMS Buses	H28DVM	Mayne
G59RND	Timeline	G230NCW	Robinsons	GBU22V	GMS Buses	H28YBV	Preston
G60RND	Timeline	G231NCW	Robinsons	GBU24V	GMS Buses	H29YBV	Preston
G61RND	Timeline	G251EHD	Wall's	GBU27V	GMS Buses	H36YCW	Hyndburn
G62RND	Timeline	G252EHD	Wall's	GBU28V	GMS Buses	H37YCW	Hyndburn
G63RND	Timeline	G253EHD	Wall's	GBU29V	GMS Buses	H38YCW	Hyndburn
G64RND	Timeline	G263TSL	Cumberland	GBV101N	Hyndburn	H39YCW	Hyndburn
G65RND	Timeline	G264TSL	Cumberland	GBV108N	Hyndburn	H51DVR	Mayne
G665ND	Timeline	G265TSL	Cumberland	GBV109N	Hyndburn	H52FDB	Mayne
G67PFR	Burnley & Pendle	G266TSL	Cumberland	GBV110N	Hyndburn	H64CCK	Fishwick
G67RND	Timeline	G267TSL	Cumberland	GCK49W	Hyndburn	H65CCK	Fishwick
G68PFR	Burnley & Pendle	G268TSL	Cumberland	GCK428W	Fishwick	H67WNN	B & D Coaches
G68RND	Timeline	G269TSL	Cumberland	GCK429W	Fishwick	H73DVM	Timeline
G69RND	Timeline	G275MWU	Bluebird	GCK430W	Fishwick	H74DVM	Timeline
G70RND	Timeline	G276MWU	Bluebird	GDZ3841	Mayne	H76DVM	Timeline
G71RND	Timeline	G277MWU	Bluebird	GFJ660N	R Bullock	H78CFV	Burnley & Pendle
G72RND	Timeline	G278MWU	Bluebird	GFR101W	Ribble	H78DVM	Timeline
G94VFP	Rossendale	G279MWU	Bluebird	GFV151W	Preston	H79CFV	Burnley & Pendle
G96MRN	Burnley & Pendle	G280MWU	Bluebird	GFV152W	Preston	H79DVM	Timeline
G97MRN	Burnley & Pendle	G293TSL	Cumberland	GFV153W	Preston	H81DVM	Timeline
G98PCK	Burnley & Pendle	G294TSL	Cumberland	GFV154W	Preston	H82DVM	Timeline
G99PCK	Burnley & Pendle	G295TSL	Cumberland	GFV155W	Preston	H83DVM	Timeline
G101NBV	Blackpool	G296TSL	Cumberland	GFV156W	Preston	H84DVM	Timeline
G102NBV	Blackpool	G297TSL	Cumberland	GFV157W	Preston	H84PTG	City Nippy
G103NBV	Blackpool	G298TSL	Cumberland	GGM76W	Wall's	H85DVM	Timeline
G104NBV	Blackpool	G299TSL	Cumberland	GGM109W	Wall's	H86DVM	Timeline
G105NBV	Blackpool	G300TSL	Cumberland	GHG341W	Blackpool	H87DVM	Timeline
G106NBV	Blackpool	G315YHJ	Wall's	GHG343W	Blackpool	H101BFR	Preston
G107NBV	Blackpool	G316YHJ	Wall's	GHG344W	Blackpool	H101VFV	Rossendale
G107RND	Timeline	G337PAO	Taylors Cs	GHG345W	Blackpool	H102BFR	Preston
G108NBV	Blackpool	G344ESC	Kirkby Lonsdale	GHG346W	Blackpool	H102VFV	Rossendale
G108RND	Timeline	G423SNF	R Bullock	GHG347W	Blackpool	H103BFR	Preston
G115SBA	Mayne	G481HNP	R Bullock	GHG348W	Blackpool	H103VFV	Rossendale
G116SBA	Mayne	G506PFM	Dennis's	GHG349W	Blackpool	H104BFR	Preston
G117SBA	Mayne	G507PFM	Dennis's	GHG350W	Blackpool	H104CHG	Rossendale
G139LRM	City Nippy	G532VND	Bluebird	GHR301W	Springfield Cs	H105CHG	Rossendale
G140LRM	City Nippy	G533SBA	Bluebird	GIB1437	Stotts	H109DVM	Timeline
G143LRM	City Nippy	G566PRM	Ribble	GIL2160	Mayne	H109YHG	Blackpool
G148LRM	Bluebird	G567PRM	Ribble	GIL3016	Shaw Hadwin	H110DVM	Timeline
G150MMA	Vale of Manchester	G568PRM	Ribble	GIL3259	Mayne	H110YHG	Blackpool
G178PAO	Cumberland	G569PRM	Ribble	GLS267S	Blue Bus	H112DVM	Timeline
G179PAO	Ribble	G570PRM	Ribble	GLS275S	Blue Bus	H112SAO	Cumberland
G180JHG	Ribble	G571PRM	Ribble	GMS276S	Blue Bus	H112YHG	Blackpool
G180PAO	Ribble	G572PRM	Ribble	GMS277S	Blue Bus	H113ABV	Burnley & Pendle
G181JHG	Ribble	G573PRM	Ribble	GMS278S	Blue Bus	H113SAO	Cumberland
G181PAO	Ribble	G574PRM	Ribble	GMS291S	Blue Bus	H113YHG	Blackpool
G182JHG	Ribble	G575PRM	Ribble	GMS294S	Blue Bus	H114ABV	Burnley & Pendle
G182PAO	Ribble	G576PRM	Ribble	GMS299S	Blue Bus	H114SAO	Cumberland
G183JHG	Ribble	G577PRM	Ribble	GMS310S	Blue Bus	H114YHG	Blackpool
G183PAO	Ribble	G578PRM	Ribble	GNC294N	Wall's	H115ABV	Burnley & Pendle
G184JHG	Ribble	G581PVU	Shaw Hadwin	GND505N	Mayne	H115SAO	Cumberland
G184PAO	Ribble	G647ONH	Titteringtons	GNF16V	G M N	H115YHG	Blackpool
G185JHG	Ribble	G665PHH	Ribble	GNF17V	G M N	H116SAO	Cumberland
G185PAO	Ribble	G690ORM	Ken Routledge	GNS672N	Atherton Bus	H116YHG	Blackpool
G186JHG	Ribble	G715TTY	GMS Buses	GRM623V	Brownrigg's	H117SAO	Cumberland
G186PAO	Ribble	G767CDU	Hyndburn	GRM625V	Cumberland	H117YHG	Blackpool
G187JHG	Ribble	G812RNC	Blackpool	GRN895W	Fishwick	H118CHG	Blackpool
G187PAO	Ribble	G813RNC	Blackpool	GSB146Y	Stotts	H118SAO	Cumberland
G188JHG	Ribble	G852NUP	Wright Bros	GSB147Y	Stotts	H119CHG	Blackpool
G188PAO	Ribble	G874DSC	Vale of Manchester	GSU551	Burnley & Pendle	H119SAO	Cumberland
G189JHG	Ribble	G888TJA	City Nippy	GSU552	Burnley & Pendle	H120CHG	Blackpool
G189PAO	Ribble	G889TJA	City Nippy	GSU553	Burnley & Pendle	H121CHG	Blackpool
G190PAO	Ribble	G915KWF	Brownrigg's	GSU554	Burnley & Pendle	H122CHG	Blackpool
G191PAO	Ribble	G963REC	Mountain Goat	GTU606X	Shaw Hadwin	H129YGG	Springfield Cs

H131GVM	GMS Buses	H493BND	Shaw Hadwin	HDB122V	G M N	J125GRN	Blackpool
H132GVM	GMS Buses	H501DVM	Shearings	HDB123V	G M N	J125XHH	Cumberland
H133GVM	GMS Buses	H522FSB	Timeline	HDB125V	G M N	J126GRN	Blackpool
H134GVM	GMS Buses	H534YCX	Wall's	HFB845X	Hyndburn	J126XHH	Cumberland
H135GVM	GMS Buses	H536YCX	Wall's	HFM804N	R Bullock	J127XHH	Cumberland
H136GVM	GMS Buses	H537YCX	Wall's	HFR507E	Blackpool	J153LRN	Royal Mail PB
H137GVM	GMS Buses	H538EVM	Sim	HHH370V	Ribble	J154LRN	Royal Mail PB
H138GVM	GMS Buses	H538SEO	Shaw Hadwin	HHH372V	Ribble	J155LRN	Royal Mail PB
H139GVM	GMS Buses	H538YCX	Wall's	HHH373V	Ribble	J158OHG	Fishwick
H140AFV	Robinsons	H539SEO	Shaw Hadwin	HIL5341	Blackpool	J176MCW	Burnley & Pendle
H140GVM	GMS Buses	H564DVM	Shearings	HIL5342	Blackpool	J177MCW	Burnley & Pendle
H142SAO	Brownrigg's	H564OOK	Timeline	HIL5943	Blackpool	J198HFR	Ribble
H147CBU	City Nippy	H575DVM	Timeline	HIL7745	Finglands	J199HFR	Ribble
H149SAO	Brownrigg's	H577DVM	Timeline	HIL7746	Finglands	J200BUL	R Bullock
H156DVM	Shearings	H580DVM	Timeline	HIL7747	Finglands	J201HFR	Ribble
H157DVM	Shearings	H588DVM	Timeline	HIL7748	Finglands	J202HFR	Ribble
H158DVM	Shearings	H611CGG	Phoenix HandyBus	HIL7923	Finglands	J203HFR	Ribble
H159DVM	Shearings	H611CVM	Wall's	HIL8915	Shaw Hadwin	J204HFR	Ribble
H160DVM	Shearings	H612CGG	Phoenix HandyBus	HIL8916	Shaw Hadwin	J205HFR	Ribble
H161DVM	Shearings	H613CGG	Phoenix HandyBus	HIL8917	Shaw Hadwin	J206HFR	Ribble
H162DVM	Shearings	H617ACK	Burnley & Pendle	HIL9152	Blue Bus	J206NNC	Shearings
H163DVM	Shearings	H618ACK	Burnley & Pendle	HIL9311	Shaw Hadwin	J207HFR	Ribble
H165DVM	Shearings	H619ACK	Burnley & Pendle	HNE253V	Cumberland	J207NNC	Shearings
H166DVM	Shearings	H620ACK	Burnley & Pendle	HPF313N	Blackburn	J208HFR	Ribble
H167DVM	Shearings	H621ACK	Burnley & Pendle	HRN98N	Blackpool	J208NNC	Shearings
H168DVM	Shearings	H622ACK	Burnley & Pendle	HRN99N	Blackpool	J209HFR	Ribble
H169DVM	Shearings	H623ACK	Burnley & Pendle	HRN100N	Blackpool	J209NNC	Shearings
H174EJU	Blackburn	H687XBV	Abbott's	HRN101N	Blackpool	J210HFR	Ribble
H176ANE	Shaw Hadwin	H691FNB	City Nippy	HRN102N	Blackpool	J210NNC	Shearings
H181DVM	Shearings	H701GVM	G M N	HRN103N	Blackpool	J211NNC	Shearings
H182DVM	Shearings	H702GVM	G M N	HSC161X	Pioneer	J212NNC	Shearings
H183DVM	Shearings	H703GVM	G M N	HSC164X	Shaw Hadwin	J215NNC	Shearings
H184DVM	Shearings	H704GVM	G M N	HSC174X	Pioneer	J217NNC	Shearings
H185DVM	Shearings	H705GVM	G M N	HUI4575	Hulme Hall	J218NNC	Shearings
H186DVM	Shearings	H706GVM	G M N	HXI311	Burnley & Pendle	J219NNC	Shearings
H187DVM	Shearings	H707GVM	G M N	IAZ4775	Mayne	J220NNC	Shearings
H191DVM	Shearings	H708GVM	G M N	IAZ4776	Mayne	J221NNC	Shearings
H191WFR	Ribble	H721CNC	GMS Buses	IIL1047	GMS Buses	J223NNC	Shearings
H192DVM	Shearings	H722CNC	G M N	IIL2257	Mayne	J224NNC	Shearings
H192WFR	Ribble	H723CNC	G M N	IIL2258	Mayne	J225NNC	Shearings
H193DVM	Shearings	H724CNC	GMS Buses	IIL3198	Shaw Hadwin	J226NNC	Shearings
H193WFR	Ribble	H724VWU	Blackburn	IIL4291	Blackpool	J227NNC	Shearings
H194DVM	Shearings	H725CNC	G M N	J6GFM	R Bullock	J228NNC	Shearings
H194WFR	Ribble	H726CNC	GMS Buses	J7JFS	Fishwick	J229NNC	Shearings
H195DVM	Shearings	H726LOL	Manchester Airport	J9JFS	Fishwick	J231NNC	Shearings
H195WFR	Ribble	H727FNC	GMS Buses	J9JPT	City Nippy	J232NNC	Shearings
H196DVM	Shearings	H728FNC	GMS Buses	J14JFS	Fishwick	J233NNC	Shearings
H196WFR	Ribble	H804SFP	Phoenix HandyBus	J20JPT	City Nippy	J234NNC	Shearings
H197DVM	Shearings	H812RWJ	Holmeswood	J23GCX	Dennis's	J235NNC	Shearings
H197WFR	Ribble	H835DNE	Bluebird	J24MCW	Burnley & Pendle	J236NNC	Shearings
H198DVM	Shearings	H882JFA	Shaw Hadwin	J25MCW	Burnley & Pendle	J237NNC	Shearings
H199DVM	Shearings	H907AHS	Finglands	J26LRN	Blackpool	J238NNC	Shearings
H199ENC	Manchester Airport	H917PTG	Wright Bros	J29LBA	Mayne	J239NNC	Shearings
H201ENC	Manchester Airport	H927DRJ	Holmeswood	J73VTG	GMS Buses	J241NNC	Shearings
H210CVU	Dennis's	H929DRJ	Holmeswood	J107KCW	Preston	J242NNC	Shearings
H220TCP	Wall's	H933DBU	Dennis's	J108KCW	Preston	J243LFR	Robinsons
H236AFV	Robinsons	HCK847S	Abbott's	J109KCW	Preston	J243NNC	Shearings
H237AFV	Robinsons	HDB102V	G M N	J110KCW	Preston	J244LFR	Robinsons
H238AFV	Robinsons	HDB104V	G M N	J112KCW	Preston	J244NNC	Shearings
H239AFV	Robinsons	HDB105V	G M N	J113KCW	Preston	J245LFR	Robinsons
H241AFV	Robinsons	HDB106V	G M N	J114KCW	Preston	J245NNC	Shearings
H242AFV	Robinsons	HDB108V	G M N	J120AAO	Cumberland	J246LFR	Robinsons
H251ANE	Shaw Hadwin	HDB109V	G M N	J120AHH	Cumberland	J246NNC	Shearings
H282WHH	Brownrigg's	HDB110V	G M N	J121AAO	Cumberland	J247LFR	Robinsons
H380XHG	Darwen Minibus	HDB111V	G M N	J121AHH	Cumberland	J247NNC	Shearings
H406BVR	Timeline	HDB113V	G M N	J122AAO	Cumberland	J248NNC	Shearings
H415BVR	Timeline	HDB114V	G M N	J122AHH	Ribble	J249NNC	Shearings
H463GVM	GMS Buses	HDB115V	G M N	J123AHH	Ribble	J251NNC	Shearings
H464GVM	GMS Buses	HDB117V	G M N	J123GRN	Blackpool	J252NNC	Shearings
H465GVM	GMS Buses	HDB118V	G M N	J123XHH	Cumberland	J253NNC	Shearings
H466GVM	GMS Buses	HDB119V	G M N	J124AHH	Ribble	J254NNC	Shearings
H467GVM	GMS Buses	HDB120V	G M N	J124GRN	Blackpool	J255NNC	Shearings
H487CEC	Mountain Goat	HDB121V	G M N	J124XHH	Cumberland	J256NNC	Shearings

Reg	Operator	Reg	Operator	Reg	Operator	Reg	Operator
J257NNC	Shearings	JCK848W	Ribble	JND256V	Timeline	K471VVR	Shearings
J258NNC	Shearings	JCW517S	Abbott's	JND259V	Brownrigg's	K472VVR	Shearings
J259NNC	Shearings	JDB121N	Finglands	JND264V	Brownrigg's	K473VVR	Shearings
J261NNC	Shearings	JDK912P	South Manchester	JPU817	Cumberland	K474VVR	Shearings
J262NNC	Shearings	JDK914P	South Manchester	JWG191P	Blackburn	K475VVR	Shearings
J263KRN	Hyndburn	JDT432N	Blackburn	JWU248N	Town Bus	K476VVR	Shearings
J263NNC	Shearings	JFR2W	Ribble	K1BLU	Blue Bus	K477VVR	Shearings
J264KRN	Hyndburn	JFR3W	Ribble	K2BLU	Bluebird	K478VVR	Shearings
J264NNC	Shearings	JFR4W	Ribble	K3BLU	Bluebird	K479VVR	Shearings
J265NNC	Shearings	JFR5W	Ribble	K3JFS	Fishwick	K481VVR	Shearings
J266NNC	Shearings	JFR6W	Ribble	K5JFS	Fishwick	K482VVR	Shearings
J267NNC	Shearings	JFR7W	Ribble	K26WBV	Burnley & Pendle	K483VVR	Shearings
J268NNC	Shearings	JFR8W	Ribble	K27WBV	Burnley & Pendle	K484VVR	Shearings
J269NNC	Shearings	JFR9W	Ribble	K28XBA	Mayne	K485VVR	Shearings
J270NNC	Shearings	JFR10W	Ribble	K29XBA	Mayne	K486VVR	Shearings
J271NNC	Shearings	JFR11W	Ribble	K36OUY	Shaw Hadwin	K487VVR	Shearings
J272NNC	Shearings	JFR12W	Ribble	K75XCW	Burnley & Pendle	K488VVR	Shearings
J273NNC	Shearings	JFR13W	Ribble	K80VVR	Shearings	K489VVR	Shearings
J274NNC	Shearings	JFS978X	Vale of Manchester	K84UND	City Nippy	K490VVR	Shearings
J275NNC	Shearings	JFT413X	R Bullock	K100BLU	Blue Bus	K491VVR	Shearings
J276NNC	Shearings	JFT414X	R Bullock	K112XHG	Ribble	K492VVR	Shearings
J277NNC	Shearings	JFV294N	Hyndburn	K113XHG	Cumberland	K493VVR	Shearings
J278NNC	Shearings	JFV295N	Hyndburn	K114XHG	Cumberland	K494VVR	Shearings
J279NNC	Shearings	JFV313S	Blue Bus	K115XHG	Ribble	K495VVR	Shearings
J281NNC	Shearings	JIB3515	Shaw Hadwin	K116XHG	Ribble	K496VVR	Shearings
J282NNC	Shearings	JIL2045	Shaw Hadwin	K117XHG	Ribble	K600BUL	R Bullock
J283NNC	Shearings	JIL2047	Shaw Hadwin	K118XHG	Ribble	K610UFR	Ribble
J284NNC	Shearings	JIL5229	City Nippy	K120XHG	Ribble	K611UFR	Ribble
J285NNC	Shearings	JIL5279	GMS Buses	K121XHG	Cumberland	K612UFR	Ribble
J286NNC	Shearings	JIL7606	GMS Buses	K123AJA	City Nippy	K613UFR	Ribble
J287NNC	Shearings	JIL7607	GMS Buses	K123TCP	Stuart's	K614UFR	Ribble
J288NNC	Shearings	JIL7608	GMS Buses	K124TCP	Stuart's	K615EEO	Shaw Hadwin
J289NNC	Shearings	JIL7609	GMS Buses	K124XHG	Ribble	K615UFR	Ribble
J290NNC	Shearings	JIL7610	GMS Buses	K125TCP	Manchester Airport	K616UFR	Ribble
J291NNC	Shearings	JIL8202	R Bullock	K126TCP	Manchester Airport	K617SBV	Abbott's
J292NNC	Shearings	JIL8204	R Bullock	K127TCP	Manchester Airport	K617UFR	Ribble
J293NNC	Shearings	JIL8205	R Bullock	K127UFV	Blackpool	K618UFR	Ribble
J294NNC	Shearings	JIL8206	R Bullock	K128DAO	Cumberland	K619UFR	Ribble
J295NNC	Shearings	JIL8207	R Bullock	K128UFV	Blackpool	K620UFR	Ribble
J296NNC	Shearings	JIL8208	R Bullock	K129DAO	Cumberland	K621UFR	Ribble
J297NNC	Shearings	JIL8209	R Bullock	K129UFV	Blackpool	K622UFR	Cumberland
J298NNC	Shearings	JIL8210	R Bullock	K130DAO	Cumberland	K623UFR	Cumberland
J299NNC	Shearings	JIL8211	R Bullock	K130UFV	Blackpool	K624UFR	Ribble
J400BUL	R Bullock	JIL8212	R Bullock	K131DAO	Cumberland	K625UFR	Ribble
J418JBV	Blackburn	JIL8213	R Bullock	K132DAO	Cumberland	K626UFR	Cumberland
J419JBV	Blackburn	JIL8214	R Bullock	K133DAO	Cumberland	K627UFR	Ribble
J420JBV	Blackburn	JIL8215	R Bullock	K134DAO	Cumberland	K628UFR	Ribble
J421JBV	Blackburn	JIL8216	R Bullock	K135DAO	Cumberland	K699ERM	Cumberland
J422JBV	Blackburn	JIL8217	R Bullock	K286ESF	Dennis's	K700BUL	R Bullock
J461OVU	G M N	JIL8303	R Bullock	K287ESF	Dennis's	K700DAO	Cumberland
J603HMF	G M N	JIL8374	GMS Buses	K289ESF	Dennis's	K701DAO	Cumberland
J604HMF	G M N	JJG907P	Blackburn	K290ESF	Dennis's	K702DAO	Cumberland
J606HMF	G M N	JKW281W	Stotts	K449YCW	Ribble	K703DAO	Cumberland
J607HMF	G M N	JKW286W	Hyndburn	K450YCW	Ribble	K704ERM	Cumberland
J608HMF	G M N	JKW288W	Rossendale	K451VVR	Shearings	K705DAO	Cumberland
J608KGB	Phoenix HandyBus	JKW290W	Rossendale	K452VVR	Shearings	K706DAO	Cumberland
J609HMF	G M N	JKW291W	Rossendale	K453VVR	Shearings	K707DAO	Cumberland
J614HMF	G M N	JKW292W	Stotts	K454VVR	Shearings	K708DAO	Cumberland
J619HMF	G M N	JKW293W	Rossendale	K455VVR	Shearings	K709DAO	Cumberland
J685PJA	City Nippy	JKW294W	Rossendale	K456VVR	Shearings	K710DAO	Cumberland
J686PJA	City Nippy	JKW296W	Rossendale	K457VVR	Shearings	K711DAO	Cumberland
J709ONF	G M N	JKW297W	Rossendale	K458VVR	Shearings	K712DAO	Cumberland
J710CWT	Holmeswood	JKW298W	Stotts	K459VVR	Shearings	K713DAO	Cumberland
J710ONF	G M N	JKW304W	Stotts	K460VVR	Shearings	K714DAO	Cumberland
J712BAO	Ken Routledge	JKW310W	Stuart's	K461VVR	Shearings	K715DAO	Cumberland
J767BHH	Sim	JKW315W	Stotts	K462VVR	Shearings	K716DAO	Cumberland
J886PNC	Bluebird	JKW316W	Stuart's	K463VVR	Shearings	K717DAO	Cumberland
J976PRW	Preston	JKW321W	Stotts	K464VVR	Shearings	K718DAO	Cumberland
JAO400V	Wright Bros	JKW322W	Stuart's	K465VVR	Shearings	K719DAO	Cumberland
JBN540N	Wall's	JKW332W	Stotts	K466VVR	Shearings	K720DAO	Cumberland
JBN948N	Dennis's	JKW335W	Stuart's	K467VVR	Shearings	K721DAO	Cumberland
JCK846W	Ribble	JMB331T	Springfield Cs	K468VVR	Shearings	K722DAO	Cumberland
JCK847W	Ribble	JNB151N	Finglands	K469VVR	Shearings	K723DAO	Cumberland

Reg	Operator	Reg	Operator	Reg	Operator	Reg	Operator
K724DAO	Cumberland	K878GHH	Cumberland	L107SDY	Ribble	L448FFR	Hyndburn
K725DAO	Cumberland	K881UDB	G M N	L114DNA	Mayne	L502FVU	City Nippy
K726DAO	Cumberland	K883UDB	G M N	L119DRN	Ribble	L510JND	Dennis's
K727DAO	Cumberland	K977JWW	Manchester Airport	L122DRN	Ribble	L543YUS	GMS Buses
K728DAO	Cumberland	K978JWW	Manchester Airport	L123DRN	Cumberland	L561FND	Shearings
K729DAO	Cumberland	KBC4V	Blackburn	L125DRN	Ribble	L562FND	Shearings
K730DAO	Cumberland	KBD21V	Robinson's	L125NAO	Cumberland	L563FND	Shearings
K731DAO	Cumberland	KBU912P	Finglands	L126DRN	Cumberland	L564FND	Shearings
K732DAO	Cumberland	KBZ5749	Shaw Hadwin	L126NAO	Cumberland	L565FND	Shearings
K733DAO	Cumberland	KDB126V	G M N	L127DRN	Ribble	L566FND	Shearings
K734DAO	Cumberland	KDB127V	G M N	L127NAO	Cumberland	L567FND	Shearings
K735DAO	Cumberland	KDB128V	G M N	L128DRN	Ribble	L568FND	Shearings
K736DAO	Cumberland	KDB129V	G M N	L138BFV	Ribble	L569FND	Shearings
K737DAO	Cumberland	KDB131V	G M N	L139BFV	Ribble	L570FND	Shearings
K738DAO	Cumberland	KDB132V	G M N	L140BFV	Ribble	L629BFV	Ribble
K739DAO	Cumberland	KDB133V	G M N	L141BFV	Ribble	L630BFV	Ribble
K740DAO	Cumberland	KDB136V	G M N	L141JVR	Timeline	L631BFV	Ribble
K741DAO	Cumberland	KDB139V	G M N	L142BFV	Ribble	L632BFV	Ribble
K742DAO	Cumberland	KDB140V	G M N	L142JVR	Timeline	L633BFV	Ribble
K743DAO	Cumberland	KDB301V	GMS Buses	L143BFV	Ribble	L634BFV	Ribble
K744DAO	Cumberland	KDB302V	GMS Buses	L144BFV	Ribble	L635BFV	Ribble
K745DAO	Cumberland	KDB303V	G M N	L145BFV	Ribble	L636BFV	Ribble
K746DAO	Cumberland	KDB686P	Finglands	L146BFV	Ribble	L660HKS	Ribble
K748DAO	Cumberland	KDW707P	South Manchester	L148BFV	Ribble	L661MSF	Ribble
K749DAO	Cumberland	KGE74T	Finglands	L149BFV	Ribble	L662MSF	Ribble
K750DAO	Cumberland	KGF306T	Brownrigg's	L150BFV	Ribble	L663MSF	Ribble
K751DAO	Cumberland	KGS493Y	GMS Buses	L151BFV	Ribble	L664MSF	Ribble
K752DAO	Cumberland	KHG194T	Hyndburn	L151DRJ	Timeline	L665MSF	Ribble
K753DAO	Cumberland	KHH375W	Ribble	L152BFV	Ribble	L667MSF	Ribble
K754DAO	Cumberland	KHH377W	Ribble	L152DRJ	Timeline	L668MSF	Ribble
K755DAO	Cumberland	KHH378W	Ribble	L153BFV	Ribble	L669MSF	Ribble
K756DAO	Cumberland	KIB7257	Hyndburn	L153DRJ	Timeline	L680GNA	Dennis's
K757DAO	Cumberland	KJA299G	R Bullock	L154BFV	Ribble	L681GNA	Dennis's
K758DAO	Cumberland	KJF3V	Blackburn	L154DRJ	Timeline	L682GNA	Dennis's
K759DAO	Cumberland	KON332P	Wall's	L155BFV	Ribble	L683GNA	Dennis's
K760DAO	Cumberland	KON336P	Town Bus	L156BFV	Ribble	L720JFA	Royal Mail PB
K761DAO	Cumberland	KRM431W	Cumberland	L157BFV	Ribble	L743MAO	Ken Routledge
K762DAO	Cumberland	KRM432W	Cumberland	L158BFV	Ribble	L749NEO	Holmeswood
K763DAO	Cumberland	KRM433W	Cumberland	L159CCW	Ribble	L800BUL	R Bullock
K764DAO	Cumberland	KRM434W	Cumberland	L160CCW	Ribble	L803FBA	Bu-Val
K765DAO	Cumberland	KRM435W	Cumberland	L161CCW	Ribble	L804FBA	Bu-Val
K766DAO	Cumberland	KRM436W	Cumberland	L178KHG	Burnley & Pendle	L813KCW	Rossendale
K767DAO	Cumberland	KRM437W	Cumberland	L179KHG	Burnley & Pendle	L814KCW	Rossendale
K768DAO	Cumberland	KRN103T	Cumberland	L196DNW	City Nippy	L911ECW	Rossendale
K769DAO	Cumberland	KRN104T	Brownrigg's	L237CCW	Ribble	L912ECW	Rossendale
K770DAO	Cumberland	KRN105T	Cumberland	L239CCW	Ribble	LAO627W	Springfield Cs
K771DAO	Cumberland	KRN113T	Cumberland	L240CCW	Ribble	LBU607V	Bluebird
K772DAO	Cumberland	KRN119T	Cumberland	L242CCK	Ribble	LBZ4071	Blue Bus
K773DAO	Cumberland	KSA189P	Blue Bus	L248JBV	Robinsons	LCB652P	Border
K774DAO	Cumberland	KSJ940P	Border	L249JBV	Robinsons	LCW411W	Holmeswood
K775DAO	Cumberland	KSU851P	Blue Bus	L250JBV	Robinsons	LDZ2951	Blue Bus
K776DAO	Cumberland	KSU857P	Border	L251CCK	Ribble	LFJ858W	Ribble
K777DAO	Cumberland	KUC969P	Mayne	L252CCK	Ribble	LFJ859W	Ribble
K778DAO	Cumberland	KUX774	Pioneer	L253CCK	Ribble	LFJ861W	Ribble
K779DAO	Cumberland	KVO142W	Mayne	L255CCK	Ribble	LFJ866W	Ribble
K780DAO	Cumberland	KVO144W	Mayne	L256CCK	Ribble	LFJ882W	Ribble
K781DAO	Cumberland	KVO145W	Mayne	L270LHH	Cumberland	LFJ883W	Ribble
K783DAO	Cumberland	L1JFS	Fishwick	L271LHH	Cumberland	LFJ884W	Ribble
K784DAO	Cumberland	L4BLU	Bluebird	L272LHH	Cumberland	LFJ885W	Ribble
K785DAO	Cumberland	L5HWD	Holmeswood	L273LHH	Cumberland	LFR127T	Blackburn
K786DAO	Cumberland	L8HWD	Holmeswood	L274LHH	Cumberland	LFR128T	Blackburn
K787DAO	Cumberland	L10BUL	R Bullock	L275JAO	Cumberland	LFR129T	Blackburn
K788DAO	Cumberland	L18HWD	Holmeswood	L276JAO	Cumberland	LFR130T	Blackburn
K815TJU	Burnley & Pendle	L20BUL	R Bullock	L277JAO	Ribble	LFR856X	Ribble
K831FEE	Ken Routledge	L26FNE	Mayne	L278JAO	Ribble	LFR857X	Ribble
K865CEH	Royal Mail PB	L27FNE	Mayne	L279JAO	Ribble	LFR858X	Ribble
K871GHH	Cumberland	L76ATA	Darwen Minibus	L281JAO	Ribble	LFR859X	Ribble
K872GHH	Cumberland	L101SDY	Ribble	L282JAO	Cumberland	LFR866X	Ribble
K873GHH	Cumberland	L102SDY	Ribble	L283JAO	Ribble	LFR868X	Ribble
K874GHH	Cumberland	L103SDY	Ribble	L435KHH	Ken Routledge	LFR870X	Ribble
K875GHH	Cumberland	L104SDY	Ribble	L445FFR	Hyndburn	LFR871X	Ribble
K876GHH	Cumberland	L105SDY	Ribble	L446FFR	Hyndburn	LFR877X	Ribble
K877GHH	Cumberland	L106SDY	Ribble	L447FFR	Hyndburn	LFV205X	Ribble

Reg	Operator	Reg	Operator	Reg	Operator	Reg	Operator
LFV206X	Ribble	M156LNC	Timeline	M406TCK	Preston	M601ORJ	Shearings
LHE254W	Blackburn	M157LNC	Timeline	M407TCK	Preston	M602ORJ	Shearings
LHL246P	Blue Bus	M158LNC	Timeline	M408TCK	Preston	M603ORJ	Shearings
LIB1180	Rossendale	M159LNC	Timeline	M409TCK	Preston	M604ORJ	Shearings
LIB1181	Rossendale	M160LNC	Timeline	M410RND	G M N	M605ORJ	Shearings
LIB1183	Rossendale	M161LNC	Timeline	M410TCK	Preston	M606ORJ	Shearings
LIB1184	Rossendale	M162LNC	Timeline	M411RND	G M N	M607ORJ	Shearings
LIB5440	Mayne	M163LNC	Timeline	M412RND	G M N	M608ORJ	Shearings
LIB6437	Mayne	M164LNC	Timeline	M413RND	G M N	M608SBA	G M N
LIB6438	Mayne	M164SCK	Ribble	M414RND	G M N	M609ORJ	Shearings
LIB6439	Mayne	M165LNC	Timeline	M415RND	G M N	M609SBA	G M N
LIJ749	Blackburn	M165SCK	Ribble	M415RRN	Finglands	M610ORJ	Shearings
LIL2830	City Nippy	M166LNC	Timeline	M416RND	G M N	M610SBA	G M N
LIL2831	City Nippy	M167LNC	Timeline	M416RRN	Finglands	M611ORJ	Shearings
LIL3317	GMS Buses	M201LNC	Timeline	M417RRN	Finglands	M611SBA	G M N
LIL4612	GMS Buses	M202LNC	Timeline	M418RRN	Finglands	M612ORJ	Shearings
LIW1323	Mayne	M203LNC	Timeline	M419RRN	Finglands	M612SBA	G M N
LIW4289	Rossendale	M204LNC	Timeline	M420RRN	Finglands	M613ORJ	Shearings
LJA473P	Wall's	M205LNC	Timeline	M421RRN	Finglands	M613SBA	G M N
LJA480P	Wall's	M206LNC	Timeline	M422RRN	Finglands	M614ORJ	Shearings
LJA484P	Wall's	M208SCK	Shaw Hadwin	M423RRN	Finglands	M614SBA	G M N
LJA611P	Finglands	M209SCK	Shaw Hadwin	M424RRN	Finglands	M615ORJ	Shearings
LJC800	Cumberland	M210NDB	Mayne	M425RRN	Finglands	M615SBA	G M N
LJY145	Cumberland	M211NDB	Mayne	M426RRN	Finglands	M616ORJ	Shearings
LNA367	Wall's	M230TBV	Ribble	M427RRN	Finglands	M616SBA	G M N
LRN552N	Blackburn	M231TBV	Ribble	M451VCW	Ribble	M617ORJ	Shearings
LSU939	Shaw Hadwin	M232TBV	Ribble	M452VCW	Ribble	M617SBA	G M N
LTE487P	G M N	M233TBV	Ribble	M453VCW	Ribble	M618ORJ	Shearings
LTE490P	G M N	M234TBV	Ribble	M454VCW	Ribble	M618SBA	G M N
LTE491P	G M N	M235TBV	Ribble	M454VHE	GMS Buses	M619ORJ	Shearings
LTE495P	G M N	M236TBV	Ribble	M455VCW	Ribble	M620ORJ	Shearings
LTF346	Shaw Hadwin	M248NNF	G M N	M455VHE	GMS Buses	M621ORJ	Shearings
LTG271X	Wright Bros	M249NNF	G M N	M456VCW	Ribble	M622ORJ	Shearings
LTK91R	Finglands	M251NVM	G M N	M456VHE	GMS Buses	M623ORJ	Shearings
LTK93R	Finglands	M252NVM	G M N	M457VCW	Ribble	M624ORJ	Shearings
LTK94R	Finglands	M253NVM	G M N	M457VHE	GMS Buses	M625ORJ	Shearings
LTK96R	Finglands	M254NVM	G M N	M458VCW	Ribble	M626ORJ	Shearings
LUA273V	Cumberland	M255NVM	G M N	M458VHE	GMS Buses	M627ORJ	Shearings
LUA275V	Cumberland	M256NVM	G M N	M459VCW	Ribble	M627WBV	Blackburn
LUA714V	Fishwick	M257NVM	G M N	M459VHE	GMS Buses	M628ORJ	Shearings
M2BLU	Blue Bus	M258NVM	G M N	M460VCW	Ribble	M628WBV	Blackburn
M2JPT	City Nippy	M259NVM	G M N	M460VHE	GMS Buses	M629ORJ	Shearings
M4HWD	Holmeswood	M260NVM	G M N	M461VCW	Ribble	M629WBV	Blackburn
M5BLU	Bluebird	M261SVU	G M N	M461VHE	GMS Buses	M630ORJ	Shearings
M5HWD	Holmeswood	M262SVU	G M N	M462VCW	Ribble	M630WBV	Blackburn
M6BLU	Bluebird	M263SVU	G M N	M462VHE	GMS Buses	M631MVU	Shearings
M6HWD	Holmeswood	M264SVU	G M N	M463VCW	Ribble	M631WFR	Blackburn
M6MGH	Mountain Goat	M265SVU	G M N	M501PNA	G M N	M632MVU	Shearings
M7JPT	City Nippy	M266SVU	G M N	M502PNA	G M N	M632WFR	Blackburn
M8BLU	Bluebird	M267SVU	G M N	M503PNA	G M N	M633MVU	Shearings
M8JPT	City Nippy	M268SVU	G M N	M504PNA	G M N	M634FJF	Glossopdale
M8MGH	Mountain Goat	M269SVU	G M N	M505PNA	G M N	M634MVU	Shearings
M9BLU	Bluebird	M270SVU	G M N	M506PNA	G M N	M635FJF	Glossopdale
M10BLU	Bluebird	M307KRY	Abbott's	M507PNA	G M N	M635MVU	Shearings
M10MGH	Mountain Goat	M337KRY	Abbott's	M508PNA	G M N	M636FJF	Glossopdale
M12BLU	Bluebird	M338EEC	Shaw Hadwin	M509PNA	G M N	M636MVU	Shearings
M15WAL	Wall's	M339EEC	Shaw Hadwin	M510PNA	G M N	M637MVU	Shearings
M16WAL	Wall's	M359OBU	Manchester Airport	M511PNA	G M N	M638MVU	Shearings
M17WAL	Wall's	M360OBU	Manchester Airport	M512PNA	G M N	M639MVU	Shearings
M18WAL	Wall's	M361OBU	Manchester Airport	M513PNA	G M N	M640MVU	Shearings
M19WAL	Wall's	M362OBU	Manchester Airport	M514PNA	G M N	M641MVU	Shearings
M20WAL	Wall's	M364SNB	Finglands	M515PNA	G M N	M642MVU	Shearings
M42ONF	Mayne	M374SCK	Blackpool	M516PNA	G M N	M643MVU	Shearings
M85DEW	Glossopdale	M375SCK	Blackpool	M517PNA	G M N	M644MVU	Shearings
M86DEW	Glossopdale	M376SCK	Blackpool	M518PNA	G M N	M645MVU	Shearings
M101RRJ	G M N	M377SCK	Blackpool	M519PNA	G M N	M646MVU	Shearings
M102RRJ	G M N	M378SCK	Blackpool	M520PNA	G M N	M646RCP	Blue Bus
M103RRJ	G M N	M379SCK	Blackpool	M529RHG	Rossendale	M647MVU	Shearings
M104RRJ	G M N	M401TCK	Preston	M530RHG	Rossendale	M647RCP	Blue Bus
M105RRJ	G M N	M402TCK	Preston	M533RCW	Blackburn	M648MVU	Shearings
M106RRJ	G M N	M403TCK	Preston	M534RCW	Blackburn	M649MVU	Shearings
M107RRJ	G M N	M404TCK	Preston	M535RCW	Blackburn	M650MVU	Shearings
M113RNK	Mayne	M405TCK	Preston	M536RCW	Blackburn	M651MVU	Shearings

M652MVU	Shearings	M903OVR	Timeline	MNC524W	G M N	MRJ407W	G M N
M653MVU	Shearings	M904OVR	Timeline	MNC525W	GMS Buses	MRJ408W	G M N
M654MVU	Shearings	M905OVR	Timeline	MNC526W	G M N	MRJ409W	GMS Buses
M655MVU	Shearings	M906OVR	Timeline	MNC527W	GMS Buses	MRJ410W	G M N
M656MVU	Shearings	M907OVR	Timeline	MNC528W	GMS Buses	MRJ411W	G M N
M657MVU	Shearings	M908OVR	Timeline	MNC529W	GMS Buses	MSL155X	Pioneer
M658MVU	Shearings	M909OVR	Timeline	MNC530W	G M N	MSU611Y	Abbott's
M659MVU	Shearings	M910OVR	Timeline	MNC531W	G M N	MTE22R	G M N
M660MVU	Shearings	M911OVR	Timeline	MNC533W	G M N	MTE23R	G M N
M661MVU	Shearings	M912OVR	Timeline	MNC534W	G M N	MTE31R	G M N
M662MVU	Shearings	M913OVR	Timeline	MNC535W	G M N	N3BLU	Blue Bus
M663MVU	Shearings	M914OVR	Timeline	MNC536W	G M N	N4BLU	Blue Bus
M664MVU	Shearings	M915OVR	Timeline	MNC537W	G M N	N5BLU	Blue Bus
M664WCK	Fishwick	M916OVR	Timeline	MNC538W	G M N	N7BLU	Bluebird
M665MVU	Shearings	M917OVR	Timeline	MNC539W	GMS Buses	N10WAL	Wall's
M665WCK	Fishwick	M924TYG	Blackpool	MNC540W	G M N	N12WAL	Wall's
M667MVU	Shearings	M949RHH	Titteringtons	MNC541W	G M N	N13BLU	Bluebird
M668MVU	Shearings	M950RHH	Titteringtons	MNC542W	G M N	N13WAL	Wall's
M669MVU	Shearings	M958VWY	Manchester Airport	MNC543W	GMS Buses	N14BLU	Bluebird
M670MVU	Shearings	MFR420T	Springfield Cs	MNC544W	G M N	N14WAL	Wall's
M671MVU	Shearings	MFV30T	Burnley & Pendle	MNC545W	G M N	N15WAL	Wall's
M672MVU	Shearings	MFV31T	Burnley & Pendle	MNC546W	G M N	N16WAL	Wall's
M673MVU	Shearings	MFV32T	Burnley & Pendle	MNC547W	G M N	N17BLU	Bluebird
M674MVU	Shearings	MFV33T	Burnley & Pendle	MNC548W	GMS Buses	N22BLU	Bluebird
M675MVU	Shearings	MFV34T	Burnley & Pendle	MNC549W	G M N	N67YVR	Mayne
M676MVU	Shearings	MFV35T	Burnley & Pendle	MNC550W	G M N	N68YVR	Mayne
M677MVU	Shearings	MFV36T	Burnley & Pendle	MRJ31W	G M N	N71YNF	G M N
M678MVU	Shearings	MFV37T	Burnley & Pendle	MRJ32W	G M N	N128VAO	Cumberland
M679MVU	Shearings	MIB920	Blackburn	MRJ33W	G M N	N129VAO	Cumberland
M680MVU	Shearings	MIW4840	Stuart's	MRJ34W	G M N	N130VAO	Cumberland
M681MVU	Shearings	MIW4841	Stuart's	MRJ35W	G M N	N131VAO	Cumberland
M682MVU	Shearings	MIW8186	Blackpool	MRJ36W	GMS Buses	N132VAO	Cumberland
M683MVU	Shearings	MIW8187	Blackpool	MRJ37W	GMS Buses	N132XND	Stuart's
M684MVU	Shearings	MIW8188	Blackpool	MRJ38W	GMS Buses	N133XND	Stuart's
M685MVU	Shearings	MIW9048	Hyndburn	MRJ39W	G M N	N134XND	Stuart's
M686MVU	Shearings	MJI5763	Mayne	MRJ40W	GMS Buses	N160GRN	Shaw Hadwin
M687MVU	Shearings	MJI5764	Mayne	MRJ41W	GMS Buses	N168WNF	Timeline
M688MVU	Shearings	MJI5765	Mayne	MRJ42W	GMS Buses	N169WNF	Timeline
M728MBU	Dennis's	MJI5766	Mayne	MRJ43W	GMS Buses	N170WNF	Timeline
M729MBU	Dennis's	MJI7846	Blackpool	MRJ44W	GMS Buses	N171WNF	Timeline
M730MBU	Dennis's	MNC486W	G M N	MRJ45W	GMS Buses	N172WNF	Timeline
M741PRS	GMS Buses	MNC489W	G M N	MRJ46W	GMS Buses	N173WNF	Timeline
M742PRS	GMS Buses	MNC490W	G M N	MRJ47W	GMS Buses	N174WNF	Timeline
M743PRS	GMS Buses	MNC491W	G M N	MRJ48W	GMS Buses	N175WNF	Timeline
M744PRS	GMS Buses	MNC492W	G M N	MRJ49W	GMS Buses	N176WNF	Timeline
M745PRS	GMS Buses	MNC493W	G M N	MRJ50W	G M N	N177WNF	Timeline
M746PRS	GMS Buses	MNC494W	GMS Buses	MRJ51W	GMS Buses	N201UHH	Cumberland
M748PRS	GMS Buses	MNC495W	GMS Buses	MRJ52W	GMS Buses	N202UHH	Cumberland
M749PRS	GMS Buses	MNC496W	GMS Buses	MRJ53W	GMS Buses	N203UHH	Cumberland
M750PRS	GMS Buses	MNC497W	GMS Buses	MRJ54W	GMS Buses	N204UHH	Cumberland
M781NBA	R Bullock	MNC498W	GMS Buses	MRJ55W	GMS Buses	N205UHH	Cumberland
M782NBA	R Bullock	MNC499W	GMS Buses	MRJ56W	G M N	N206UHH	Cumberland
M782PRS	Ribble	MNC504W	GMS Buses	MRJ57W	G M N	N207UHH	Cumberland
M783NBA	R Bullock	MNC505W	G M N	MRJ58W	G M N	N207WBA	Timeline
M783PRS	Ribble	MNC506W	G M N	MRJ59W	G M N	N208UHH	Cumberland
M784NBA	R Bullock	MNC507W	GMS Buses	MRJ60W	G M N	N208WBA	Timeline
M785NBA	R Bullock	MNC508W	G M N	MRJ61W	G M N	N209UHH	Cumberland
M785PAO	Robinson's	MNC509W	GMS Buses	MRJ62W	G M N	N209WBA	Timeline
M788NBA	R Bullock	MNC510W	G M N	MRJ63W	G M N	N210UHH	Cumberland
M789NBA	R Bullock	MNC511W	G M N	MRJ64W	G M N	N210WBA	Timeline
M790NBA	R Bullock	MNC512W	GMS Buses	MRJ66W	GMS Buses	N211UHH	Cumberland
M792RHH	Ken Routledge	MNC513W	G M N	MRJ67W	GMS Buses	N211WBA	Timeline
M794NBA	Ribble	MNC514W	GMS Buses	MRJ68W	G M N	N212UHH	Cumberland
M795PRS	Ribble	MNC515W	G M N	MRJ69W	G M N	N212WBA	Timeline
M796PRS	Ribble	MNC516W	G M N	MRJ70W	G M N	N213UHH	Cumberland
M797PRS	Ribble	MNC517W	GMS Buses	MRJ71W	GMS Buses	N214UHH	Cumberland
M798PRS	Ribble	MNC518W	G M N	MRJ275W	Cumberland	N215UHH	Cumberland
M799PRS	Ribble	MNC519W	GMS Buses	MRJ401W	G M N	N257DUR	Dennis's
M832HVC	Finglands	MNC520W	G M N	MRJ402W	GMS Buses	N258DUR	Dennis's
M846HDF	GMS Buses	MNC521W	GMS Buses	MRJ403W	G M N	N259DUR	Dennis's
M847PRS	GMS Buses	MNC522W	G M N	MRJ404W	GMS Buses	N298VRM	Sim
M901OVR	Timeline	MNC523W	G M N	MRJ405W	G M N	N300EST	Rossendale
M902OVR	Timeline	MNC523W	GMS Buses	MRJ406W	GMS Buses	N301WNF	Timeline

The latest deliveries carry the N-prefix and while these are currently allocated on a yearly basis commencing in August, there is debate as to whether the system will continue. One of the latest arrivals in the region is Timeline 302, N302WNF seen arriving at Harwood having passed through Affetside. *Bill Potter*

N302WNF	Timeline	N425GBV	Preston	N544WVR	G M N	N711UVR	Shearings
N303WNF	Timeline	N425WVR	GMS Buses	N545WVR	G M N	N712UVR	Shearings
N304WNF	Timeline	N426GBV	Preston	N546WVR	G M N	N713UVR	Shearings
N305WNF	Timeline	N426WVR	GMS Buses	N547WVR	G M N	N714UVR	Shearings
N306WNF	Timeline	N427GBV	Preston	N548WVR	G M N	N715UVR	Shearings
N320YNC	Dennis's	N427WVR	GMS Buses	N549WVR	G M N	N716UVR	Shearings
N321YNC	Dennis's	N428GBV	Preston	N550WVR	G M N	N717UVR	Shearings
N322YNC	Dennis's	N428WVR	GMS Buses	N551WVR	G M N	N718UVR	Shearings
N401WVR	GMS Buses	N429GBV	Preston	N552WVR	G M N	N719UVR	Shearings
N402WVR	GMS Buses	N429WVR	GMS Buses	N553WVR	G M N	N720UVR	Shearings
N403WVR	GMS Buses	N430GBV	Preston	N554WVR	G M N	N721UVR	Shearings
N404WVR	GMS Buses	N430WVR	GMS Buses	N585GRN	Blackpool	N722UVR	Shearings
N405WVR	GMS Buses	N431GBV	Preston	N586GRN	Blackpool	N723UVR	Shearings
N406WVR	GMS Buses	N47ANE	Finglands	N587GRN	Blackpool	N724UVR	Shearings
N407WVR	GMS Buses	N521WVR	G M N	N588GRN	Blackpool	N725UVR	Shearings
N408WVR	GMS Buses	N522WVR	G M N	N589GRN	Blackpool	N726UVR	Shearings
N409WVR	GMS Buses	N523WVR	G M N	N590GRN	Blackpool	N727UVR	Shearings
N410WVR	GMS Buses	N524WVR	G M N	N591GRN	Blackpool	N728UVR	Shearings
N411WVR	GMS Buses	N525WVR	G M N	N592GRN	Blackpool	N729UVR	Shearings
N412WVR	GMS Buses	N526WVR	G M N	N599XRJ	Manchester Airport	N730UVR	Shearings
N413WVR	GMS Buses	N527WVR	G M N	N601XRJ	Manchester Airport	N731UVR	Shearings
N414WVR	GMS Buses	N528WVR	G M N	N602XRJ	Manchester Airport	N732UVR	Shearings
N415WVR	GMS Buses	N529WVR	G M N	N620XBU	R Bullock	N733UVR	Shearings
N416WVR	GMS Buses	N530WVR	G M N	N630XBU	R Bullock	N734UVR	Shearings
N417WVR	GMS Buses	N531WVR	G M N	N631XBU	R Bullock	N735UVR	Shearings
N418WVR	GMS Buses	N532WVR	G M N	N632XBU	R Bullock	N740VBA	Finglands
N419WVR	GMS Buses	N533WVR	G M N	N633XBU	R Bullock	N741VBA	Finglands
N420GBV	Preston	N534WVR	G M N	N701UVR	Shearings	N742VBA	Finglands
N420WVR	GMS Buses	N535WVR	G M N	N702UVR	Shearings	N743VBA	Finglands
N421GBV	Preston	N536WVR	G M N	N703UVR	Shearings	N744ANE	Finglands
N421WVR	GMS Buses	N537WVR	G M N	N704UVR	Shearings	N745ANE	Finglands
N422GBV	Preston	N538WVR	G M N	N705UVR	Shearings	N746ANE	Finglands
N422WVR	GMS Buses	N539WVR	G M N	N706UVR	Shearings	N746YVR	Glossopdale
N423GBV	Preston	N540WVR	G M N	N707UVR	Shearings	N748ANE	Finglands
N423WVR	GMS Buses	N541WVR	G M N	N708UVR	Shearings	N748YVR	Glossopdale
N424GBV	Preston	N542WVR	G M N	N709UVR	Shearings	N781PEC	Shaw Hadwin
N424WVR	GMS Buses	N543WVR	G M N	N710UVR	Shearings	N789NRM	Cumberland

Reg	Operator	Reg	Operator	Reg	Operator	Reg	Operator
N790NRM	Cumberland	OCW15X	Blackburn	ORJ84W	G M N	OTK802	GMS Buses
N796XRA	B & D Coaches	OED201	Mayne	ORJ85W	G M N	OVR409W	Shaw Hadwin
N962WJA	Manchester Airport	OEH930W	Wright Bros	ORJ86W	G M N	OWO234Y	Blue Bus
N963WJA	Manchester Airport	OEM788S	Border	ORJ87W	G M N	OXK373	GMS Buses
N964WJA	Manchester Airport	OEX799W	Blue Bus	ORJ88W	G M N	OZ4688	Titteringtons
NAO64W	Apex Travel	OFJ870	Borderbus	ORJ89W	G M N	PBV637P	Abbott's
NCW747T	Abbott's	OFV14X	Ribble	ORJ90W	G M N	PCB24	Blackburn
NFN62M	Dennis's	OFV15X	Ribble	ORJ91W	GMS Buses	PCK335	Cumberland
NFR487M	Abbott's	OFV16X	Ribble	ORJ92W	GMS Buses	PCW115P	Blackburn
NFR497M	Abbott's	OFV17X	Ribble	ORJ93W	GMS Buses	PCW680P	Mayne
NFR558T	Fishwick	OFV18X	Ribble	ORJ94W	GMS Buses	PEC345V	Hulme Hall
NFR559T	Fishwick	OFV19X	Ribble	ORJ95W	GMS Buses	PFC514W	Hulme Hall
NFR560T	Fishwick	OFV20X	Ribble	ORJ96W	G M N	PFC515W	Hulme Hall
NFR747T	Hyndburn	OFV21X	Ribble	ORJ97W	G M N	PFS561M	Timeline
NFR748T	Hyndburn	OFV22X	Ribble	ORJ98W	GMS Buses	PHF559T	South Manchester
NHH358W	Manchester Airport	OFV23X	Ribble	ORJ99W	G M N	PHH24W	Taylors Cs
NHH359W	Manchester Airport	OFV467G	Abbott's	ORJ100W	GMS Buses	PJI5632	Blackpool
NHH380W	Ribble	OFV620X	Fishwick	ORJ351W	G M N	PJI6069	Pioneer
NIB3261	Mayne	OFV621X	Fishwick	ORJ352W	GMS Buses	PJI9170	Rossendale
NIB4162	Mayne	OGE9Y	Rossendale	ORJ353W	G M N	PJI9171	Rossendale
NIB7625	Mayne	OHG33T	Blackpool	ORJ354W	G M N	PJI9172	Border
NIW1673	GMS Buses	OHG34T	Blackpool	ORJ355W	G M N	PJI9173	Border
NIW1676	GMS Buses	OIB1285	Bluebird	ORJ356W	G M N	PJI9174	Border
NIW2399	GMS Buses	OIB1287	Rossendale	ORJ357W	G M N	PJI9175	Rossendale
NIW6492	Blackpool	OIB3604	Rossendale	ORJ358W	G M N	PJI9176	Rossendale
NIW6514	Rossendale	OIB3608	Rossendale	ORJ359W	G M N	PJI9177	Rossendale
NIW6517	Rossendale	OIB5403	Rossendale	ORJ360W	G M N	PJI9178	Rossendale
NIW6518	Rossendale	OIB6205	Rossendale	ORJ361W	G M N	PJI9179	Rossendale
NIW6519	Rossendale	OIB6207	Rossendale	ORJ362W	GMS Buses	PJT267R	Blackburn
NJA568W	GMS Buses	OIB8606	Timeline	ORJ363W	G M N	PKA724S	South Manchester
NJI5504	Blackpool	OIB9379	Blue Bus	ORJ364W	G M N	PKA725S	Border
NJI5505	Blackpool	OIJ201	Burnley & Pendle	ORJ365W	GMS Buses	PNW606W	G M N
NLG926T	Border	OIW1317	GMS Buses	ORJ366W	G M N	PRA114R	Blue Bus
NLS986W	Ribble	OIW1318	GMS Buses	ORJ367W	G M N	PRA115R	Blue Bus
NLS988W	Ribble	OIW1319	GMS Buses	ORJ368W	GMS Buses	PRJ485R	Border
NMX643	Mayne	OIW1608	GMS Buses	ORJ369W	G M N	PRN909	Preston
NNH187Y	Timeline	OIW5801	Rossendale	ORJ370W	G M N	PSU775	Ribble
NNH191Y	Vale of Manchester	OJD131R	Mayne	ORJ371W	G M N	PSU787	Cumberland
NOC450R	Town Bus	OJD163R	Mayne	ORJ372W	G M N	PSU788	Ribble
NOC603R	Stotts	OJD457R	R Bullock	ORJ373W	G M N	PTD415S	Border
NRG155M	Border	OJI4371	Blackpool	ORJ374W	G M N	PTD416S	Border
NRG160M	Border	OJI4372	Blackpool	ORJ375W	GMS Buses	PTD417S	Rossendale
NRG161M	Border	OJI4373	Blackpool	ORJ376W	GMS Buses	PTD642S	G M N
NRG165M	Border	OJI4374	Blackpool	ORJ377W	GMS Buses	PTD648S	G M N
NRG167M	Border	OJI9451	GMS Buses	ORJ378W	G M N	PTD650S	G M N
NRN383P	Hyndburn	OJI9452	GMS Buses	ORJ379W	G M N	PTD654S	G M N
NRN390P	Hyndburn	OJI9455	GMS Buses	ORJ380W	GMS Buses	PUS158W	Blackburn
NRN397P	Finglands	ONF653R	Finglands	ORJ381W	GMS Buses	PVS830	Bluebird
NRN402P	Hyndburn	ONF659R	South Manchester	ORJ382W	G M N	PWK7W	Brownrigg's
NRN404P	Hyndburn	ONF660R	Blackpool	ORJ383W	G M N	PXI7915	GMS Buses
NSU181	Rossendale	ONF663R	Finglands	ORJ384W	G M N	PXI8916	GMS Buses
NUS333Y	Robinson's	ONF664R	South Manchester	ORJ385W	G M N	Q580GRJ	Manchester Airport
NUT16W	Blackpool	ONF667R	South Manchester	ORJ386W	G M N	RBJ36W	Hyndburn
NXI414	Burnley & Pendle	ONF669R	Blackpool	ORJ387W	G M N	RBU179R	G M N
NXI812	Burnley & Pendle	ONF673R	Blackpool	ORJ388W	G M N	RDV419H	Pioneer
OBV158X	Preston	ONF684R	Rossendale	ORJ389W	G M N	RGV37W	Hyndburn
OBV159X	Preston	ONF685R	G M N	ORJ390W	G M N	RGV38W	Hyndburn
OBV160X	Preston	ONF691R	G M N	ORJ391W	G M N	RGV39W	Hyndburn
OBV161X	Preston	ONF692R	Rossendale	ORJ392W	G M N	RGV40W	Hyndburn
OBV162X	Preston	ONF695R	Finglands	ORJ393W	GMS Buses	RHG95T	Blackpool
OBV163X	Preston	ONF698R	G M N	ORJ394W	G M N	RHG878X	Ribble
OBV164X	Preston	ORJ72W	GMS Buses	ORJ395W	GMS Buses	RHG879X	Ribble
OBV165X	Preston	ORJ73W	GMS Buses	ORJ396W	GMS Buses	RHG881X	Ribble
OCS114R	Town Bus	ORJ74W	GMS Buses	ORJ398W	G M N	RHG884X	Ribble
OCW6X	Blackburn	ORJ75W	GMS Buses	ORJ399W	G M N	RHG886X	Ribble
OCW7X	Blackburn	ORJ76W	GMS Buses	ORJ400W	G M N	RIB4089	Blackpool
OCW8X	Blackburn	ORJ77W	GMS Buses	ORY640	Cumberland	RIB4323	Shaw Hadwin
OCW9X	Blackburn	ORJ78W	GMS Buses	OSJ607R	Blue Bus	RIB5093	Shaw Hadwin
OCW10X	Blackburn	ORJ79W	GMS Buses	OSR193R	Burnley & Pendle	RIB6590	Blackpool
OCW11X	Blackburn	ORJ80W	GMS Buses	OSR195R	Burnley & Pendle	RIW3364	GMS Buses
OCW12X	Blackburn	ORJ81W	GMS Buses	OSR196R	Burnley & Pendle	RJA701R	GMS Buses
OCW13X	Blackburn	ORJ82W	G M N	OSR197R	Burnley & Pendle	RJA703R	Finglands
OCW14X	Blackburn	ORJ83W	G M N	OSR205R	Burnley & Pendle	RJA705R	Rossendale

Half-opentop double-deck buses are a rarity, but here we see WRH294J in Blackpool's Blue Buses fleet. Photographed outside the famous Blackpool Tower it is destined for Pontins holiday camp adjacent to Blackpool airport. *Paul Wigan*

Reg	Operator	Reg	Operator	Reg	Operator	Reg	Operator
RJA706R	G M N	RWU52R	Stotts	SJI4560	GMS Buses	SND124X	GMS Buses
RJA708R	G M N	RYV77	Finglands	SJI5407	Hyndburn	SND125X	GMS Buses
RJA719R	G M N	SAO466X	Wright Bros	SKB650T	Apex Travel	SND126X	G M N
RJA721R	G M N	SAO467X	Wright Bros	SKB650T	Stotts	SND127X	G M N
RJA724R	G M N	SBV16X	Blackburn	SKF8T	G M N	SND128X	G M N
RJA725R	G M N	SBV17X	Blackburn	SKF9T	G M N	SND129X	G M N
RJA726R	G M N	SCH149X	Mayne	SKN905R	Border	SND130X	G M N
RJA729R	GMS Buses	SCH151X	Bluebird	SMK828	Borderbus	SND131X	G M N
RJA802R	G M N	SCH152X	Bluebird	SND27X	Rossendale	SND132X	GMS Buses
RJA803R	G M N	SCK224X	Ribble	SND28X	Rossendale	SND133X	G M N
RJA805R	G M N	SCK225X	Ribble	SND82X	GMS Buses	SND134X	G M N
RJA809R	G M N	SCK226X	Ribble	SND83X	Shaw Hadwin	SND135X	G M N
RJA815R	GMS Buses	SCS360M	Blue Bus	SND86X	GMS Buses	SND136X	G M N
RJI2161	Blue Bus	SDA613S	Stuart's	SND101X	G M N	SND137X	G M N
RJI4082	Hulme Hall	SDZ9026	GMS Buses	SND102X	G M N	SND138X	G M N
RJI4083	Hulme Hall	SFR127J	Abbott's	SND103X	G M N	SND139X	G M N
RJI8613	Hyndburn	SGA710N	Stuart's	SND104X	G M N	SND140X	G M N
RJI8720	Rossendale	SHH387X	Ribble	SND105X	G M N	SND141X	GMS Buses
RJI8721	Rossendale	SHH388X	Ribble	SND106X	GMS Buses	SND142X	GMS Buses
RJI8722	Rossendale	SHH390X	Ribble	SND107X	GMS Buses	SND143X	GMS Buses
RJI8723	Rossendale	SHH391X	Ribble	SND108X	GMS Buses	SND144X	GMS Buses
RJI8918	Hulme Hall	SHH393X	Ribble	SND109X	GMS Buses	SND145X	GMS Buses
RJX318	Springfield Cs	SHH394X	Ribble	SND110X	GMS Buses	SND146X	G M N
RMA432V	Hulme Hall	SIA6180	Finglands	SND111X	GMS Buses	SND147X	G M N
RPB955X	Pioneer	SIB1361	GMS Buses	SND112X	G M N	SND148X	G M N
RRC485R	Border	SIB1832	GMS Buses	SND113X	G M N	SND149X	G M N
RRM383X	Ribble	SIB2014	GMS Buses	SND114X	G M N	SND150X	G M N
RRM384X	Ribble	SIB2632	Robinson's	SND115X	G M N	SND288X	Hulme Hall
RRM386X	Ribble	SIB4631	Blackpool	SND116X	GMS Buses	SND289X	Hyndburn
RRM915M	Wright Bros	SIB6614	Finglands	SND117X	GMS Buses	SND412X	GMS Buses
RRP858R	Ribble	SIB6615	Finglands	SND118X	GMS Buses	SND413X	G M N
RUF41R	GMS Buses	SIB8405	Blackpool	SND119X	GMS Buses	SND414X	G M N
RUF44R	Manchester Airport	SJI1887	Bluebird	SND120X	GMS Buses	SND415X	G M N
RVB977S	Wall's	SJI2054	GMS Buses	SND121X	GMS Buses	SND416X	G M N
RWM576T	Apex Travel	SJI4558	GMS Buses	SND122X	G M N	SND417X	G M N
RWM576T	Stotts	SJI4559	GMS Buses	SND123X	GMS Buses	SND418X	GMS Buses

SND419X	G M N	SND493X	G M N	THX555S	Mayne	UNA762S	G M N
SND420X	G M N	SND494X	G M N	THX566S	Town Bus	UNA766S	GMS Buses
SND421X	GMS Buses	SND495X	GMS Buses	THX569S	Town Bus	UNA767S	G M N
SND422X	GMS Buses	SND496X	GMS Buses	THX579S	Mayne	UNA769S	G M N
SND423X	G M N	SND497X	G M N	THX594S	Mayne	UNA771S	G M N
SND424X	G M N	SND498X	G M N	THX601S	Mayne	UNA773S	G M N
SND425X	GMS Buses	SND499X	G M N	THX619S	Mayne	UNA779S	G M N
SND426X	G M N	SND500X	G M N	TJI2488	GMS Buses	UNA782S	G M N
SND427X	G M N	SND501X	GMS Buses	TJN505R	Blackburn	UNA783S	G M N
SND428X	G M N	SND502X	G M N	TKH266H	Blackpool	UNA785S	G M N
SND429X	GMS Buses	SND503X	G M N	TKU462K	Blackpool	UNA787S	G M N
SND430X	GMS Buses	SND504X	G M N	TKU465K	Blackpool	UNA797S	G M N
SND431X	G M N	SND505X	GMS Buses	TKU466K	Blackpool	UNA819S	Finglands
SND433X	G M N	SND506X	GMS Buses	TKU469K	Blackpool	UNA820S	GMS Buses
SND434X	G M N	SND507X	G M N	TKU540	Mayne	UNA821S	G M N
SND434X	GMS Buses	SND508X	G M N	TNA161J	Timeline	UNA822S	G M N
SND435X	GMS Buses	SND509X	G M N	TOF649S	Blackburn	UNA828S	G M N
SND436X	G M N	SND510X	G M N	TPL762X	Vale of Manchester	UNA829S	G M N
SND437X	GMS Buses	SND511X	G M N	TPX884	GMS Buses	UNA831S	GMS Buses
SND438X	G M N	SND512X	GMS Buses	TRN476V	Ribble	UNA833S	G M N
SND439X	G M N	SND513X	GMS Buses	TRN478V	Ribble	UNA834S	G M N
SND440X	GMS Buses	SND514X	GMS Buses	TRN480V	Ribble	UNA838S	GMS Buses
SND441X	G M N	SND515X	G M N	TRN481V	Ribble	UNA839S	G M N
SND442X	G M N	SND516X	G M N	TRN482V	Ribble	UNA843S	GMS Buses
SND443X	G M N	SND517X	G M N	TRN772	Blackpool	UNA844S	Finglands
SND444X	G M N	SND518X	GMS Buses	TRN802V	Ribble	UNA847S	G M N
SND445X	G M N	SND519X	GMS Buses	TRN806V	Ribble	UNA848S	Finglands
SND446X	G M N	SND520X	G M N	TRN810V	Cumberland	UNA852S	G M N
SND447X	G M N	SND521X	GMS Buses	TRN812V	Ribble	UNA860S	GMS Buses
SND448X	G M N	SND522X	G M N	TSD571S	Blackpool	UNA862S	GMS Buses
SND449X	GMS Buses	SND523X	G M N	TSJ57S	Blue Bus	UNA866S	G M N
SND450X	GMS Buses	SND524X	G M N	TSU639W	Blackburn	UOL337	Mayne
SND451X	GMS Buses	SND525X	G M N	TSU640W	Blackburn	UPB336S	Dennis's
SND452X	GMS Buses	SND526X	GMS Buses	TSU641W	Blackburn	URA604S	Bluebird
SND452X	GMS Buses	SND527X	GMS Buses	TSV807	Wright Bros	URF662S	Ribble
SND453X	GMS Buses	SND528X	G M N	TWH701T	G M N	URM801Y	Cumberland
SND454X	GMS Buses	SND529X	G M N	TWH702T	G M N	URM802Y	Cumberland
SND455X	GMS Buses	SND530X	GMS Buses	TYS256W	Stotts	URN12V	Vale of Manchester
SND456X	G M N	SND550X	Rossendale	TYS257W	Stotts	URN166Y	Preston
SND457X	G M N	SND551X	Rossendale	TYS258W	Stotts	URN167Y	Preston
SND458X	G M N	SPR35	Shearings	TYS259W	Stotts	URN168Y	Preston
SND459X	G M N	SPR124	Shearings	TYT653	Titteringtons	URN169Y	Preston
SND460X	G M N	SRJ734R	Finglands	UCE665	Mayne	URN170Y	Preston
SND461X	G M N	SRJ740R	Rossendale	UDT178S	Border	URN171Y	Preston
SND463X	G M N	SRJ744R	Border	UDX921	Wright Bros	URN172Y	Preston
SND464X	G M N	SRJ756R	Blackpool	UFG62S	Manchester Airport	URN322V	Blackpool
SND465X	GMS Buses	SRJ757R	Blackpool	UGE807W	Wright Bros	URN323V	Blackpool
SND466X	G M N	SRJ759R	GMS Buses	UHG141V	Preston	URN324V	Blackpool
SND468X	GMS Buses	SRN103P	Fishwick	UHG142V	Preston	URN325V	Blackpool
SND469X	G M N	SSV269	Mayne	UHG143V	Preston	URN326V	Blackpool
SND470X	G M N	SSX599V	Vale of Manchester	UHG144V	Preston	URN327V	Blackpool
SND471X	G M N	SSX601V	Pioneer	UHG145V	Preston	URN328V	Blackpool
SND472X	GMS Buses	STE18S	Rossendale	UHG147V	Preston	URN329V	Blackpool
SND473X	GMS Buses	STE19S	Rossendale	UHG148V	Preston	URN330V	Blackpool
SND474X	G M N	SWH127T	Hyndburn	UHG149V	Preston	USU641	Borderbus
SND475X	G M N	SWH271T	R Bullock	UHG150V	Preston	USU642	Borderbus
SND476X	GMS Buses	SWS768S	Robinson's	UHG351Y	Blackpool	USU643	Borderbus
SND477X	GMS Buses	SXI3627	Stuart's	UHG352Y	Blackpool	UTF736M	Brownrigg's
SND478X	G M N	SXI9033	Stuart's	UHG353Y	Blackpool	UWR294	Shaw Hadwin
SND479X	GMS Buses	SXI9034	Stuart's	UHG354Y	Blackpool	UWV610S	Cumberland
SND480X	GMS Buses	SXI9037	Stuart's	UIA7087	Shaw Hadwin	UWV612S	Cumberland
SND481X	G M N	SXI9039	Stuart's	UIB4751	Shaw Hadwin	UWV618S	Cumberland
SND482X	G M N	SYG437W	Apex Travel	UIB4752	Shaw Hadwin	UWV620S	Cumberland
SND483X	GMS Buses	TCK200X	Ribble	ULS316T	Blue Bus	UWV622S	Cumberland
SND484X	GMS Buses	TCK212X	Ribble	ULS318T	Blue Bus	UWV622S	Ribble
SND485X	G M N	TCK841	Cumberland	ULS322T	Blue Bus	UWW5X	Blackpool
SND486X	G M N	TCW868T	Blackburn	ULS329T	Blue Bus	UWW11X	Blackpool
SND487X	GMS Buses	TET746S	Stotts	ULS334T	Blue Bus	UWW15X	Blackpool
SND488X	GMS Buses	TET747S	Stotts	ULS614X	Stuart's	VBA151S	G M N
SND489X	GMS Buses	THH288X	Shaw Hadwin	ULS663T	Mayne	VBA152S	GMS Buses
SND490X	G M N	THX303S	Mayne	ULS666T	Mayne	VBA153S	GMS Buses
SND491X	G M N	THX322S	Mayne	UMR194T	Fishwick	VBA155S	G M N
SND492X	G M N	THX515S	Mayne	UMR196T	Fishwick	VBA156S	GMS Buses

Reg	Operator	Reg	Operator	Reg	Operator	Reg	Operator
VBA157S	GMS Buses	VFV907R	Abbott's	WVM870S	GMS Buses	XSU908	Burnley & Pendle
VBA158S	G M N	VGU443	Mayne	WVM872S	GMS Buses	XSU909	Burnley & Pendle
VBA159S	G M N	VKW999S	Town Bus	WVM879S	GMS Buses	XSU910	Burnley & Pendle
VBA160S	G M N	VNB132L	GMS Buses	WVM885S	GMS Buses	XTB728N	Fishwick
VBA162S	GMS Buses	VNH157W	Hyndburn	WVM886S	G M N	XTB729N	Fishwick
VBA163S	G M N	VNN54Y	Bluebird	WVM891S	GMS Buses	XTJ4W	G M N
VBA164S	GMS Buses	VOY182X	Border	WVM895S	GMS Buses	XTJ5W	G M N
VBA165S	G M N	VRM73S	Wright Bros	WVM896S	GMS Buses	XTJ7W	G M N
VBA166S	GMS Buses	VRN827Y	Ribble	WVM897S	South Manchester	YCD78T	Manchester Airport
VBA167S	G M N	VRN828Y	Ribble	WWH94T	G M N	YCD81T	Border
VBA168S	GMS Buses	VRN829Y	Ribble	WWM576W	Hyndburn	YCD88T	Manchester Airport
VBA169S	GMS Buses	VRN830Y	Ribble	WWM905W	G M N	YDG616	Cumberland
VBA170S	GMS Buses	VRR447	Cumberland	WWM920W	Hyndburn	YDN921V	Borderbus
VBA171S	G M N	VUA472X	Hulme Hall	WWM922W	Hyndburn	YEL95Y	Stuart's
VBA174S	GMS Buses	VUP514V	Blue Bus	WWM928W	South Manchester	YEV317S	Blackburn
VBA175S	GMS Buses	VVU229S	Border	WWM932W	South Manchester	YEV324S	Blackburn
VBA177S	G M N	WAO396Y	Ribble	WWM933W	Hyndburn	YFG333	Shaw Hadwin
VBA178S	GMS Buses	WAO398Y	Ribble	WXI5865	Sim	YFR496R	Hyndburn
VBA179S	G M N	WAO645Y	Ribble	WYJ164S	Manchester Airport	YHG15V	Bluebird
VBA180S	G M N	WAO646Y	Ribble	XAP956	Titteringtons	YKA8W	Hyndburn
VBA181S	G M N	WBN466T	GMS Buses	XBF58S	Springfield Cs	YNA281M	Stotts
VBA182S	GMS Buses	WBN474T	GMS Buses	XBF63S	Brownrigg's	YNA282M	South Manchester
VBA183S	G M N	WBN955L	G M N	XBU3S	G M N	YNA284M	Stotts
VBA184S	G M N	WCK213Y	Ribble	XBU4S	G M N	YNA287M	Stotts
VBA186S	GMS Buses	WCK215Y	Ribble	XBU7S	G M N	YNA300M	Stotts
VBA187S	GMS Buses	WDA680T	Stuart's	XBU12S	G M N	YNA303M	Stotts
VBA188S	GMS Buses	WDA975T	Stotts	XBU13S	G M N	YNA307M	Wall's
VBA189S	G M N	WDA980T	Stuart's	XBU16S	G M N	YNA328M	Mayne
VBA190S	GMS Buses	WDA981T	Stuart's	XBU18S	G M N	YNA345M	Stotts
VBA191S	G M N	WFR147K	Abbott's	XCW955R	Fishwick	YNA354M	R Bullock
VBA192S	G M N	WFR167K	Abbott's	XCW957R	Fishwick	YNJ434	Blackpool
VBA193S	GMS Buses	WIA4122	GMS Buses	XDO32	Shaw Hadwin	YPF771T	Dennis's
VBA194S	G M N	WIB1364	Brownrigg's	XFK305	Burnley & Pendle	YPL764	Mayne
VBA195S	GMS Buses	WIB1366	Brownrigg's	XHG96V	Blackpool	YRN507R	Abbott's
VBA196S	G M N	WIB4053	Blue Bus	XJA549L	Stotts	YRN813V	Ribble
VBA197S	G M N	WIB4054	Blue Bus	XJF386	Shaw Hadwin	YRN814V	Ribble
VBA198S	G M N	WL9475	Darwen Minibus	XLV163W	G M N	YRN815V	Ribble
VBA200S	GMS Buses	WLT706	Cumberland	XNK206X	Manchester Airport	YRN817V	Ribble
VBG80V	G M N	WLT824	Cumberland	XNK209X	Manchester Airport	YRN818V	Ribble
VBG81V	G M N	WLT848	Blackpool	XNK212X	Manchester Airport	YRN819V	Ribble
VBG82V	G M N	WLT879	Blackpool	XNK215X	Manchester Airport	YRN820V	Ribble
VBG83V	G M N	WLT980	Cumberland	XOU692	Titteringtons	YRN822V	Ribble
VBG85V	G M N	WPH134Y	Blackburn	XRJ201S	G M N	YSF97S	Blue Bus
VBG86V	G M N	WPH137Y	Blackburn	XRJ202S	G M N	YSF99S	Blue Bus
VBG95V	G M N	WPH138Y	Blackburn	XRJ203S	GMS Buses	YSG651W	Vale of Manchester
VBG97V	G M N	WPH141Y	Blackburn	XRJ204S	GMS Buses	YSU991	Holmeswood
VBG98V	G M N	WRH291J	Blackpool	XRJ205S	G M N	YSV205	Wall's
VBG99V	G M N	WRH294J	Blackpool	XRJ206S	G M N	YSV426	Wall's
VBV18Y	Blackburn	WRH295J	Blackpool	XRN29V	Blackpool	YSV589	Wall's
VBV19Y	Blackburn	WRN133V	Blackburn	XRN44V	Burnley & Pendle	YSV605	Wall's
VBV20Y	Blackburn	WRN134V	Blackburn	XRN45V	Burnley & Pendle	YSV662	Wall's
VBV21Y	Blackburn	WRN135V	Blackburn	XRN46V	Burnley & Pendle	YTE584V	G M N
VBV22Y	Blackburn	WRN136V	Blackburn	XRN47V	Burnley & Pendle	YTE585V	G M N
VCW196V	Hyndburn	WRN137V	Blackburn	XRN48V	Burnley & Pendle	YTE586V	G M N
VCW197V	Hyndburn	WRN138V	Blackburn	XRN49V	Burnley & Pendle	YTE589V	G M N
VCW596Y	Pioneer	WRN139V	Blackburn	XRN50V	Burnley & Pendle	YTE590V	G M N
VCW598Y	Bluebird	WRN140V	Blackburn	XRR175S	Cumberland	YTE592V	G M N
VDY528T	Rossendale	WRN141V	Blackburn	XSJ652T	Stotts	YTE593V	G M N
VDY529T	Rossendale	WRN142V	Blackburn	XSU905	Burnley & Pendle	YTP749	Shearings
VDY530T	Rossendale	WRN412V	Fishwick	XSU906	Burnley & Pendle	YTY887	Holmeswood
VDY531T	Rossendale	WRN413V	Fishwick	XSU907	Burnley & Pendle	YUC765	Mayne
VFV7V	Burnley & Pendle	WTU490W	Hulme Hall				

ISBN 1 897990 13 8

Published by *British Bus Publishing Ltd*
The Vyne, 16 St Margarets Drive, Wellington,
Telford, Shropshire, TF1 3PH
Answerphone/Fax - (+44) (0) 1952 255669

Printed by Graphics & Print Ltd
Unit A1, Stafford Park 15
Telford, Shropshire, TF3 3BB

British Bus Publishing

BUS HANDBOOKS

Also available!

The Leyland Lynx - £8.95
The 1996 FirstBus Handbook - £9.95
The 1996 Stagecoach Bus Handbook - £9.95
The North East Bus Handbook - £9.95
The Yorkshire Bus Handbook - £9.95
The Merseyside and Cheshire Bus Handbook - £9.95
The Scottish Bus Handbook - £9.95
The Welsh Bus Handbook - £9.95
The East Midlands Bus Handbook - £8.95
The South Midlands Bus Handbook - £8.95
The Model Bus Handbook - £9.95
The Fire Brigade Handbook - £8.95

Coming Soon

The North and West Midlands Bus Handbook - £9.95

Get the best!
Buy today from your local bookseller,
or order direct from:

**British Bus Publishing
The Vyne, 16 St Margaret's Drive, Wellington
Telford, Shropshire TF1 3PH
*Fax and Credit Card orders: 01952 255669***